Gnostic Gospels

Edition.

Modern Translation Including Thomas, Judas, Mary, Philip, Truth, Q, Infancy Gospels, and Acts of Pilate

HOLY APOCRYPHA

2024 Edition

CONTENTS

CONTENTS

GOSPEL OF THOMAS

Prologue

These are the hidden sayings that the living Jesus spoke and Didymos Judas Thomas wrote down.

True Meaning

And he said, "Whoever discovers the meaning of these sayings won't taste death."

Seek and Find

Jesus said, "Whoever seeks shouldn't stop until they find. When they find, they'll be disturbed. When they're disturbed, they'll be [...] amazed, and reign over the All."

Seeking Within

Jesus said, "If your leaders tell you, 'Look, the kingdom is in heaven,' then the birds of heaven will precede you. If they tell you, 'It's in the sea,' then the fish will precede you. Rather, the kingdom is within you and outside of you.
"When you know yourselves, then you'll be known, and you'll realize that you're the children of the living Father. But if you don't know yourselves, then you live in poverty, and you are the poverty."

First and Last

Jesus said, "The older person won't hesitate to ask a little seven-day-old child about the place of life, and they'll live, because many who are first will be last, and they'll become one."

Hidden and Revealed

Jesus said, "Know what's in front of your face, and what's hidden from you will be revealed to you, because there's nothing hidden that won't be revealed."

Public Ritual

His disciples said to him, "Do you want us to fast? And how should we pray? Should we make donations? And what food should we avoid?"
Jesus said, "Don't lie, and don't do what you hate, because everything is revealed in the sight of heaven; for there's nothing hidden that won't be revealed, and nothing covered up that will stay secret."

The Lion and the Human

Jesus said, "Blessed is the lion that's eaten by a human and then becomes human, but how awful for the human who's eaten by a lion, and the lion becomes human."

The Parable of the Fish

He said, "The human being is like a wise fisher who cast a net into the sea and drew it up from the sea full of little fish. Among them the wise fisher found a fine large fish and cast all the little fish back down into the sea, easily choosing the large fish. Anyone who has ears to hear should hear!"

The Parable of the Sower

Jesus said, "Look, a sower went out, took a handful of seeds, and scattered them. Some fell on the roadside; the birds came and gathered them. Others fell on the rock; they didn't take root in the soil and ears of grain didn't rise toward heaven. Yet others fell on thorns; they choked the seeds and worms ate them. Finally, others fell on good soil; it produced fruit up toward heaven, some sixty times as much and some a hundred and twenty."

Jesus and Fire

Jesus said, "I've cast fire on the world, and look, I'm watching over it until it blazes."

Those Who Are Living Won't Die

Jesus said, "This heaven will disappear, and the one above it will disappear too. Those who are dead aren't alive, and those who are living won't die. In the days when you ate what was dead, you made it alive. When you're in the light, what will you do? On the day when you were one, you became divided. But when you become divided, what will you do?"

James the Just

The disciples said to Jesus, "We know you're going to leave us. Who will lead us then?" Jesus said to them, "Wherever you are, you'll go to James the Just, for whom heaven and earth came into being."

Thomas' Confession

Jesus said to his disciples, "If you were to compare me to someone, who would you say I'm like?" Simon Peter said to him, "You're like a just angel." Matthew said to him, "You're like a wise philosopher." Thomas said to him, "Teacher, I'm completely unable to say whom you're like." Jesus said, "I'm not your teacher. Because you've drunk, you've become intoxicated by the bubbling spring I've measured out." He took him aside and told him three things. When Thomas returned to his companions, they asked, "What did Jesus say to you?" Thomas said to them, "If I tell you one of the things he said to me, you'll pick up stones and cast them at me, and fire will come out of the stones and burn you up."

Public Ministry

Jesus said to them, "If you fast, you'll bring guilt upon yourselves; and if you pray, you'll be condemned; and if you make donations, you'll harm your spirits. If they welcome you when you enter any land and go around in the countryside, heal those who are sick among them and eat whatever they give you, because it's not what goes into your mouth that will defile you. What comes out of your mouth is what will defile you."

Worship

Jesus said, "When you see the one who wasn't born of a woman, fall down on your face and worship that person. That's your Father."

Not Peace, but War

Jesus said, "Maybe people think that I've come to cast peace on the world, and they don't know that I've come to cast divisions on the earth: fire, sword, and war. Where there are five in a house, there'll be three against two and two against three, father against son and son against father. They'll stand up and be one."

Divine Gift

Jesus said, "I'll give you what no eye has ever seen, no ear has ever heard, no hand has ever touched, and no human mind has ever thought."

Beginning and End

The disciples said to Jesus, "Tell us about our end. How will it come?"

Jesus said, "Have you discovered the beginning so that you can look for the end? Because the end will be where the beginning is. Blessed is the one who will stand up in the beginning. They'll know the end, and won't taste death."

Five Trees in Paradise

Jesus said, "Blessed is the one who came into being before coming into being. If you become my disciples and listen to my message, these stones will become your servants; because there are five trees in paradise which don't change in summer or winter, and their leaves don't fall. Whoever knows them won't taste death."

The Parable of the Mustard Seed

The disciples asked Jesus, "Tell us, what can the kingdom of heaven be compared to?" He said to them, "It can be compared to a mustard seed. Though it's the smallest of all the seeds, when it falls on tilled soil it makes a plant so large that it shelters the birds of heaven."

The Parables of the Field, the Bandits, and the Reaper

Mary said to Jesus, "Whom are your disciples like?" He said, "They're like little children living in a field which isn't theirs. When the owners of the field come, they'll say, 'Give our field back to us.' They'll strip naked in front of them to let them have it and give them their field. So I say that if the owner of the house realizes the bandit is coming, they'll watch out beforehand and won't let the bandit break into the house of their domain and steal their possessions. You, then, watch out for the world! Prepare to defend yourself so that the bandits don't attack you, because what you're expecting will come. May there be a wise person among you! When the fruit ripened, the reaper came quickly, sickle in hand, and harvested it. Anyone who has ears to hear should hear!"

Making the Two into One

Jesus saw some little children nursing. He said to his disciples, "These nursing children can be compared to those who enter the kingdom." They said to him, "Then we'll enter the kingdom as little children?" Jesus said to them, "When you make the two into one, and make the inner like the outer and the outer like the inner, and the upper like the lower, and so make the male and the female a single one so that the male won't be male nor the female female; when you make eyes in the place of an eye, a hand in the place of a hand, a foot in the place of a foot, and an image in the place of an image; then you'll enter [the kingdom]."

Those Who are Chosen

Jesus said, "I'll choose you, one out of a thousand and two out of ten thousand, and they'll stand as a single one."

Light

His disciples said, "Show us the place where you are, because we need to look for it." He said to them, "Anyone who has ears to hear should hear! Light exists within a person of light, and they light up the whole world. If they don't shine, there's darkness."

Love and Protect

Jesus said, "Love your brother as your own soul. Protect them like the pupil of your eye."

Speck and Beam

Jesus said, "You see the speck that's in your brother's eye, but you don't see the beam in your own eye. When you get the beam out of your own eye, then you'll be able to see clearly to get the speck out of your brother's eye."

Fasting and Sabbath

"If you don't fast from the world, you won't find the kingdom. If you don't make the Sabbath into a Sabbath, you won't see the Father."

The World is Drunk

Jesus said, "I stood in the middle of the world and appeared to them in the flesh. I found them all drunk; I didn't find any of them thirsty. My soul ached for the children of humanity, because they were blind in their hearts and couldn't see. They came into the world empty and plan on leaving the world empty. Meanwhile, they're drunk. When they shake off their wine, then they'll change."

Spirit and Body

Jesus said, "If the flesh came into existence because of spirit, that's amazing. If spirit came into existence because of the body, that's really amazing! But I'm amazed at how [such] great wealth has been placed in this poverty."

Divine Presence

Jesus said, "Where there are three deities, they're divine. Where there are two or one, I'm with them."

Prophet and Doctor

Jesus said, "No prophet is welcome in their own village. No doctor heals those who know them."

The Parable of the Fortified City

Jesus said, "A city built and fortified on a high mountain can't fall, nor can it be hidden."

The Parable of the Lamp

Jesus said, "What you hear with one ear, listen to with both, then proclaim from your rooftops. No one lights a lamp and puts it under a basket or in a hidden place. Rather, they put it on the stand so that everyone who comes and goes can see its light."

The Parable of Those Who Can't See

Jesus said, "If someone who's blind leads someone else who's blind, both of them fall into a pit."

The Parable of Binding the Strong

Jesus said, "No one can break into the house of the strong and take it by force without tying the hands of the strong. Then they can loot the house."

Anxiety

Jesus said, "Don't be anxious from morning to evening or from evening to morning about what you'll wear."

Seeing Jesus

His disciples said, "When will you appear to us? When will we see you?" Jesus said, "When you strip naked without being ashamed, and throw your clothes on the ground and stomp on them as little children would, then [you'll] see the Son of the Living One and won't be afraid."

Finding Jesus

Jesus said, "Often you've wanted to hear this message that I'm telling you, and you don't have anyone else from whom to hear it. There will be days when you'll look for me, but you won't be able to find me."

The Keys of Knowledge

Jesus said, "The Pharisees and the scholars have taken the keys of knowledge and hidden them. They haven't entered, and haven't let others enter who wanted to. So be wise as serpents and innocent as doves."

A Grapevine

Jesus said, "A grapevine has been planted outside of the Father. Since it's malnourished, it'll be pulled up by its root and destroyed."

More and Less

Jesus said, "Whoever has something in hand will be given more, but whoever doesn't have anything will lose even what little they do have."

Passing By

Jesus said, "Become passersby."

The Tree and the Fruit

His disciples said to him, "Who are you to say these things to us?" "You don't realize who I am from what I say to you, but you've become like those Judeans who either love the tree but hate its fruit, or love the fruit but hate the tree."

Blasphemy

Jesus said, "Whoever blasphemes the Father will be forgiven, and whoever blasphemes the Son will be forgiven, but whoever blasphemes the Holy Spirit will not be forgiven, neither on earth nor in heaven."

Good and Evil

Jesus said, "Grapes aren't harvested from thorns, nor are figs gathered from thistles, because they don't produce fruit. [A person who's good] brings good things out of their treasure, and a person who's [evil] brings evil things out of their evil treasure. They say evil things because their heart is full of evil."

Greater than John the Baptizer

Jesus said, "From Adam to John the Baptizer, no one's been born who's so much greater than John the Baptizer that they shouldn't avert their eyes. But I say that whoever among you will become a little child will know the kingdom and become greater than John."

The Parables of Divided Loyalties, New Wine in Old Wineskins, and New Patch on Old Cloth

Jesus said, "It's not possible for anyone to mount two horses or stretch two bows, and it's not possible for a servant to follow two leaders, because they'll respect one and despise the other. No one drinks old wine and immediately wants to drink new wine. And new wine isn't put in old wineskins, because they'd burst. Nor is old wine put in new wineskins, because it'd spoil. A new patch of cloth isn't sewn onto an old coat, because it'd tear apart."

Unity

Jesus said, "If two make peace with each other in a single house, they'll say to the mountain, 'Go away,' and it will."

Those Who Are Chosen

Jesus said, "Blessed are those who are one – those who are chosen, because you'll find the kingdom. You've come from there and will return there."

Our Origin and Identity

Jesus said, "If they ask you, 'Where do you come from?' tell them, 'We've come from the light, the place where light came into being by itself, [established] itself, and appeared in their image.' If they ask you, 'Is it you?' then say, 'We are its children, and we're chosen by our living Father.' If they ask you, 'What's the sign of your Father in you?' then say, 'It's movement and rest.'"

The New World

His disciples said to him, "When will the dead have rest, and when will the new world come?" He said to them, "What you're looking for has already come, but you don't know it."

Twenty-Four Prophets

His disciples said to him, "Twenty-four prophets have spoken in Israel, and they all spoke of you." He said to them, "You've ignored the Living One right in front of you, and you've talked about those who are dead."

True Circumcision

His disciples said to him, "Is circumcision useful, or not?" He said to them, "If it were useful, parents would have children who are born circumcised. But the true circumcision in spirit has become profitable in every way."

Those Who Are Poor

Jesus said, "Blessed are those who are poor, for yours is the kingdom of heaven."

Discipleship

Jesus said, "Whoever doesn't hate their father and mother can't become my disciple, and whoever doesn't hate their brothers and sisters and take up their cross like I do isn't worthy of me."

The World is a Corpse

Jesus said, "Whoever has known the world has found a corpse. Whoever has found a corpse, of them the world isn't worthy."

The Parable of the Weeds

Jesus said, "My Fathers' kingdom can be compared to someone who had [good] seed. Their enemy came by night and sowed weeds among the good seed. The person didn't let anyone pull out the weeds, 'so that you don't pull out the wheat along with the weeds,' they said to them. 'On the day of the harvest, the weeds will be obvious. Then they'll be pulled out and burned.'"

Finding Life

Jesus said, "Blessed is the person who's gone to a lot of trouble. They've found life."

The Living One

Jesus said, "Look for the Living One while you're still alive. If you die and then try to look for him, you won't be able to."

Don't Become a Corpse

They saw a Samaritan carrying a lamb to Judea. He said to his disciples, "What do you think he's going to do with that lamb?" They said to him, "He's going to kill it and eat it." He said to them, "While it's living, he won't eat it, but only after he kills it and it becomes a corpse." They said, "He can't do it any other way." He said to them, "You, too, look for a resting place, so that you won't become a corpse and be eaten."

Jesus and Salome

Jesus said, "Two will rest on a couch. One will die, the other will live." Salome said, "Who are you, Sir, to climb onto my couch and eat off my table as if you're from someone?" Jesus said to her, "I'm the one who exists in equality. Some of what belongs to my Father was given to me." "I'm your disciple." "So I'm telling you, if someone is /equal, they'll be full of light; but if they're divided, they'll be full of darkness."

Mysteries

Jesus said, "I tell my mysteries to [those who are worthy of my] mysteries. Don't let your left hand know what your right hand is doing."

The Parable of the Rich Fool

Jesus said, "There was a rich man who had much money. He said, 'I'll use my money to sow, reap, plant, and fill my barns with fruit, so that I won't need anything.' That's what he was thinking to himself, but he died that very night. Anyone who has ears to hear should hear!"

The Parable of the Dinner Party

Jesus said, "Someone was planning on having guests. When dinner was ready, they sent their servant to call the visitors. "The servant went to the first and said, 'My master invites you.' "They said, 'Some merchants owe me money. They're coming tonight. I need to go and give them instructions. Excuse me from the dinner.' "The servant went to another one and said, 'My master invites you.' "They said, "I've just bought a house and am needed for the day. I won't have time.' "The servant went to another one and said, 'My master invites you.' "They said, 'My friend is getting married and I'm going to make dinner. I can't come. Excuse me from the dinner.' "The servant went to another one and said, 'My master invites you.' "They said, "I've just bought a farm and am going to collect the rent. I can't come. Excuse me.' "The servant went back and told the master, 'The ones you've invited to the dinner have excused themselves.' "The master said to their servant, 'Go out to the roads and bring whomever you find so that they can have dinner.' "Buyers and merchants won't [enter] the places of my Father."

The Parable of the Sharecroppers

He said, "A [creditor] owned a vineyard. He leased it out to some sharecroppers to work it so he could collect its fruit. He sent his servant so that the sharecroppers could give him the fruit of the vineyard. They seized his servant, beat him, and nearly killed him. The servant went back and told his master. His master said, 'Maybe he just didn't know them.' He sent another servant, but the tenants beat that one too. Then the master sent his son, thinking, 'Maybe they'll show some respect to my son.' Because they knew that he was the heir of the vineyard, the sharecroppers seized and killed him. Anyone who has ears to hear should hear!"

The Rejected Cornerstone

Jesus said, "Show me the stone the builders rejected; that's the cornerstone."

Knowing Isn't Everything

Jesus said, "Whoever knows everything, but is personally lacking, lacks everything."

Persecution

Jesus said, "Blessed are you when you're hated and persecuted, and no place will be found where you've been persecuted."

Those Who Are Persecuted

Jesus said, "Blessed are those who've been persecuted in their own hearts. They've truly known the Father. Blessed are those who are hungry, so that their stomachs may be filled."

Salvation is Within

Jesus said, "If you give birth to what's within you, what you have within you will save you. If you don't have that within [you], what you don't have within you [will] kill you."

Destroying the Temple

Jesus said, "I'll destroy [this] house, and no one will be able to build it [...]"

Not a Divider

[Someone said to him], "Tell my brothers to divide our inheritance with me." He said to him, "Who made me a divider?" He turned to his disciples and said to them, "Am I really a divider?"

Workers for the Harvest

Jesus said, "The harvest really is plentiful, but the workers are few. So pray that the Lord will send workers to the harvest."

The Empty Well

He said, "Lord, many are gathered around the well, but there's nothing to drink."

The Bridal Chamber

Jesus said, "Many are waiting at the door, but those who are one will enter the bridal chamber."

The Parable of the Pearl

Jesus said, "The Father's kingdom can be compared to a merchant with merchandise who found a pearl. The merchant was wise; they sold their merchandise and bought that single pearl for themselves. You, too, look for the treasure that doesn't perish but endures, where no moths come to eat and no worms destroy."

Jesus is the All

Jesus said, "I'm the light that's over all. I am the All. The All has come from me and unfolds toward me. Split a log; I'm there. Lift the stone, and you'll find me there."

Into the Desert

Jesus said, "What did you go out into the desert to see? A reed shaken by the wind? A [person] wearing fancy clothes, [like your] rulers and powerful people? They (wear) fancy [clothes], but can't know the truth."

Listening to the Message

A woman in the crowd said to him, "Blessed is the womb that bore you, and the breasts that nourished you." He said to [her], "Blessed are those who have listened to the message of the Father and kept it, because there will be days when you'll say, 'Blessed is the womb that didn't conceive and the breasts that haven't given milk.'"

The World is a Body

Jesus said, "Whoever has known the world has found the body; but whoever has found the body, of them the world isn't worthy."

Riches and Renunciation

Jesus said, "Whoever has become rich should become a ruler, and whoever has power should renounce it."

Jesus and Fire

Jesus said, "Whoever is near me is near the fire, and whoever is far from me is far from the kingdom."

Light and Images

Jesus said, "Images are revealed to people, but the light within them is hidden in the image of the Father's light. He'll be revealed, but his image will be hidden by his light."

Our Previous Images

Jesus said, "When you see your likeness, you rejoice. But when you see your images that came into being before you did – which don't die, and aren't revealed – how much you'll have to bear!"

Adam Wasn't Worthy

Jesus said, "Adam came into being from a great power and great wealth, but he didn't become worthy of you. If he had been worthy, [he wouldn't have tasted] death."

Foxes and Birds

Jesus said, "[The foxes have dens] and the birds have nests, but the Son of Humanity has nowhere to lay his head and rest."

Body and Soul

Jesus said, "How miserable is the body that depends on a body, and how miserable is the soul that depends on both."

Angels and Prophets

Jesus said, "The angels and the prophets will come to you and give you what belongs to you. You'll give them what you have and ask yourselves, 'When will they come and take what is theirs?'"

Inside and Outside

Jesus said, "Why do you wash the outside of the cup? Don't you know that whoever created the inside created the outside too?"

Jesus' Yoke is Easy

Jesus said, "Come to me, because my yoke is easy and my requirements are light. You'll be refreshed."

Reading the Signs

They said to him, "Tell us who you are so that we may trust you." He said to them, "You read the face of the sky and the earth, but you don't know the one right in front of you, and you don't know how to read the present moment."

Look and Find

Jesus said, "Look and you'll find. I didn't answer your questions before. Now I want to give you answers, but you aren't looking for them."

Don't Throw Pearls to Pigs

"Don't give what's holy to the dogs, or else it might be thrown on the manure pile. Don't throw pearls to the pigs, or else they might [...]"

Knock and It Will Be Opened

Jesus [said], "Whoever looks will find, [and whoever knocks], it will be opened for them."

Giving Money

[Jesus said], "If you have money, don't lend it at interest. Instead, give [it to] someone from whom you won't get it back."

The Parable of the Yeast

Jesus [said], "The Father's kingdom can be compared to a woman who took a little yeast and [hid] it in flour. She made it into large loaves of bread. Anyone who has ears to hear should hear!"

The Parable of the Jar of Flour

Jesus said, "The Father's kingdom can be compared to a woman carrying a jar of flour. While she was walking down [a] long road, the jar's handle broke and the flour spilled out behind her on the road. She didn't know it, and didn't realize there was a problem until she got home, put down the jar, and found it empty."

The Parable of the Assassin

Jesus said, "The Father's kingdom can be compared to a man who wanted to kill someone powerful.

He drew his sword in his house and drove it into the wall to figure out whether his hand was strong enough. Then he killed the powerful one."

Jesus' True Family

The disciples said to him, "Your brothers and mother are standing outside." He said to them, "The people here who do the will of my Father are my brothers and mother; they're the ones who will enter my Father's kingdom."

Give to Caesar What Belongs to Caesar

They showed Jesus a gold coin and said to him, "Those who belong to Caesar demand tribute from us." He said to them, "Give to Caesar what belongs to Caesar, give to God what belongs to God, and give to me what belongs to me."

Discipleship (2)

"Whoever doesn't hate their [father] and mother as I do can't become my [disciple], and whoever [doesn't] love their [father] and mother as I do can't become my [disciple]. For my mother [...], but [my] true [Mother] gave me Life."

The Dog in the Feeding Trough

Jesus said, "How awful for the Pharisees who are like a dog sleeping in a feeding trough for cattle, because the dog doesn't eat, and [doesn't let] the cattle eat either."

The Parable of the Bandits

Jesus said, "Blessed is the one who knows where the bandits are going to enter. [They can] get up to assemble their defenses and be prepared to defend themselves before they arrive."

Prayer and Fasting

They said to [Jesus], "Come, let's pray and fast today." Jesus said, "What have I done wrong? Have I failed? "Rather, when the groom leaves the bridal chamber, then people should fast and pray."

Knowing Father and Mother

Jesus said, "Whoever knows their father and mother will be called a bastard."

Unity (2)

Jesus said, "When you make the two into one, you'll become Children of Humanity, and if you say 'Mountain, go away!', it'll go."

The Parable of the Lost Sheep

Jesus said, "The kingdom can be compared to a shepherd who had a hundred sheep. The largest one strayed. He left the ninety-nine and looked for that one until he found it. Having gone through the trouble, he said to the sheep: 'I love you more than the ninety-nine.'"

Becoming Like Jesus

Jesus said, "Whoever drinks from my mouth will become like me, and I myself will become like them; then,

14

what's hidden will be revealed to them."

The Parable of the Hidden Treasure

Jesus said, "The kingdom can be compared to someone who had a treasure [hidden] in their field. [They] didn't know about it. After they died, they left it to their son. The son didn't know it either. He took the field and sold it. The buyer plowed the field, [found] the treasure, and began to loan money at interest to whomever they wanted."

Riches and Renunciation (2)

Jesus said, "Whoever has found the world and become rich should renounce the world."

Those Who are Living Won't Die (2)

Jesus said, "The heavens and the earth will roll up in front of you, and whoever lives from the Living One won't see death. Doesn't Jesus say,

'Whoever finds themselves, of them the world isn't worthy'?"

Flesh and Soul

Jesus said, "How awful for the flesh that depends on the soul. How awful for the soul that depends on the flesh."

The Kingdom is Already Present

His disciples said to him, "When will the kingdom come?" "It won't come by looking for it. They won't say, 'Look over here!' or 'Look over there!' Rather, the Father's kingdom is already spread out over the earth, and people don't see it."

Peter and Mary

Simon Peter said to them, "Mary should leave us, because women aren't worthy of life." Jesus said, "Look, am I to make her a man? So that she may become a living spirit too, she's equal to you men, because every woman who makes herself manly will enter the kingdom of heaven."

Gospel of Philip

Gentiles, Hebrews, and Christians

A Hebrew creates a Hebrew, and [those] of this kind are called "a proselyte." But a [proselyte] doesn't create (another) proselyte. They're like [...] and they create others [...] it's good enough for them that they come into being.

The slave seeks only freedom; they don't seek their master's property. But the son isn't just a son; he claims his father's inheritance for himself. Those who inherit the dead are themselves dead, and they inherit the dead. Those who inherit the living are themselves alive, and they inherit (both) the living and the dead. The dead can't inherit anything, because how can the dead inherit? If the dead inherits the living they won't die, but the dead will live even more! A gentile doesn't die, because they've never lived in order that they may die. Whoever has believed in the Truth has lived, and is at risk of dying, because they're alive since the day Christ came. The world is created, the cities gentrified, and the dead carried out.

When we were Hebrews, we were fatherless – we had (only) our mother. But when we became Christians, we gained both father and mother.

Life, Death, Light, and Darkness

Those who sow in the winter reap in the summer. The winter is the world, the summer the other age. Let's sow in the world so that we may reap in the summer. Because of this, it's not right for us to pray in the winter. The summer follows the winter. But if someone reaps in the winter they won't reap, but uproot, as this kind won't produce fruit [...] it doesn't just come out [...] but in the other Sabbath [...] it's fruitless.

Christ came to buy some, but to save others, and to redeem yet others. He bought those who were strangers, made them his own, and set them apart as a pledge as he wanted to. It wasn't just when he appeared that he laid down his life when he wanted to, but since the day the world came into being he laid down his life when he wanted to. Then he came first to take it, since it had been pledged. It was dominated by the robbers that had captured it, but he saved it; and those who are good in the world he redeemed, as well as those who are bad.

The light and the darkness, the right and the left, are brothers of each other. They're inseparable. So, those who are good aren't good, those who are bad aren't bad, nor is life (really) life, nor is death (really) death. Because of this, each one will be dissolved into its origin from the beginning. But those who are exalted above the world are indissoluble and eternal.

Names

The names that are given to those who are worldly are very deceptive, because they turn the heart away from what's right to what's not right, and someone who hears "God" doesn't think of what's right but thinks of what's not right. So also with "the Father," "the Son," "the Holy Spirit," "the life," "the light," "the resurrection," "the church," and all the others – they don't think of [what's right] but think of what's [not] right, [unless] they've learned what's right. The [names that were heard] exist in the world [...] [deceive. If they existed] in the (eternal) age they wouldn't have been used as names in the world, nor would they have been placed among worldly things. They have an end in the (eternal) age.

There's one name that isn't uttered in the world: the name which the Father gave to the Son. It's exalted over everything; it's the Father's name, because the Son wouldn't have become father unless he had taken the name of the Father. Those who have this name know it, but

don't say it; and those who don't have it, don't know it. But Truth brought names into the world for us, because it's impossible for us to learn it (Truth) without these names. There's only one Truth, but it's many things for us, to teach this one thing in love through many things.

The Rulers

The rulers wanted to deceive humanity, because they (the rulers) saw that they (humanity) had a kinship with those that are truly good. They took the name of those that are good and gave it to those that aren't good, to deceive them (humanity) by the names and bind them to those that aren't good; and then, what a favor they do for them! They take them from those that aren't good and place them among those that are good. They knew what they were doing, because they wanted to take those who were free and place them in slavery forever. There are powers that exist [...] humanity, not wanting them to be [saved], so that they may be [...] because if humanity [was saved], sacrifices [wouldn't] happen [...] and animals offered up to the powers, because those to whom offerings were made were animals. They were offered up alive, but when they were offered up they died. A human was offered up to God dead, and he lived.

Before Christ came, there wasn't any bread in the world – just as Paradise, where Adam was, had many trees to feed the animals but no wheat to feed humanity. Humanity used to eat like the animals, but when Christ, the perfect human, came, he brought bread from heaven so that humanity would be fed with the food of humanity.

The rulers thought they did what they did by their own power and will, but the Holy Spirit was secretly accomplishing everything it wanted to through them. Truth, which has existed from the beginning, is sown everywhere; and many see it being sown, but few see it being reaped.

The Virgin Birth

Some say that "Mary conceived by the Holy Spirit." They're wrong; they don't know what they're saying. When did a woman ever conceive by a woman? "Mary is the virgin whom no power defiled" is the great testimony of those Hebrews who became (the first) apostles and (the) apostolic (successors). The virgin whom no power defiled [...] the powers defiled themselves.

And the Lord [wouldn't] have said, "my [Father who is in] heaven" unless [he] had another father. Instead, he would simply have said ["my Father."] The Lord said to the [disciples, "...] [from] every [house] and bring into the Father's house, but don't steal (anything) from the Father's house or carry it away."

Jesus, Christ, Messiah, Nazarene

"Jesus" is a hidden name; "Christ" is a revealed name. So "Jesus" is not translated, but he's called by his name "Jesus." But the name "Christ" in Syriac is "Messiah," in Greek "Christ," and all the others have it according to their own language.

"The Nazarene" reveals what's hidden. Christ has everything within himself, whether human or angel or mystery, and the Father.

The Resurrection

Those who say that the Lord died first and then arose are wrong, because he arose first and (then) he died. Anyone who doesn't first acquire the resurrection won't die. As God lives, that one would /die

No one will hide something great and valuable in a great thing, but often someone has put countless thousands into something worth (only) a penny. It's the same with the soul; a valuable thing came to be in a contemptible body.

Some are afraid that they'll arise naked. So they want to arise in the flesh, and [they] don't know that those who wear the [flesh] are naked. Those [...] to strip themselves naked [are] not naked. "Flesh [and blood won't] inherit [God's] kingdom." What is it that won't inherit? That which is on us. But what is it, too, that will inherit? It is Jesus' (flesh) and blood. Because of this, he said, "Whoever doesn't eat my flesh and drink my blood doesn't have life in them." What's his flesh? It's the Word, and his blood is the Holy Spirit. Whoever has received these have food, drink, and clothing.

(So) I myself disagree with the others who say, "It won't arise." Both (sides) are wrong. You who say, "the flesh won't arise," tell me what will arise, so that we may honor you. You say, "the spirit in the flesh and this other light in the flesh." (But) this saying is in the flesh too, because whatever you say, you can't say apart from the flesh. It's necessary to arise in this flesh, since everything exists in it. In this world, people are better than the clothes they wear. In the kingdom of heaven, the clothes are better than the people who wear them.

Everything is purified by water and fire – the visible by the visible, the hidden by the hidden. Some things are hidden by things that are visible. There's water in water, and fire in chrism.

Seeing Jesus

Jesus took all of them by stealth, because he didn't appear as he was, but he appeared as [they'd] be able to see him. He appeared to them (in) [all these] (ways): he [appeared] to [the] great as great. He [appeared] to the small as small. He [appeared] [to the] angels as an angel, and to humans as a human. So his Word hid itself from everyone. Some did see him, thinking they were seeing themselves. But when he appeared to his disciples in glory on the mountain, he wasn't small. He became great, but he made the disciples great (too) so that they would be able to see him as great.

He said on that day in the Eucharist, "You who've united the perfect light with the Holy Spirit, unite the angels with us too, with the images!"

Don't despise the lamb, because without him it's impossible to see the door. No one will be able to approach the king naked.

Father, Son, and Holy Spirit

The children of the heavenly human are more numerous than those of the earthly human. If Adam has so many children, even though they die, how many children does the perfect human have – those who don't die, but are begotten all the time?

The father makes a son, but it's impossible for a son to make a son, because it's impossible for someone who's been born to beget (sons); the son begets brothers, not sons. All who are begotten in the world are begotten physically, and the others in [...] are begotten by him [...] out there to the human [...] in the [...] heavenly place [...] it from the mouth [...] the Word came out from there they would be nourished from the mouth [and] become perfect. The perfect are conceived and begotten through a kiss. Because of this we kiss each other too, conceiving from the grace within each other.

There were three who traveled with the Lord all the time: His mother Mary, her sister, and Magdalene, who is called his companion; because Mary is his sister, his mother, and his partner.

"The Father" and "The Son" are single names; "the Holy Spirit" is a double name, because they're everywhere. They're in heaven, they're below, they're hidden, and they're revealed. The Holy Spirit is revealed below and hidden in heaven.

Those who are holy are served through the evil powers, because the Holy Spirit has blinded them so that they think they're serving a (regular) human when they're (really) working for the holy ones. So a disciple asked the Lord one day about a worldly thing. He told him, "Ask your Mother, and she'll give you from someone else."

The apostles said to the disciples, "May our entire offering acquire salt." They called [...] "salt." Without it, the offering doesn't [become] acceptable. But Wisdom [is] childless; because of this [she's] called [...], this of salt, the place they'll [...] in their own way. The Holy Spirit [...] [...] many children.

What belongs to the father belongs to the son, and he himself – the son – as long as he's little, is not entrusted with what's his. When he becomes a man, his father gives him everything that belongs to him.

Those who've been begotten by the Spirit and go astray, go astray through it too. Because of this, through this one Spirit it blazes, that is, the fire, and it's extinguished.

Echamoth is one thing and Echmoth another. Echamoth is simply Wisdom, but Echmoth is the Wisdom of Death, which knows death. This is called "the little Wisdom."

Humans and Animals

There are animals that submit to humans, like the calf, the donkey, and others of this kind. Others are not submissive, and live alone in the wilderness. Humanity ploughs the field with the submissive animals, and consequently nourishes itself and the animals, whether submissive or not. That's what it's like with the perfect human: they plough with the submissive powers, preparing for everyone that will exist. So because of this the whole place stands, whether the good or the evil, and the right and the left. The Holy Spirit shepherds everyone and rules all the powers – those that are submissive, those that [aren't], and those that are alone – because truly it [...] confines them [so that ...] want to, they won't be able to [leave].

[The one who's been] formed [is beautiful, but] you'd find his children being noble forms. If he weren't formed but begotten, you'd find that his seed was noble. But now he was formed, and he begot. What nobility is this? First there was adultery, and then murder; and he (Cain) was begotten in adultery, because he was the son of the serpent. Because of this he became a murderer like his father too, and he killed his brother (Abel). Every partnership between those who are dissimilar is adultery.

Becoming Christians

God is a dyer. Like the good dyes – they're called true – die with what's been dyed in them, so it is with those who were dyed by God. Because his dyes are immortal, they become immortal by means of his colors. But God baptizes in water.

It's impossible for anyone to see anything that really exists unless they become like them. It's not like the person in the world who sees the sun without becoming a sun, and who sees heaven and earth and everything else without becoming them. That's the way it is. But you've seen something of that place, and have become them. You saw the Spirit, you became spirit; you saw Christ, you became Christ; you saw [the Father, you] will become father. Because of this, [here] you see everything and don't [see yourself], but you see yourself [there], because you'll [become] what you see.

Faith receives; love gives. [No one will be able to] [receive] without faith, and no one will be able to give without love. So we believe in order that we may receive, but we give in order that we may love, since anyone who doesn't give with love doesn't get anything out of it. Whoever hasn't received the Lord is still a Hebrew.

The apostles before us called (him) "Jesus the Nazarene Messiah," that is, "Jesus the Nazarene Christ." The last name is "Christ," the first is "Jesus," the middle one is "the Nazarene." "Messiah" has two meanings: both "Christ" and "the measured." "Jesus" in Hebrew is "the redemption." "Nazara" is "the truth." So "the Nazarene" is "the truth." "Christ" is the one who was measured. "The Nazarene" and "Jesus" are the ones who were measured.

A pearl doesn't become less valuable if it's cast down into the mud, nor will it become more valuable if it's anointed with balsam; but it's valuable to its owner all the time. That's what it's like with God's children: no matter where they are, they're still valuable to their Father. If you say, "I'm a Jew," no one will be moved. If you say, "I'm a Roman," no one will be disturbed. If you say, "I'm a Greek," "a Barbarian," "a slave," ["a free person,"] no one will be troubled. [If] you [say,] "I'm a Christian," the [...] will tremble. If

only [... of] this kind, this one [who ...] won't be able to endure [hearing] his name.

God is a human-eater. Because of this, the human is [sacrificed] to him. Before the human was sacrificed, animals were sacrificed, because those to whom they were sacrificed weren't gods.

Vessels of glass and pottery come into being by means of fire. But if glass vessels break they're remade, because they came into being by means of a breath, but if pottery vessels break they're destroyed, because they came into being without breath.

A donkey turning a millstone traveled a hundred miles. When it was released, it still found itself in the same place. Many people travel, but don't get anywhere. When evening came, they saw neither city nor village, nor anything created or natural, nor power nor angel. The wretches worked in vain.

The Eucharist is Jesus, because in Syriac he's called "Pharisatha," that is, "the one who's spread out," because Jesus came to crucify the world.

The Lord went into Levi's place of dyeing. He took seventy-two colors and threw them into the vat. He brought all of them out white and said, "That's the way the Son of Humanity has come [as] a dyer."

The Wisdom who is called "the barren" is the Mother [of the angels] and [the] companion of the [... Mary] Magdalene [... loved her] more than the disciples [... he] kissed her on her [... many] times. The rest of [...] [...] they said to him, "Why do you love her more than all of us?" The Savior said to them in reply, "Why don't I love you like her? When a person who's blind and one who sees are both in the dark, they're no different from one another. When the light comes, the one who sees will see the light, and the one who's blind will remain in the dark."

The Lord said, "Blessed is the one who exists before existing, because they who exist did exist, and will exist."

The superiority of humanity isn't revealed, but exists in what's hidden. So it (humanity) masters animals that are stronger, that are greater in terms of that which is revealed and that which is hidden. This allows them to survive; but if humanity separates from them (the animals), they kill, bite, and eat each other, because they didn't find food. But now they've found food because humanity has worked the earth.

If someone goes down into the water and comes up without having received anything, and says, "I'm a Christian," they've borrowed the name at interest. But if they receive the Holy Spirit, they have the gift of the name. Whoever has received a gift doesn't have it taken away, but whoever has borrowed it at interest has to give it back. That's what it's like when someone comes into being in a mystery.

The Mystery of Marriage

[The] mystery of marriage [is] great, because [without] it the world would [not exist]; because [the] structure of [the world ...], but the structure [... the marriage]. Think about the [intimate ...] defiled, because it has [...] power. Its image exists in a [defilement].

The impure spirits take male and female [forms]. The males are those that are intimate with the souls which dwell in a female form, and the females are those that mingle with those in a male form through disobedience. No one will be able to escape being bound by them without receiving a male power and a female one – the groom and the bride – in the image of the bridal chamber. When the foolish females see a male sitting alone, they jump on him, play with him, and defile him. In the same way, when the foolish males see a beautiful female sitting alone, they seduce and coerce her, wanting to defile her. But if they see the husband and his wife sitting together, the females can't go inside the husband, nor the males inside the wife. That's what it's like when the image unites with the angel; no one will be able to dare to go inside the [male] or the female.

Overcoming the World

Whoever comes out of the world can no longer be bound because they were in the world. They're revealed to be above the desire of the [... and] fear. They're master over [...] they're better than envy. If [...] come, they (the powers) bind and choke [them]. How will [they] be able to escape the [great powers ...]? How will they be able to [...]? There are some who [say], "We're faithful," in order that [...] [impure spirit] and demon, because if they had the Holy Spirit, no impure spirit would cling to them. Don't fear the flesh, nor love it. If you fear it, it'll master you; if you love it, it'll swallow and choke you.

Someone exists either in this world, or in the resurrection, or in the middle places. May I never be found there! There's both good and evil in this world. Its good things aren't good, and its evil things aren't evil. But there's an evil after this world which is truly evil: that which is called "the middle." It's death. While we're in this world, it's right for us to acquire the resurrection for ourselves, so that when we're stripped of the flesh we'll be found in the rest and not travel in the middle, because many stray on the way.

It's good to come out of the world before one sins. There are some who neither want to nor can, but others who, if they wanted to, (still) wouldn't benefit, because they didn't act. The wanting makes them sinners. But (even) if they don't want, justice will (still) be hidden from them. It's not the will, and it's not the act.

An apostle saw [in a] vision some people confined in a burning house, and bound with burning [...], thrown [...] of the burning [...] them in [...] and they said to them [... able] to be saved [...] they didn't want to, and they received [...] punishment, which is called "the [outer] darkness," because it [...].

The soul and the spirit came into being from water and fire. The offspring of the bridal chamber was from water and fire and light. The fire is the chrism, the light is the fire. I'm not talking about that formless fire, but of the other one whose form is white, which is bright and beautiful, and which gives beauty.

Truth didn't come into the world naked, but it came in types and images. It (the world) won't receive it in any other way. There's a rebirth, and an image of rebirth. It's truly necessary to be begotten again through the image. What's the resurrection and the image? Through the image it's necessary for it to arise. The bridal chamber and the image? Through the image it's necessary for them to enter the truth, which is the restoration. It's not only necessary for those who acquire the name of the Father and the Son and the Holy Spirit, but they too have been acquired for you. If someone doesn't acquire them, the name will also be taken from them. But they're received in the chrism of the [...] of the power of the cross. The apostles called this "[the] right and the left," because this person is no longer a [Christian], but a Christ.

The Lord [did] everything in a mystery: a baptism, a chrism, a Eucharist, a redemption, a bridal chamber [...] he [said], "I came to make [the below] like the [above and the outside] like the [inside, and to unite] them in the place." [...] here through [types ...] Those who say, "[...] there's one above [...]," they're wrong, because] what's revealed is that [...], that [which] is called "what's below," and what's hidden is to it what's above it, because it's good, and they say "inside and what's outside and what's outside the outside." So the Lord called destruction "the outer darkness." There's nothing outside it.

He said, "My Father who's hidden." He said, "Enter your closet, shut the door behind you, and pray to your Father who's hidden," that is, the one who's within all of them. But the one who's within all of them is the fullness. Beyond that, there's nothing else within. This is what's called "that which is above them."

Before Christ, some came from where they were no longer able to enter, and they went where they were no longer able to come out. Then Christ came. He brought out those who entered, and brought in those who went out.

Adam, Eve, and the Bridal Chamber

When Eve was [in] Adam, death didn't exist. When she separated from him, death came into being. If he [enters] again and receives it for himself, there will be no death.

"[My] God, my God, why, Lord, [have] you forsaken me?" He said this on the cross, because he was divided in that place. [...] that he was begotten through that which [...] from God. The [...] from the dead [...] exists, but [...] he's perfect [...] of flesh, but this [...] is true flesh [...] isn't true, [but ...] image of the true. A bridal chamber isn't for the animals, nor for the slaves, nor for the impure, but it's for free people and virgins.

We're begotten again through the Holy Spirit, but we're begotten through Christ by two things. We're anointed through the Spirit. When we were begotten, we were united. Without light, no one can see themselves in water or in a mirror; nor again will you be able to see in light without water or mirror. Because of this, it's necessary to baptize in both: in the light and in the water, but the light is the chrism.

There were three houses of offering in Jerusalem. The one which opens to the west is called "the Holy." The other one, which opens to the south, is called "the Holy of the Holy." The third, which opens to the east, is called "the Holy of the Holies," the place where the high priest enters alone. Baptism is "the Holy" house. [Redemption] is "the Holy of the Holy." "The [Holy] of the Holies" is the bridal chamber. The [baptism] includes the resurrection [with] the redemption. The redemption is in the bridal chamber. But [the] bridal chamber is better than [...] You won't find its [...] those who pray [...] Jerusalem. [...] Jerusalem who [... Jerusalem], being seen [...] these that are called "[the Holies] of the Holies" [... the] veil torn [...] bridal chamber except the image [... which] [is above. So] its veil was torn from top to bottom, because it was necessary for some from below to go up above.

The powers can't see those who have put on the perfect light, and they can't bind them. But one will put on that light in the mystery of the union.

If the female wouldn't have been separated from the male, she wouldn't have died with the male. His separation was the beginning of death. Because of this, Christ came to repair the separation that existed since the beginning by uniting the two again. He'll give life to those who died as a result of the separation by uniting them. Now, the wife unites with her husband in the bridal chamber, and those who have united in the bridal chamber won't be separated any longer. Because of this, Eve separated from Adam, because she didn't unite with him in the bridal chamber.

It was through a breath that Adam's soul came into being. Its partner was the spirit. That which was given to him was his mother. His soul was [taken] and he was given [life] (Eve) in its place. When he was united [...] words that were better than the powers, and they envied him [...] spiritual partner [...] hidden [...] that is, the [...] themselves [...] bridal chamber so that [...] Jesus appeared [... the] Jordan, the [fullness of the kingdom] of heaven. He who [was begotten] before everything was begotten again. He [who was anointed] first was anointed again. He who was redeemed, redeemed again.

If it's necessary to speak of a mystery: the Father of everything united with the virgin who came down, and a fire enlightened him on that day. He revealed the great bridal chamber, so his body came into being on that day. He came out of the bridal chamber like the one who came into being from the groom and the bride. That's the way Jesus established everything within himself. It's also necessary for each of the disciples to enter into his rest through these things.

Adam came into being from two virgins: from the Spirit and from the virgin earth. So Christ was begotten from a virgin, to rectify the fall that occurred in the beginning.

There are two trees growing in Paradise. One begets [animals], the other begets humans. Adam [ate] from the tree that begot animals, [and he] became an animal, and he begot [animals]. So Adam's children worship the [animals]. The tree [...] is fruit [...] this they [...] ate the [...] fruit of the [...] beget humans [...] of the human of [...] God makes the human, [... humans] make [God]. That's what it's like in the world: humans make gods and worship their creation. It would be better for the gods to worship humans!

The truth is that the work of humankind comes from their power, so they're called "the powers." Their works are their children, who come into being through rest; so their power exists in their works, but the rest is revealed in their children. And you'll find that this extends to the image. And this is the person in the image: they do their works through their power, but they beget their children through rest.

In this world, the slaves work for the free. In the kingdom of heaven, the free will serve the slaves. The children of the bridal chamber will serve the children of the [marriage. The] children of the bridal chamber have a [single] name: "Rest." [Being] together they don't need to take form, [because they have] contemplation [...] they're many [...] with those who are in the [...] the glories of the [...] not [...] them [...] go down to the [water ...] they'll redeem themselves [...] that is, those who have [...] in his name, because he said: "[That's the way] we'll fulfill all righteousness."

Baptism, Chrism, Eucharist, Bridal Chamber

Those who say that they'll die first and (then) they'll rise are wrong. If they don't first receive the resurrection while they're living, they won't receive anything when they die. It's the same when they talk about baptism and they say "Baptism is a great thing," because those who receive it will live.

Philip the apostle said, "Joseph the carpenter planted a garden because he needed wood for his trade. It was he who made the cross from the trees he planted, and his offspring hung from what he planted. His offspring was Jesus, and the plant was the cross." But the Tree of Life is in the middle of Paradise, and from the olive tree came the chrism, and from that the resurrection.

This world eats corpses. All that are eaten in it die also. Truth eats life, so no one nourished by [Truth] will die. Jesus came from that place, he brought food from there, and to those who wanted, he gave them [to eat, so that] they won't die.

[God ...] a Paradise, [human ...] Paradise, there are [...] and [...] of God [...] those in [it ...] I wish that [Paradise ...] they'll say to me, "[... eat] this," or "don't eat [that ...] wish." The tree of knowledge is the place where I'll eat everything. It killed Adam, but here it makes humanity live. The Law was the tree. It has the power to give the knowledge of good and evil. It neither kept them from evil nor placed them in the good, but it created death for those who ate from it; because when it said, "Eat this, don't eat that," it became the beginning of death.

The chrism is better than baptism, since we're called "Christians" because of the chrism, not because of baptism. And it was because of the chrism that Christ was named, because the Father anointed the Son, and the Son anointed the apostles, and the apostles anointed us. Whoever is anointed has everything: the resurrection, the light, the cross, the Holy Spirit. The Father gave this to him in the bridal chamber, and he received it. The Father was in the Son and the Son in the Father. This is [the kingdom] of heaven.

The Lord said [it] well: "Some went to the kingdom of heaven laughing and they came out [...] a Christian [...] and as soon as [... went down] into the water and he [...] everything about [...] it's [a] game, [but ... disregard] this [...] to the kingdom of [heaven ...] if they disregard [...] and if they scorn it as a game, [... out] laughing. It's the same way with the bread and the cup and the oil, though there's one better than these.

The world came into being through a transgression, because the one who created it wanted to create it imperishable and immortal. He fell away and didn't get what he wanted, because the world wasn't imperishable, and the one who created it wasn't imperishable; because things aren't imperishable, but rather children. Nothing will be able to receive imperishability without becoming a child. But whoever can't receive, how much more will they be unable to give?

The cup of prayer has wine and water, since it's laid down as the type of the blood over which they give thanks. It fills with the Holy Spirit, and it belongs to the completely perfect human. Whenever we drink this, we'll receive the perfect human. The living water is a body. It's necessary for us to put on the living human. So coming down to the water, they strip themselves so that they'll put on that one.

A horse begets a horse, a human begets a human, and a god begets god. It's the same way with [the groom] and [brides too]. They [come into being] from the [...] No Jew [...] from [...] exists and [...] from the Jews [...] the Christians [...] called these [...] "the chosen race of [...]" and "the true human" and "the Son of the Human" and "the seed of the Son of the Human." This true race is known in the world. These are the places where the children of the bridal chamber exist.

In this world, union is between male and female, the place of power and weakness; in the (eternal) age, the union is like something else, but we refer to them by the same names. There are other names, however, that are above every name that's named, and they're better than the strong, because where there's force, there are those who are even more powerful. They're not (two) different things, but they're both the same thing. This is what won't be able to come down upon the fleshly heart.

Isn't it necessary for everyone who has everything to know themselves completely? Some who don't know themselves won't be able to enjoy what they have, but those who've come to understand themselves will enjoy them.

Not only won't they be able to bind the perfect human, they won't be able to see them (the perfect human), because if they see them they'll bind them. There's no other way for someone to acquire this grace for themselves [except by] putting on the perfect light [and] becoming the perfect [light. Whoever has put it on] themselves will go [...] this is the perfect [...] for us to become [...] before we came to [...] whoever receives everything [...] these places, they'll be able to [...] that place, but they'll [... the middle] as incomplete. Only Jesus knows the end of this one.

The holy man (priest) is completely holy, down to his (very) body, because if he receives the bread he'll make it holy, or the cup, or anything else that he takes and purifies. Why won't he purify the body too?

As Jesus perfected the water of baptism, that's the way he poured out death. So we go down into the water, but we don't go down into death, so that we won't be poured out into the spirit of the world. When it blows, the winter comes. When the Holy Spirit breathes, the summer comes. Whoever knows the truth is a free person, and the free person doesn't sin, because "whoever sins is the slave of sin." Truth is the Mother, but knowledge is the joining. Those who aren't given to sin are called "free" by the world. These who aren't given to sin are made proud by the knowledge of the truth. That's what makes them free and exalts them over everything. But "love

28

builds up," and whoever has been made free through knowledge is a slave because of love for those who aren't yet able to attain [the] freedom of knowledge, [but] knowledge makes them able [to] become free. Love [...] anything its own [...] it [...] its own. It never [says "..."] or "this is mine," [but "..."] are yours." Spiritual love is wine with fragrance. All those who will anoint themselves with it enjoy it. While those who are anointed stay around, those who are nearby also enjoy it. If those who are anointed with ointment leave them and go, those who aren't anointed but are only nearby remain in their stench. The Samaritan didn't give anything to the wounded man except wine with oil. It wasn't anything but the ointment, and it healed the wounds, because "love covers a multitude of sins."

The children to whom a woman gives birth will look like the man she loves. If it's her husband, they look like her husband; if it's an adulterer, they look like the adulterer. Often, if a woman sleeps with her husband because she has to, but her heart is with the adulterer with whom she is intimate and she bears a child, the child she bears looks like the adulterer. But you who exist with the Son of God, don't love the world; rather, love the Lord, so that those you'll beget may not come to look like the world, but will come to look like the Lord.

The human unites with the human, the horse unites with the horse, the donkey unites with the donkey. Species unite [with] similar species. That's what it's like when spirit unites with spirit, the [Word] is intimate with the Word, [and light is] intimate [with light. If you] become human, [it's the human who will] love you. If you become [spirit], it's the Spirit who will unite with you. [If] you become Word, it's the Word that will unite with you. If [you] become light, it's the light which will be intimate with you. If you become one of those from above, those from above will rest upon you. If you become horse or donkey or calf or dog or sheep or any other of the animals which are outside or below, neither human nor spirit nor Word nor light nor those from above nor those inside will be able to love you. They won't be able to rest within you, and you'll have no part in them.

Whoever is an unwilling slave will be able to be made free. Whoever has become free by the grace of their master and has sold themselves (back) into slavery won't be able to be made free any longer.

Spiritual Growth

The world is farmed through four things. They gather into barns through water, earth, wind, and light. And in the same way, God farms through four things too: through faith, hope, love, and knowledge. Our earth is the faith in which we're rooted. [And] the [water] is the hope through which [we're] nourished. The wind is the love through which we grow. And the light [is] the knowledge through which we [ripen]. Grace exists in [four kinds. It's] earthly, it's [heavenly, ...] the heaven of the heaven [...] through [....] Blessed is the one who hasn't [...] a soul. This one is Jesus Christ. He went all over the place and didn't burden anyone. So, blessed is someone like this; they're a perfect person, because the Word tells us about how hard it is to keep up. How will we be able to achieve such a great thing? How will he give rest to everyone? First and foremost, it's not right to cause anyone grief – whether great or small, or faithless or faithful – and then give rest to those who are (already) at rest among those who are well off. There are some who benefit from giving rest to the one who's well off. Whoever does good can't give rest to them because they can't just do whatever they want; they can't cause grief because they can't cause distress, but sometimes the one who's well off causes them grief. They're not like that, but it's their (own) evil that causes them grief. Whoever has the nature (of the perfect person) gives joy to the one who's good, but some grieve terribly at this.

A householder acquired everything, whether child or slave or cattle or dog or pig or wheat [or] barley or straw or hay or [...] or meat and acorn. [But they're] wise and understand what to feed each [one]. To the children they served bread [...] but [... the] slaves they served [...], and to the cattle [they threw barley] and straw and hay. To [the] dogs they threw bones [and] to [the pigs] they threw acorns and slops. That's what it's like with the disciple of God. If they're wise, they understand what it means to be a disciple. The bodily forms won't deceive them, but they'll look at the condition of the soul of each one and speak with them. There are many animals in the world that are made in human form. They (the disciple) recognizes them. To the pigs they'll throw acorns, but to the cattle they'll throw barley with straw and hay. To the dogs they'll throw bones, to the slaves they'll give the appetizer, and to the children they'll give the perfect (food).

There's the Son of Humanity, and there's the son of the Son of Humanity. The Lord is the Son of Humanity, and the son of the Son of Humanity is the one who creates through the Son of Humanity. The Son of Humanity received from God the ability to create. He (also) has the ability to beget. The one who received the ability to create is a creature; the one who received the ability to beget is begotten. The one who creates can't beget; the one who begets can create. They say, "The one who creates, begets." But what they beget is a creature. [So] their begotten aren't their children, but they're [...]. The one who creates works [publicly], and are themselves [revealed]. The one who begets, begets [secretly], and they're hidden [...] the image. [Again], the one who [creates, creates] publicly, but the one who begets, [begets] children secretly.

No [one will be able to] know [when the husband] and the wife are intimate with each other, except they themselves, because the marriage of the world is a mystery for those who have married. If the defiled marriage is hidden, how much more is the undefiled marriage a true mystery! It's not fleshly, but pure. It isn't of desire, but of the will. It isn't of the darkness or the night, but it's of the day and the light. If a marriage is stripped naked, it becomes pornography – not only if the bride receives the seed of another man, but even if she leaves the chamber and is seen, she commits adultery. Let her reveal herself to her father, her mother, the best man, and the groom's children. They're allowed to enter the bridal chamber every day. But let the others yearn just to hear her voice and enjoy her perfume, and, like dogs, let them eat the crumbs that fall from the table. Grooms and brides belong to the bridal chamber. No one will be able to see the groom and the bride unless [they become] such.

Uprooting Evil

When Abraham [...] to see what he was going to see, [he] circumcised the flesh of the foreskin, [telling] us that it's necessary to destroy the flesh.

[Most (things)] of [the] world can stand up and live as long as their [insides are hidden. If they're revealed], they die, as [illustrated] by the visible human. [As long as] the human's guts are hidden, the human is alive. If their guts are exposed and come out of them, the human will die. It's the same way with the tree. While its root is hidden, it blossoms and grows. If its root is exposed, the tree dries up. That's what it's like with everything that's born in the world, not only the revealed, but also the hidden; because as long as the root of evil is hidden, it's strong. But if it's recognized, it dissolves, and if it's revealed, it dies. So the Word says, "Already the axe is laid at the root of the trees." It won't (just) cut, (because) that which will be cut blossoms again. Rather, the axe digs down into the ground until it brings up the root. Jesus plucked out the root completely, but others did so partially. As for us, let every one of us dig down to the root of the evil within and pluck it out from its root in us. It'll be uprooted if we recognize it. But if we don't recognize it, it takes root within us and bears its fruit in us. It masters us, and we're forced to serve it. It captures us so that we do what we do [not] want to; and we do [not] do what we want to. [It's] powerful because we haven't recognized it. It's active as long as [it exists]. [Ignorance] is the mother of [all evil]. Ignorance will cause [death, because] what exists from [ignorance] neither did exist nor [does exist], nor will they come into being [...] they'll be perfected when the whole truth is revealed, because the truth is like ignorance. When it's hidden, it rests within itself, but if it's revealed and recognized, it's glorified inasmuch as it's stronger than ignorance and error. It gives freedom. The Word says, "If you'll know the truth, the truth will make you free." Ignorance is slavery; knowledge is freedom. If we know the truth, we'll find the fruits of truth within us. If we unite with it, it'll receive our fullness.

Now we have what's revealed of creation. We say, "Those who are strong are honorable, but those who are hidden are weak and scorned." That's what it's like with those who are revealed of the truth; they're weak and scorned, but the hidden are strong and honorable. But the mysteries of the truth are revealed in types and images.

The chamber is hidden, however; it's the Holy in the Holy. At first, the veil concealed how God managed the creation, but when the veil is torn and what's inside is revealed, then this house will be left behind [like] a desert, or rather, will be [destroyed]. And all divinity will flee [from] these places, not into the Holies [of the] Holies, because it won't be able to unite with the pure [light] and the [flawless] fullness, [but] it'll come to be under the wings of the cross [and under] its arms. This ark will [become their] salvation when the flood of water surges over them. If some belong to the priesthood, they'll be able to enter inside the veil with the high priest. So the veil wasn't torn only at the top, since it would've been open only to those at the top; nor was it torn only at the bottom, since it would've been revealed only to those at the bottom; but it was torn from the top to the bottom. Those at the top opened to us the bottom, so that we'll enter the secret of the truth. This truly is what's honorable, what's strong, but we'll enter there through scorned types and weaknesses. They're humbled in the presence of the perfect glory. There's glory that's better than glory; there's power that's better than power. So the perfect was opened to us with the secrets of the truth, and the Holies of the Holies were revealed, and the chamber invited us in.

As long as it's hidden, evil is inactive, but it hasn't been removed from among the Holy Spirit's seed. They're slaves of evil. But whenever it's revealed, then the perfect light will flow out upon everyone, and all of them who are in it will [receive the chrism]. Then the slaves will be made free and the captives will be redeemed. "[Every] plant [which] my Father who's in heaven [hasn't] planted [will be] uprooted." Those who are separated will unite [...] will be filled.

Conclusion

Everyone who will [enter] the chamber will kindle their [lamp], because [it's] like the marriages which are [...] happen at night, the fire [...] at night and is put out. But the mysteries of this marriage are fulfilled in the day and the light. Neither that day nor its light ever sets.

If anyone becomes a child of the bridal chamber, they'll receive the light. If anyone doesn't receive it while they're here, they won't be able to receive it in the other place. Whoever will receive that light won't be seen or bound, and no one will be able to trouble someone like this even while they dwell in the world. Moreover, when they leave the world, they've already received the Truth in the images. The world has become the (eternal) ages, because the (eternal) age is the fullness for them, and it's like this: it's revealed to them alone. It's not hidden in the darkness and the night, but it's hidden in a perfect day and a holy light.

GOSPEL OF MARY

An Eternal Perspective

"Then will [matter] be [destroyed], or not?"

The Savior said, "Every nature, every form, every creature exists in and with each other, but they'll dissolve again into their own roots, because the nature of matter dissolves into its nature alone. Anyone who has ears to hear should hear!"

Peter said to him, "Since you've explained everything to us, tell us one more thing. What's the sin of the world?"

The Savior said, "Sin doesn't exist, but you're the ones who make sin when you act in accordance with the nature of adultery, which is called 'sin.' That's why the Good came among you, up to the things of every nature in order to restore it within its root."

Then he continued and said, "That's why you get sick and die, because [you love what tricks you. Anyone who] can understand should understand!

"Matter [gave birth to] a passion that has no image because it comes from what's contrary to nature. Then confusion arises in the whole body. That's why I told you to be content at heart. If you're discontented, find contentment in the presence of the various images of nature. Anyone who has ears to hear should hear!"

The Gospel

When the Blessed One said these things, he greeted them all and said, "Peace be with you! Acquire my peace. Be careful not to let anyone mislead you by saying, 'Look over here!' or 'Look over there!' Because the Son of Humanity exists within you. Follow him! Those who seek him will find him.

"Go then and preach the gospel about the kingdom. Don't lay down any rules beyond what I've given you, nor make a law like the lawgiver, lest you be bound by it." When he said these things, he left.

But they grieved and wept bitterly. They said, "How can we go up to the Gentiles to preach the gospel about the kingdom of the Son of Humanity? If they didn't spare him, why would they spare us?"

Mary and Jesus

Then Mary arose and greeted them all. She said to her brothers (and sisters), "Don't weep and grieve or let your hearts be divided, because his grace will be with you all and will protect you. Rather we should praise his greatness because he's prepared us and made us Humans."

When Mary said these things, she turned their hearts [toward] the Good and they [started] to debate the words of [the Savior].

10 Peter said to Mary, "Sister, we know the Savior loved you more than all other women. Tell us the words of the Savior that you remember – the things which you know that we don't, and which we haven't heard."

In response Mary said, "I'll tell you what's hidden from you." So she started to tell them these words: "I," she said, "I saw the Lord in a vision and I said to him, 'Lord, I saw you in a vision today.'

"In response he said to me, 'You're blessed because you didn't waver at the sight of me. For where the mind is, there is the treasure.'

"I said to him, 'Lord, now does the one who sees the vision see it in the soul or in the spirit?'

"In response the Savior said, 'They don't see in the soul or in the spirit, but the mind which [exists] between the two is [what] sees the vision [and] it [that ...]

Overcoming the Powers

"And Desire said, 'I didn't see you going down, but now I see you're go-

ing up. So why are you lying, since you belong to me?'

"In response the soul said, 'I saw you, but you didn't see me or know me. I was to you just a garment, and you didn't recognize me.' When it said these things, it left, rejoicing greatly.

"Again, it came to the third power, which is called 'Ignorance.' [It] interrogated the soul and [said], 'Where are you going? In wickedness you're bound. Since you're bound, don't judge!'

"[And] the soul said, 'Why do you judge me, since I haven't judged? I was bound, even though I haven't bound. They didn't recognize me, but I've recognized that everything will dissolve – both the things of the [earth] and the things of [heaven].'

"When the soul had overcome the third power, it went up and saw the fourth power, which took seven forms:

The first form is Darkness; The second, Desire; The third, Ignorance; The fourth, Zeal for Death; The fifth, the Kingdom of the Flesh; The sixth, the Foolish 'Wisdom' of Flesh; The seventh, the 'Wisdom' of Anger.

"These are the seven powers of Wrath.

"They ask the soul, 'Where do you come from, you murderer, and where are you going, conqueror of space?'

"In response the soul said, 'What binds me has been killed, what surrounds me has been overcome, my desire is gone, and ignorance has died. In a [world] I was released from a world, [and] in a type from a type which is above, and from the chain of forgetfulness which exists only for a time. From now on I'll receive the rest of the time of the season of the age in silence.'"

When Mary said these things, she fell silent because the Savior had spoken with her up to this point.

Conflict over Authority

In response Andrew said to the brothers (and sisters), 'Say what you will about what she's said, I myself don't believe that the Savior said these things, because these teachings seem like different ideas."

In response Peter spoke out with the same concerns. He asked them concerning the Savior: "He didn't speak with a woman without our knowledge and not publicly with us, did he? Will we turn around and all listen to her? Did he prefer her to us?"

Then Mary wept and said to Peter, "My brother Peter, what are you thinking? Do you really think that I thought this up by myself in my heart, or that I'm lying about the Savior?"

In response Levi said to Peter, "Peter, you've always been angry. Now I see you debating with this woman like the adversaries. But if the Savior made her worthy, who are you then to reject her? Surely the Savior knows her very well. That's why he loved her more than us.

"Rather we should be ashamed, clothe ourselves with perfect Humanity, acquire it for ourselves as he instructed us, and preach the gospel, not laying down any other rule or other law beyond what the Savior said."

When [Levi said these things], they started to go out to teach and to preach.

GOSPEL OF JUDAS

Introduction

This is the secret message of judgment Jesus spoke with Judas Iscariot over a period of eight days, three days before he celebrated Passover. When he appeared on earth, he did signs and great wonders for the salvation of humanity. Some [walked] in the way of righteousness, but others walked in their transgression, so the twelve disciples were called. He started to tell them about the mysteries beyond the world and what would happen at the end. Often he didn't reveal himself to his disciples, but you'd find him in their midst as a child.

Jesus Criticizes the Disciples

One day he was with his disciples in Judea. He found them sitting together practicing their piety. When he [came up to] his disciples sitting together praying over the bread, [he] laughed.

The disciples said to him, "Master, why are you laughing at [our] prayer? What have we done? [This] is what's right."

He answered and said to them, "I'm not laughing at you. You're not do-ing this because you want to, but because through this your God [will be] praised."

They said, "Master, you [...] are the Son of our God!"

Jesus said to them, "How do [you] know me? Truly [I] say to you, no generation of the people among you will know me."

When his disciples heard this, [they] started to get angry and furious and started to curse him in their hearts.

But when Jesus noticed their ignorance, [he said] to them, "Why are you letting your anger trouble you? Has your God within you and [his stars] become angry with your souls? If any of you is [strong enough] among humans to bring out the perfect Humanity, stand up and face me."

All of them said, "We're strong enough." But their spirits weren't brave enough to stand before [him] – except Judas Iscariot. He was able to stand before him, but he couldn't look him in the eye, so he looked away.

Judas [said] to him, "I know who you are and where you've come from. You've come from the immortal realm of Barbelo, and I'm not worthy to utter the name of the one who's sent you."

Then Jesus, knowing that he was thinking about what's exalted, said to him, "Come away from the others and I'll tell you the mysteries of the kingdom. Not so that you'll go there, but you'll grieve much because someone else will replace you to complete the twelve [elements] before their God."

Judas said to him, "When will you tell me these things, and when will the great day of light dawn for the generation [...]?"

But when he said these things, Jesus left him.

Another Generation

The next morning, he appeared to his disciples. [And] they said to him, "Master, where did [you] go and what did you do when you left us?"

Jesus said to them, "I went to another great and holy generation."

His disciples said to him, "Lord, what great generation is better and holier than us, that's not in these realms?"

Now when Jesus heard this, he laughed. He said to them, "Why are you wondering in your hearts about the strong and holy generation? Truly I say to you, no one born [of] this realm will see that [generation], no army of angels from the stars will rule over it, and no person of mortal birth will be able to join it, because that generation doesn't come from [...] that has become [...] the generation of the people among [them] is from the generation of the great people [...] the powerful au-

thorities who [...] nor the powers [...] those by which you rule."

When his disciples heard these things, they were each troubled in their spirit. They couldn't say a thing.

The Disciples' Vision

Another day Jesus came up to them. They said to him, "Master, we've seen you in a dream, because we had great [dreams last] night."

But Jesus said, "Why [...] hidden yourselves?"

And they [said, "We saw] a great [house, with a great] altar [in it, and] twelve people – we'd say they were priests – and a name. And a crowd of people was waiting at the altar [until] the priests [finished receiving] the offerings. We kept waiting too."

[Jesus said], "What were they like?"

And they said, "[Some] fast [for] two weeks. Others sacrifice their own children; others their wives, praising and humbling themselves among each other. Others sleep with men; others murder; yet others commit many sins and do criminal things. [And] the people standing [before] the altar invoke your [name]! And in all their sacrificing, they fill the [altar] with their offerings." When they said this, [they] fell silent because they were troubled.

Jesus said to them, "Why are you troubled? Truly I say to you, all the priests standing before that altar invoke my name. And [again], I say to you, my name has been written on this [house] of the generations of the stars by the human generations. [And they] have shamefully planted fruitless trees in my name." Jesus said to them, "You're the ones receiving the offerings on the altar you've seen. That's the God you serve, and you're the twelve people you've seen. And the animals you saw brought in to be sacrificed are the crowd you lead astray before that altar. [Your minister] will stand up and use my name like that, and [the] generations of the pious will be loyal to him. After him, another person will present [those who sleep around], and another those who murder children, and another those who sleep with men, and those who fast, and the rest of impurity, crime, and error. And those who say, 'We're equal to the angels' – they're the stars that finish everything. It's been said to the human generations, 'Look, God has accepted your sacrifice from the hands of priests,' that is, the minister of error. But the Lord who commands is the Lord over everything. On the last day, they'll be found guilty."

Jesus said [to them], "Stop [sacrificing animals]. You've [offered them] over the altar, over your stars with your angels where they've already been completed. So let them become [...] with you and let them [become] clear."

His disciples [said to him], "Cleanse us from our [sins] that we've committed through the deceit of the angels."

Jesus said to them, "It's not possible [...], nor [can] a fountain quench the fire of the entire inhabited world. Nor can a [city's] well satisfy all the generations, except the great, stable one. A single lamp won't illuminate all the realms, except the second generation, nor can a baker feed all creation under [heaven]."

And [when the disciples heard] these [things], they said to [him], "Master, help us and save us!"

Jesus said to them, "Stop struggling against me. Each one of you has his own star, [and ...] of the stars will [...] what belongs to it [...] I wasn't sent to the corruptible generation, but to the strong and incorruptible generation, because no enemy has ruled [over] that generation, nor any of the stars. Truly I say to you, the pillar of fire will fall quickly and that generation won't be moved by the stars."

Jesus and Judas

Jesus and Judas
And when Jesus [said] these things, he left, [taking] Judas Iscariot with him. He said to him, "The water on the exalted mountain is [from] [...] it didn't come to [water ... the well] of the tree of [the fruit ...] of this realm [...] after a time [...], but came to water God's paradise and the enduring [fruit], because [it] won't corrupt that generation's [walk of life], but [it will exist] for all eternity."

Judas said to [him, "Tell] me, what kind of fruit does this generation have?"

Jesus said, "The souls of every human generation will die; however, when these people have completed the time in the kingdom and the spirit leaves them, their bodies will die but their souls will live, and they'll be taken up."

Judas said, "What will the rest of the human generations do?"

Jesus said, "It's not possible to sow on [rock] and harvest its fruit. In the same way, it's [not possible to sow on] the [defiled] race along with the perishable wisdom [and] the hand which created mortal humans so that their souls may go up to the realms above. [Truly] I say to you, [no ruler], angel, [or] power will be able to see the [places] that [this great], holy generation [will see]."

When Jesus said this, he left.

Judas said, "Master, just as you've listened to all of them, now listen to me too, because I've seen a great vision."

But Jesus laughed when he heard this. He said to him, "Why are you all worked up, you thirteenth demon? But speak up, and I'll bear with you."

Judas said to him, "In the vision, I saw myself. The twelve disciples are stoning me and chasing [me rapidly]. And I also came to the place where [I had followed] you. I saw [a house in this place], and my eyes couldn't [measure] its size. Great people surrounded it, and that house had a roof of greenery. In the middle of the house was [a crowd ...]. Master, take me in with these people!"

[Jesus] answered and said, "Your star has led you astray, Judas," and that "no person of mortal birth is worthy to enter the house you've seen, because that place is reserved for those who are holy. Neither the sun nor the moon will rule there, nor the day, but those who are holy will always stand in the realm with the holy angels. Look, I've told you the mysteries of the kingdom and I've taught you about the error of the stars and [...] sent [on high] over the twelve realms."

Judas said, "Master, surely my seed doesn't dominate the rulers, does it?"

Jesus answered and said to him, "Come, let me [tell] you [about the holy generation. Not so that you'll go there], but you'll grieve much when you see the kingdom and all its generation."

When Judas heard this, he said to him, "What good has it done me that you've separated me from that generation?"

Jesus answered and said, "You'll become the thirteenth, and will be cursed by the other generations and will rule over them. In the last days they'll [...] to you and you won't go up to the holy generation."

Jesus Reveals Everything to Judas

Jesus said, "[Come] and I'll teach you about the [mysteries that no] human [will] see, because there exists a great and boundless realm whose horizons no angelic generation has seen, [in] which is a [great] invisible Spirit, which no [angelic] eye has ever seen, no heart has ever comprehended, and it's never been called by any name.

"And a luminous cloud appeared there. And he (the Spirit) said, 'Let an angel come into being to attend me.' And a great angel, the Self-Begotten, the God of the Light, emerged from the cloud. And because of him, another four angels came into being from another cloud, and they attended the angelic

Self-Begotten. And said the [Self-Begotten], 'Let [a realm] come into being,' and it came into being [just as he said]. And he [created] the first luminary to rule over it. And he said, 'Let angels come into being to serve [it,' and myriads] without number came into being. And he said, '[Let a] luminous realm come into being,' and it came into being. He created the second luminary to rule over it, along with myriads of angels without number to offer service. And that's how he created the rest of the realms of light. And he made them to be ruled, and created for them myriads of angels without number to assist them.

"And Adamas was in the first cloud of light that no angel could ever see among all those called 'God.' And [Adamas begat Seth in] that [place after the] image [of ...] and after the likeness of [this] angel. He made the incorruptible [generation] of Seth appear to the twelve androgynous [luminaries. And then] he made seventy-two luminaries appear in the incorruptible generation according to the Spirit's will. Then the seventy-two luminaries themselves made three hundred sixty luminaries appear in the incorruptible generation according to the Spirit's will so that there'd be five for each. And the twelve realms of the twelve luminaries make up their father, with six heavens for each realm so there are seventy-two heavens for the seventy-two luminaries, and for each one [of them five] firmaments [for a total of] three hundred sixty [firmaments. They] were given authority and a [great] army of angels without number for honor and service, along with virgin spirits [too] for the honor and [service] of all the realms and the heavens with their firmaments.

"Now the crowd of those immortals is called 'cosmos' – that is, 'perishable' – by the father and the seventy-two luminaries with the Self-Begotten and his seventy-two realms. That's where the first human appeared with his incorruptible powers. In the realm that appeared with his generation is the cloud of knowledge and the angel who's called [Eleleth ...] After these things [Eleleth] said, 'Let twelve angels come into being [to] rule over Chaos and [Hades]. And look, from the cloud there appeared an [angel] whose face flashed with [fire] and whose likeness was [defiled] by blood. His name was Nebro, which means 'Rebel.' Others call him Yaldabaoth. And another angel, Saklas, came from the cloud too. So Nebro created six angels – and Saklas (did too) – to be assistants. They brought out twelve angels in the heavens, with each of them receiving a portion in the heavens.

"And the twelve rulers spoke with the twelve angels: 'Let each of you [...] and let them [...] generation [... five] angels:
The first [is Yaoth], who's called 'the Good One.' The second is Harmathoth, [the eye of fire]. The [third] is Galila. The fourth [is] Yobel. The fifth is Adonaios.

"These are the five who ruled over Hades and are the first over Chaos.

"Then Saklas said to his angels, 'Let's create a human being after the likeness and the image.' And they fashioned Adam and his wife Eve, who in the cloud is called 'Life,' because by this name all the generations seek him, and each of them calls her by their names. Now Saklas didn't [command ...] give birth, except [...] among the generations [...] which this [...] and the [angel] said to him, 'Your life will last for a limited time, with your children.'"

Then Judas said to Jesus, "[How] long can a person live?"

Jesus said, "Why are you amazed that the lifespans of Adam and his generation are limited in the place he's received his kingdom with his ruler?"

Judas said to Jesus, "Does the human spirit die?"

Jesus said, "This is how it is. God commanded Michael to loan spirits to people so that they might serve. Then the Great One commanded Gabriel to give spirits to the great generation with no king – the spirit along with the soul. So the [rest] of the souls [...] light [... the] Chaos [...] seek [the] spirit within you which you've made to live in this flesh from the angelic generations. Then God caused knowledge to be brought to Adam and those with him, so that the kings of Chaos and Hades might not rule over them."

[Then] Judas said to Jesus, "So what will those generations do?"

Jesus said, "Truly I say to you, the stars complete all these things. When Saklas completes the time span that's been determined for him, their first star will appear with the generations, and they'll finish what's been said. Then they'll sleep around in my name, murder their children, and [they'll ...] evil and [...] the realms, bringing the genera-

tions and presenting them to Saklas. [And] after that [...] will bring the twelve tribes of [Israel] from [...], and the [generations] will all serve Saklas, sinning in my name. And your star will [rule] over the thirteenth realm." Then Jesus [laughed]. [Judas] said, "Master, why [are you laughing at me?"

Jesus] answered [and said], "I'm not laughing [at you but] at the error of the stars, because these six stars go astray with these five warriors, and they'll all be destroyed along with their creations."

Then Judas said to Jesus, "What will those do who've been baptized in your name?"

The Betrayal

Jesus said, "Truly I say [to you], this baptism [which they've received in] my name [...] will destroy the whole generation of the earthly Adam. Tomorrow they'll torture the one who bears me. Truly I [say] to you, no hand of a mortal human [will fall] upon me. Truly [I say] to you, Judas, those who offer sacrifices to Saklas [...] everything that's evil. But you'll do more than all of them, because you'll sacrifice the human who bears me. Your horn has already been raised, your anger has been kindled, your star has ascended, and your heart has [strayed]. Truly [I say to you], your last [... and] the [... the thrones] of the realm have [been defeated], the kings have grown weak, the angelic generations have grieved, and the evil [they sowed ...] is destroyed, [and] the [ruler] is wiped out. [And] then the [fruit] of the great generation of Adam will be exalted, because before heaven, earth, and the angels, that generation from the realms exists. Look, you've been told everything. Lift up your eyes and see the cloud with the light in it and the stars around it. And the star that leads the way is your star." Then Judas looked up and saw the luminous cloud, and he entered it. Those standing on the ground heard a voice from the cloud saying, "[. . . the] great [generation . . .] and [. . .]." And Judas didn't see Jesus anymore.

Immediately there was a disturbance among [the] Jews, more than

[...] Their high priests grumbled because he'd gone into the guest room to pray. But some scribes were there watching closely so they could arrest him during his prayer, because they were afraid of the people, since they all regarded him as a prophet.

And they approached Judas and said to him, "What are you doing here? Aren't you Jesus' disciple?"

Then he answered them as they wished. Then Judas received some money and handed him over to them.

GOSPEL OF TRUTH

Prologue

The Gospel of Truth is a joy for those who've received grace from the Father of Truth, that they might know him through the power of the Word that came from the fullness – the one who's in the thought and mind of the Father. They call him "Savior." That's the name of the work he'll do to redeem those who had become ignorant of the Father. And the term "the Gospel" is the revelation of hope, the discovery of those who search for him.

Error and Forgetfulness

Since all searched for the one from whom they had come – all were within him, the uncontainable, inconceivable one who's beyond every thought – (and) since ignorance of the Father caused anguish and terror, and the anguish grew thick like a fog, so that no one could see – Error was strengthened. It worked on its own matter in vain, not knowing the Truth.

It happened in a deluding way, as it (Error) prepared with power, in beauty, a substitute for the Truth. Now this wasn't humiliating for the uncontainable, inconceivable one, because the anguish and forgetfulness and delusion of deceit were like nothing, whereas the Truth is established, unchangeable, unperturbed, beyond beauty. Because of this, disregard Error, since it has no root.

It happened in a fog concerning the Father. It happens (now) since it (Error) prepares works in forgetfulness and terror, so that with them it (Error) might attract those in the middle and imprison them.

The forgetfulness of Error wasn't revealed; it wasn't a [thought] from the Father. Forgetfulness didn't come into being from the Father, though it did come into being because of him. What comes into being within him is the knowledge, which was revealed so that forgetfulness might be dissolved, and the Father might be known. Forgetfulness came into being because the Father was unknown, so when the Father comes to be known, forgetfulness won't exist anymore.

45

The Gospel

This is the Gospel of the one they search for, revealed to those who are complete through the mercies of the Father, the hidden mystery. Through it (the Gospel), Jesus Christ enlightened those who were in darkness through forgetfulness. He enlightened them; he showed them a Way, and the Way is the Truth which he taught them.

As a result, Error was angry. It pursued him. It was threatened by him and brought to nothing. They nailed him (Jesus) to a tree, and he became the fruit of the Father's knowledge. However, it (the fruit) didn't cause destruction when it was eaten, but those who ate it were given joy in the discovery. He discovered them in himself and they discovered him in themselves.

As for the uncontainable, inconceivable one – the Father, the complete one who made all – all are within him, and all need him. Although he kept their completion within himself which he didn't give to all, the Father wasn't jealous. Indeed, what jealousy is there between him and his members? For if, like this, the generation [received the completion,] they couldn't have come [...] the Father. He keeps their completion within himself, giving it to them to return to him with a unitary knowledge in completion. He's the one who made all, and all are within him, and all need him.

Like someone who's unknown, he wants to be known and loved – because what did all need if not the knowledge of the Father?

He became a guide, peaceful and leisurely. He came and spoke the Word as a teacher in places of learning. Those who were wise in their own estimation came up to him to test him, but he confounded them because they were vain. They hated him because they weren't wise in Truth. After all of them, all the little children came too; theirs is the knowledge of the Father. When they were strengthened, they received teaching about the Father's expressions. They knew and they were known; they received glory and they gave glory. In their hearts the living Book of the Living was revealed, which was written in the thought and mind [of the] Father, and before the [foundation] of all within his incomprehensibility. This (book) is impossible to take, since it permits the one who takes it to be killed. No one could've been revealed among those who'd been entrusted with salvation unless the book had appeared. Because of this, the merciful and faithful Jesus patiently suffered until he took that book, since he knows that his death is life for many.

When a will hasn't yet been opened, the wealth of the deceased master of the house is hidden; so too all were hidden while the Father of all was invisible. They were from him, from whom every realm comes. Because of this:

Jesus was revealed, put on that book, was nailed to a tree, and published the Father's edict on the cross.

Oh, what a great teaching!

Drawing himself down to death, he clothed himself in eternal life, stripped himself of the perishable rags, and clothed himself in incorruptibility, which no one can take from him.

When he entered the empty realms of terror, he passed through those who were stripped by forgetfulness, being knowledge and completion, proclaiming the things that are in the heart [...] teach those who will [receive teaching].

The Book of the Living

Now those who will receive teaching [are] the living who are written in the Book of the Living. They receive teaching about themselves, and they receive it from the Father, returning to him again.

Since the completion of all is in the Father, it's necessary for all to go up to him. Then, if someone has knowledge, they receive what are their own, and he draws them to himself, because the one who's ignorant is in need. And it's a great need, since they need what will complete them. Since the completion of all is in the Father, it's necessary for all to go up to him, and for each one to receive what are their own. He inscribed these things beforehand, having prepared them to give to those who came out from him.

Those whose names he knew beforehand were called at the end, so that the one who has knowledge is the one whose name the Father has called, because those whose name hasn't been spoken are ignorant. Indeed, how can someone hear if their name hasn't been called? For the one who's ignorant until the end is a delusion of forgetfulness, and they'll dissolve with it. Otherwise, why do these miserable ones have no name? Why do they have no voice?

So if someone has knowledge, they're from above. If they're called, they hear, they reply, and they turn to the one who calls them. And they go up to him, and they know how they are called. Having knowledge, they do the will of the one who called them, they want to please him, and they receive rest. Each one's name becomes their own. The one who has knowledge like this knows where they come from and where they're going. They know like one who, having been drunk, turns from their drunkenness, and having returned to themselves, restores what are their own.

He's returned many from Error. He went before them to the realms from which they had moved away. They had received Error because of the depth of the one who surrounds every realm, though nothing surrounds him. It's a great wonder that they were in the Father, not knowing him, and that they were able to come out by themselves, since they weren't able to grasp and know the one in whom they were. He revealed his will as knowledge in harmony with all that emanated from him.

This is the knowledge of the living book which he revealed to the generations at the end, letters from him revealing how they're not vowels or consonants, so that one might read them and think they're meaningless, but they're letters of the Truth – they speak and know themselves. Each letter is a complete thought, like a book that's complete, since they're letters written by the Unity, the Father having written them so that the generations, by means of his letters, might know the Father.

The Return to Unity

His Wisdom meditates on the Word, his teaching speaks it, his knowledge has revealed it, his patience is a crown upon it, his joy is in harmony with it, his glory has exalted it, his image has revealed it, his rest has received it, his love made a body around it, his faith embraced it.

In this way, the Word of the Father goes out in all, as the fruit [of] his heart and an expression of his will. But it supports all. It chooses them and also takes the expression of all, purifying them, returning them to the Father and to the Mother, Jesus of infinite sweetness.

The Father reveals his bosom, and his bosom is the Holy Spirit. He reveals what's hidden of himself; what's hidden of himself is his Son – so that through the mercies of the Father, the generations may know him and cease their work in searching for the Father, resting in him and knowing that this is the rest. He's filled the need and dissolved its appearance – its appearance is the world in which it served, because where there's envy and strife there's need, but where there's Unity there's completion. Since need came into being because the Father wasn't known, when the Father is known, from then on, need will no longer exist. As someone's ignorance dissolves when they gain knowledge, and as darkness dissolves when the light appears, so also need dissolves in completion. So the appearance is revealed from then on, but it'll dissolve in the harmony of Unity.

For now, their works lie scattered. In time, Unity will complete the realms. Within Unity each one will receive themselves, and within knowledge they'll purify themselves from multiplicity into Unity, consuming matter within themselves like fire, and darkness by light, death by life. If indeed these things have happened to each one of us, then it's right for us to think about all, so that this house will be holy and silent for the Unity.

The Parable of the Jars

It's like some who've left their home, having jars that weren't any good in places. They broke them, but the master of the house doesn't suffer any loss. Instead he rejoices, because in place of the bad jars are ones that are full and complete. For this is the judgment that's come from above; it's judged everyone. It's a drawn, two-edged sword which cuts both ways. The Word, which is in the hearts of those who speak it, appeared. It isn't just a sound, but it was incarnated (embodied).

A great disturbance arose among the jars, because some were empty, others filled; some provided for, others poured out; some purified, others broken. All the realms were shaken and disturbed, because they didn't have order or stability. Error was anxious. It didn't know what to do; it grieved, mourned, and hurt itself, because it knew nothing. The knowledge, which is its (Error's) destruction, approached it (Error) and all that emanated from it. Error is empty, with nothing inside it.

Truth came into their midst, and all that emanated knew it. They welcomed the Father in Truth with a complete power that joins them with the Father. Truth is the Father's mouth; the Holy Spirit is his tongue. Everyone who loves the Truth and are joined to the Truth are joined to the Father's mouth. By his tongue they'll receive the Holy Spirit. This is the revelation of the Father and his manifestation to his generations. He revealed what was hidden of himself; he explained it, because who has anything, if not the Father alone?

Coming into Being

Every realm emanates from him. They know they've come out from him like children who are from someone who's completely mature. They knew they hadn't yet received form or a name. The Father gives birth to each one. Then, when they receive form from his knowledge, although they're really within him, they don't know him. But the Father is complete, knowing every realm that's within him. If he wants to, he reveals whomever he wants, giving them a form and a name. He gives a name to them, and causes those to come into being who, before they come into being, are ignorant of the one who made them.

I'm not saying, then, that those who haven't yet come into being are nothing, but they exist in the one who will want them to come into being when he wants, like a later time. Before everything is revealed, he knows what he'll produce. But the fruit which he hasn't yet revealed doesn't yet know anything, nor does it do anything. In addition, every realm which is itself in the Father is from the one who exists, who establishes them from what doesn't exist. For those who have no root have no fruit either. They think to themselves, "I've come into being," but they'll dissolve by themselves. Because of this, those who didn't exist at all won't exist.

The Parable of the Nightmares

What, then, did he want them to think of themselves? He wanted to them to think, "I've come into being like the shadows and phantoms of the night." When the light shines on the terror which they received, they know that it's nothing. In this way, they were ignorant of the Father, whom they didn't see. Since it was terror and disturbance and instability and doubt and division, many illusions were at work among them, and vain ignorance, like they were deep in sleep and found themselves in nightmares. Either they're running somewhere, or unable to run away from someone; or they're fighting, or being beaten; or they've fallen from heights, or fly through the air without wings. Sometimes, too, it's like someone is killing them, even though no one's chasing them; or they themselves are killing those around them, covered in their blood. Until those who are going through all these nightmares can wake up, they see nothing, because these things are nothing.

That's the way it is with those who've cast off ignorance like sleep. They don't regard it as anything, nor do they regard its other works as real, but they abandon them like a dream in the night. They value the knowledge of the Father like they value the light. The ignorant have acted like they're asleep; those who've come to knowledge have acted like they've awakened. Good for the one who returns and awakens! Blessed is the one who's opened the eyes of those who can't see! The Holy Spirit hurried after them to revive them. Having given a hand to the one who lay on the ground, it set them up on their feet, because they hadn't yet arisen. It gave them the knowledge of the Father and the revelation of the Son, because when they saw him and heard him, he granted them to taste him and to grasp the beloved Son.

The Revelation of the Son

When he was revealed, he taught them about the Father, the uncontainable one, and breathed into them what's in the thought, doing his will. When many had received the light, they turned to him. For the material ones were strangers, who didn't see his form or know him. For he came by means of fleshly form, and nothing could block his path, because incorruptibility can't be grasped. Moreover, he said new things while he spoke about what's in the Father's heart and brought out the complete Word. When the light spoke through his mouth, and by his voice gave birth to life, he gave them thought, wisdom, mercy,

salvation, and the Spirit of power from the infinity and sweetness of the Father. He caused punishments and torments to cease, because they led astray into Error and bondage those who needed mercy. He dissolved and confounded them with knowledge. He became:
a Way for those who were led astray, knowledge for those who were ignorant, a discovery for those who were searching, strength for those who were wavering, and purity for those who were impure.

The Parable of the Sheep

He's the shepherd who left behind the ninety-nine sheep which weren't lost. He went and searched for the one which was lost. He rejoiced when he found it, because ninety-nine is a number expressed with the left hand. However, when the one is found, the numerical sum moves to the right hand. In this way, what needs the one – that is, the whole right hand – draws what it needs, takes it from the left hand, and moves it to the right, so the number becomes one hundred. This is a symbol of the sound of these numbers; this is the Father.
Even on the Sabbath, he worked for the sheep which he found fallen in the pit. He saved the life of the sheep, having brought it up from the pit, so that you may know in your hearts – you're children of the knowledge of the heart – what is the Sabbath, on which it isn't right for salvation to be idle, so that you may speak of the day which is above, which has no night, and of the light that doesn't set, be-

cause it's complete. Speak then from the heart, because you're the completed day, and the light that doesn't cease dwells within you. Speak of the Truth with those who search for it, and of knowledge with those who've sinned in their Error.

Doing the Father's Will

Strengthen the feet of those who stumble, and reach out to those who are sick. Feed those who are hungry, and give rest to those who are weary. Raise up those who want to arise, and awaken those who sleep, because you're the understanding that's unsheathed. If strength is like this, it becomes stronger.

Be concerned about yourselves. Don't be concerned about other things which you've rejected from yourselves. Don't return to eat your vomit. Don't be eaten by worms, because you've already shaken it off. Don't become a dwelling-place for the devil, because you've already brought him to naught. Don't strengthen your obstacles which are collapsing, as though you're a support. For the lawless one is nothing, to be treated more harshly than the just, doing his works among others.

Do then the Father's will, because you're from him. For the Father is sweet, and goodness is in his will. He knows what's yours, that you may find rest in them. For by the fruits they know what's yours, because the children of the Father are his fragrance, since they're from the grace of his expression. Because of this, the Father loves his fragrance, and reveals it in every place. And

when it mixes with matter, it gives his fragrance to the light, and in tranquility he causes it to rise above every form and every sound. For it's not the ears that smell the fragrance, but it's the Spirit that smells, and draws the fragrance to itself, and sinks down into the Father's fragrance. He shelters it, then, and takes it to the place from which it came, from the first fragrance which has grown cold. It's something in a soul-endowed delusion, like cold water sunk into loose earth. Those who see it think that it's just earth. Afterwards, it dissolves again. If a breath draws it, it becomes warm. So the fragrances which are cold are from the division. Because of this, faith came. It dissolved the division, and it brought the fullness that's warm with love, so that the cold may not return, but rather the unitary thought of completion.

Restoring what was Needed

This is the Word of the Gospel of the discovery of the fullness, which comes for those who are awaiting the salvation which is coming from above. The hope for which they're waiting is waiting for those whose image is light with no shadow in it. If at that time the fullness comes, the need of matter doesn't come through the infinity of the Father, who comes to give time to the need – although no one can say that the incorruptible one will come like this. But the depth of the Father multiplied, and the thought of Error didn't exist with him. It's something that's fallen, which is easily set upright in the discovery of the one who's to come to what he'll return, because the return is called "repentance."

Because of this, incorruptibility breathed out. It followed after the one who sinned, so that they might rest, because forgiveness is what remains for the light in need, the Word of fullness. For the doctor hurries to the place where there's sickness, because that's what he (or she) wants to do. The one in need, then, doesn't hide it, because one (the doctor) has what they need. In this way the fullness, which has no need but fills the need, is what he provided from himself to fill up what's needed, so that they might receive grace; because when they were in need, they didn't have grace. Because of this, a diminishing took place where there is no grace. When what was diminished was restored, what they needed was revealed as fullness. This is the discovery of the light of Truth which enlightened them, because it doesn't change.

Because of this, they spoke of Christ in their midst: "Seek, and those who were disturbed will receive a return – and he'll anoint them with ointment." The ointment is the mercy of the Father, who will have mercy on them. But those whom he anointed are those who have been completed, because full jars are the ones that are anointed. But when the anointing of one dissolves, it empties, and the cause of the need is the place where the ointment leaks, because a breath and its power draws it. But from the one who has no need, no seal is removed, nor is anything emptied, but what it needs

is filled again by the Father, who's complete.

The Father's Paradise

He's good. He knows his plants, because he planted them in his paradise. Now his paradise is a place of rest. This is the completion in the Father's thought, and these are the words of his meditation. Each of his words is the work of his one will in the revelation of his Word. When they were still in the depths of his thought, the Word – which was the first to come out – revealed them along with a mind that speaks the one Word in a silent grace. He was called "the Thought," since they were in it before being revealed. It happened, then, that he was the first to come out at the time when it pleased the one who wanted it. Now the Father rests in his will, and is pleased with it.

Nothing happens without him, nor does anything happen without the will of the Father, but his will is incomprehensible. His trace is the will, and no one can know him, nor does he exist for people to scrutinize so that they might grasp him, but when he wills, what he wills is this – even if the sight doesn't please them in any way before God – the will of the Father, because he knows the beginning of all of them, and their end, for in the end he'll greet them directly. Now the end is receiving knowledge of the one who's hidden; this is the Father, from whom the beginning has come, and to whom all who've come out from him will return. They were revealed for the glory and the joy of his name.

The Father's Name

Now the name of the Father is the Son. He's the one who first gave a name to the one who comes out from him, who was himself, and he gave birth to him as a Son. He gave him his name which belonged to him. He's the one to whom everything around the Father belongs. The name and the Son are his. It's possible for him to be seen; the name, however, is invisible, because it alone is the mystery of the invisible which comes to ears that are filled completely with it by him. For indeed, the Father's name isn't spoken, but it's revealed through a Son.

In this way, then, the name is great. Who, then, will be able to utter a name for him, the great name, except him alone to whom the name belongs, and the children of the name, those in whom the Father's name rests, and who themselves, in turn, rest in his name? Since the Father is unbegotten, it's he alone who gave birth to him for himself as a name, before he had made the generations, so that the Father's name might be over their head as Lord, which is the true name, confirmed in his command in complete power. For the name isn't from words and naming; the name, rather, is invisible.

He gave a name to him alone. He alone sees him, he alone having the power to give him a name, because whoever doesn't exist has no name. For what name will they give one who doesn't exist? But the one who exists, exists also with his name, and he alone knows it, and he's given a name to him alone. This is the Father; his name is the Son. He didn't hide it within, then, but it existed. The Son alone gave a name. The name, then, belongs to the Father, as the name of the Father is the beloved Son. Where, indeed, would he find a name, except from the Father?

But doubtless one will ask their neighbor, "Who is it who'll give a name to the one who existed before them, as if offspring didn't receive a name from those who gave them birth?" First, then, it's right for us to consider what the name is. It's the true name, the name from the Father, because it's the proper name. So he didn't receive the name on loan, the way others do, according to the form in which each one will be produced. This, then, is the proper name. There's no one else who gave it to him. But he's unnameable, indescribable, until the time when he who's complete spoke of him alone. And it's he who has the power to speak his name and to see him.

So when it pleased him that his beloved name should be his Son, and he gave the name to him who came out from the depth, he disclosed his secrets, knowing that the Father is without evil. Because of this, he brought him out so that he might speak about the place, and his resting place from which he had come, and to glorify the fullness, the greatness of his name, and the Father's sweetness.

The Place of Rest

Each one will speak about the place from which they came, and they'll hurry to return again to the place where they received their restoration to receive from the place where they were, receiving a taste from that place and receiving nourishment, receiving growth.

And their place of rest is their fullness. All that have emanated from the Father, then, are fullnesses, and the roots of all that have emanated from him are within the one who caused them all to grow. He gave them their destinies. Then each one was revealed, so that through their own thought [...] for the place to which they send their thought is their root, which takes them up through all the heights, up to the Father. They embrace his head, which is rest for them, and they're grasped, approaching him, as though to say that they receive his expression by means of kisses. But they're not revealed in this way, because they neither exalted themselves, nor wanted the Father's glory, nor did they think of him as trivial or harsh or wrathful; but he's without evil, unperturbed, and sweet. He knows every realm before they've come into existence, and he has no need to be instructed.

This is the way of those who possess something of the immeasurable greatness from above, as they wait for the complete one alone, who's a Mother for them. And they don't go down to Hades, nor do they have envy or groaning, nor death within them, but they rest in the one who rests, not striving nor twisting around in the search for Truth. But they themselves are the Truth, and the Father is within them, and they're in the Father, being complete. They're undivided from the truly good one. They don't need anything, but they rest, refreshed in the Spirit. And they'll listen to their root. They'll devote themselves to those things that they'll find in their root and not suffer loss to their soul. This is the place of the blessed; this is their place.

Conclusion

As for the others, then, may they know, where they're at, that it's not right for me, having come to the place of rest, to say anything else, but I'll come to be in it, and will devote myself continually to the Father of all and the true brothers (and sisters), those upon whom the Father's love is emptied and in whose midst there is no need. They're the ones who are revealed in Truth; they exist in the true eternal life, and they speak of the light that's complete and that's filled with the Father's seed, and that's in his heart and in the fullness. His Spirit rejoices in it, and glorifies the one in whom it existed, because he's good. And his children are complete, and worthy of his name, because he's the Father. It's children like this that he loves.

GOSPEL OF PETER

Pilate and Herod

1 But of the Jews no one washed the hands, neither Herod nor one of his judges, and when they didn't want to wash Pilate stood up. 2 And then Herod the king, commanding the Lord to be brought, said to them, "Do whatever I commanded you to do to him."

Joseph Requests Jesus' Body

3 And Joseph stood there, the friend of Pilate and the Lord. And seeing that they were about to crucify him, he went to Pilate and asked for the body of the Lord for burial. 4 And Pilate, having sent to Herod, asked him for the body.

5 And Herod said, "Brother Pilate, even if someone hadn't asked for him, we would've buried him, since also Sabbath is beginning, because it's written in the Law, 'The sun shouldn't set on one who's been killed.'"

The Lord is Tortured and Mocked

And he handed him over to the people before the first day of their festival of the Unleavened Bread. 6 And those having taken the Lord were running, pushing him, and saying, "Let's drag the Son of God, having authority over him!"

7 And they were clothing him with purple, and sat him on the seat of judgment, saying, "Judge justly, king of Israel!" 8 And one of them brought a thorn crown and placed it on the Lord's head.

9 And other bystanders were spitting in his face, and others slapped his cheeks. Others were piercing him with a reed, and some were scourging him, saying, "With this honor, let's honor the Son of God!"

The Lord is Crucified

10 And they brought two wrongdoers and crucified the Lord in the middle of them, but he was silent as if having no pain. 11 And when they set up the cross, they wrote that "This is the king of Israel." 12 And having laid the clothes in front of him, they divided them and cast lots for them.

13 But one of those wrongdoers rebuked them, saying, "We, because of the wrong that we did, are suffering this way, but this one, having

become Savior of humanity, what wrong has he done to you?"

14 And they were angry at him. They commanded that the legs not be broken, so that he might die tortured.

The Lord Dies

15 And it was mid-day, and darkness held fast over all Judea. And they were troubled and distressed lest the sun set, since he was still living. It's written to them, "The sun shouldn't set on one who's been killed." 16 And one of them said, "Give him bile with sour wine to drink." And having mixed it, they gave it to him to drink. 17 And they fulfilled all things and accumulated the sins on their head. 18 And many were going around with lanterns, thinking it was night, and some fell down. 19 And the Lord cried out, saying, "My Power, the Power, you've left me!" And when he said this, it was taken up. 20 And that very hour, the veil of the temple in Jerusalem was torn in two.

The Lord is Buried

21 And then they drew the nails from the Lord's hands and placed him on the earth. And the whole earth was shaken, and great fear came.

22 Then the sun shone and it was found to be the ninth hour. 23 And the Jews rejoiced, and gave Joseph his body to bury, since he had seen all the good he had done. 24 And having taken the Lord, he washed him and wrapped him in linen, and brought him into his own tomb, which was known as "Joseph's Garden."

People React

25 Then the Jews, the elders, and the priests, knowing how much wrong they had done to themselves, began to mourn and say, "Woe to our sins. The judgment and the end of Jerusalem is near!"

26 But I with my companions was grieved, and being wounded in mind, we were hiding, because we were being sought by them as wrongdoers and as wanting to burn the temple. 27 On top of all this, we were fasting, sitting, mourning, and weeping night and day until the Sabbath.

The Tomb is Secured

28 And the scribes, the Pharisees, and the elders gathered together with one another, having heard that all the people were grumbling, beating their chests, and saying, "If at his death these greatest signs have happened, see how just he was!"

29 The elders were afraid, and went to Pilate, begging him and saying, 30 "Give us soldiers, that we may guard his grave for three days, lest his disciples come and steal him, and the people think that he rose from the dead, and do us wrong."

31 And Pilate gave them Petronius the centurion, with soldiers to guard the tomb. And elders and scribes went with them to the grave. 32 And having rolled a great stone to the centurion and the soldiers, all who were there placed it at the door of the grave. 33 And they put seven

seals on it, and having pitched a tent there, they kept watch.

Men Descend from Heaven

34 Now when the morning of the Sabbath dawned, a crowd from Jerusalem and the surrounding countryside went that they might see the grave that had been sealed. 35 But during the night before the Lord's day dawned, while the soldiers were watching two by two as guards, there was a great voice in heaven. 36 And they saw the heavens being opened, and two men descended from there, having much radiance, and they approached the tomb. 37 But that stone which had been placed at the door rolled away by itself, and made way in part, and the tomb was opened, and both the young men went in.

Emerging from the Tomb

38 Then those soldiers seeing it woke up the centurion and the elders, because they were there too, keeping guard. 39 And while they were explaining to them what they saw, again they saw three men coming out of the tomb, with the two supporting the one, and a cross following them. 40 And the heads of the two reached as far as heaven, but that of the one being led by them reached beyond the heavens.

41 And they heard a voice from the heavens, saying, "Have you proclaimed to those who sleep?"

42 And a response was heard from the cross: "Yes!"

Reporting to Pilate

43 Then those men decided to go with each other and report these things to Pilate. 44 And while they were still considering, again the heavens were seen being opened, and a certain man descended and went into the grave. 45 Having seen these things, those with the centurion hurried by night to Pilate, having left the tomb they were watching, and described all that they saw, being greatly distressed, and saying, "Truly he was the Son of God!"

46 In response Pilate said, "I'm clean of the blood of the Son of God, and this is clear to us."

47 Then all who came were begging him, and encouraging him to command the centurion and the soldiers to say nothing about what they saw. 48 "It's better for us," they said, "to be guilty of a great sin in front of God than to fall into the hands of the Jewish people and be stoned." 49 So Pilate commanded the centurion and the soldiers to say nothing.

Mary Magdalene Goes to the Tomb

50 Now at dawn on the Lord's day, Mary Magdalene, a disciple of the Lord, afraid because of the Jews (since they were inflamed by anger), had not done at the Lord's grave what women are accustomed to do for their loved ones who've died.

51 Taking her friends with her, she went to the grave where he was laid. 52 And they were afraid lest the Jews might see them, and were saying, "If on the day he was crucified we weren't able to weep and

mourn, even now we might do this on his grave. 53 But who will roll away for us the stone that has been placed at the door of the grave so that we might go in, sit by him, and do our duties? 54 Because the stone is great, and we're afraid lest someone sees us. And if we aren't able, at least let's place at the door what we're bringing in memory of him, and we'll weep and mourn until we return to our house."

Encounter at the Tomb

55 And having gone, they found the tomb had been opened. And having approached, they bent down and saw there a certain young man sitting in the middle of the tomb. He was beautiful, having clothed himself with a long, shining robe. He said to them, 56 "Why did you come? Whom do you seek? Not that one who was crucified? He arose and went away. But if you don't believe, bend down and see where he was lying, that he's not there, because he arose and went to where he came from."

57 Then the women were afraid, and fled.

The Disciples Depart

58 Now it was the last day of the Unleavened Bread, and many people were leaving, returning to their houses, the festival being over. 59 But we, the twelve disciples of the Lord, were weeping and grieving, and each of us grieving because of what had happened, returned home. 60 But I, Simon Peter, and my brother Andrew, having taken our nets, went off to the sea. And with us was Levi, the son of Alphaeus, whom the Lord...

GOSPEL OF Q

Chapter 3

2 John [...] 3 [...] the entire region around the Jordan [...]

7 He told the crowds who went out to be baptized, "You offspring of vipers, who warned you to flee from the fury to come? 8 So bear fruit worthy of change! Don't start to say to yourselves, 'We have Abraham for our ancestor,' because I tell you that God is able to raise up children for Abraham from these stones.

9 "Even now the axe lies at the root of the trees! So every tree that doesn't bear good fruit is cut down and thrown into the fire.

16 "I baptize you in water, but one who's greater than I will come, the thong of whose sandals I'm not worthy to loosen. He'll baptize you in holy Spirit and fire. 17 His pitchfork is in his hand to clean out his threshing floor, and to gather the wheat into his barn; but he'll burn up the chaff with a fire that can't be put out."

21 [...] Jesus [...] baptized [...] heaven opened 22 and [...] the Spirit [...] on him [...] Son [...]

Chapter 4

1 Jesus was led by the Spirit into the desert 2 to be tested by the devil. He didn't eat anything for forty days [...] he was hungry.

3 And the devil told him, "If you're God's Son, tell these stones to turn into bread."

4 And Jesus replied, "It's written, 'A person shouldn't live on bread alone.'"

9 The devil led him to Jerusalem, set him on the pinnacle of the temple, and said, "If you're God's Son, throw yourself down, 10 because it's written, 'God will put God's angels in charge of you,' 11 and 'On their hands they'll bear you up, so that you don't dash your foot against a stone.'"

12 And in reply Jesus told him, "It's been said, 'Don't test the Lord, your God.'"

5 Then the devil took him to a very high mountain and showed him all the empires of the world and their glory and told him, 6 "I'll give you all these, 7 if you'll bow to me."

8 And in reply Jesus told him, "It's written: 'Bow to the Lord your God, and serve God only.'"

13 And the devil left him.

16 [...] Nazareth [...]

Chapter 6

20 He looked up at his disciples and said:

Blessed are you who are poor, because yours is God's reign.

21 Blessed are you who are hungry, because you'll be full.

Blessed are you who mourn, because you'll be comforted.

22 "Blessed are you when they criticize you, persecute you, and spread lies about you because of the Son of Humanity. 23 Rejoice and be glad, because your heavenly reward is great; for that's how they persecuted the prophets before you.

27 "Love your enemies, 28 and pray for those who persecute you. 35 You'll become children of your Father, who makes the sun rise on those who are evil and those who are good, and sends rain on those who are just and those who are unjust.

29 "When someone slaps you on the cheek, offer the other one too. When someone sues you for your shirt, give them your coat too. (QMt 5:41) When someone makes you go one mile, go an extra mile. (QLk 6:30) Give to everyone who asks you, and when someone borrows your things, don't ask for them back.

31 "Treat people how you want them to treat you. 32 If you love those who love you, why should you be rewarded? Don't even toll collectors do that? 34 And if you lend to those from whom you expect repayment, why should you be rewarded?

Don't even gentiles do that? 36 Be merciful, just like your Father.

37 "Don't judge, and you won't be judged; (QMt 7:2) because you'll be judged the way that you judge. (QLk 6:38) And you'll be measured the way that you measure.

39 "Can someone who can't see guide another person who can't see? Won't they both fall into a pit? 40 A disciple isn't greater than their teacher. It's enough for the disciple to become like their teacher.

41 "Why do you see the speck that's in your brother's eye, but don't consider the beam that's in your own eye? 42 How can you tell your brother, 'Let me get that speck out of your eye,' when you don't see the beam that's in your own eye? You hypocrite! First get the beam out of your own eye, and then you'll see clearly to get the speck out of your brother's eye.

43 "No good tree bears rotten fruit, nor does a rotten tree bear good fruit. 44 Every tree is known by its own fruit. Are figs gathered from thorns, or grapes from thistles? 45 The person who's good brings good things out of their good treasure, and the person who's evil brings evil things out of evil treasure, because one's mouth speaks from the overflow of the heart.

46 "Why do you call me, 'Master, Master,' and don't do what I say? 47 Everyone who hears my words and acts on them 48 can be compared to someone building a house on bedrock. When the rain poured, and the floods came, and the winds blew and pounded that house, it didn't collapse, because it was founded on bedrock. 49 But everyone who hears

my words and doesn't act on them is like someone who built a house on the sand. When the rain poured, and the floods came, and the winds blew and pounded that house, it collapsed immediately. How great was its fall!"

Chapter 7

1 And so when it happened that he had finished saying these things, he went to Capernaum. 3 A centurion approached and begged him and said, "My boy is sick."

And Jesus told him, "I'll go heal him."

6 And the centurion replied, "Master, I'm not worthy for you to come under my roof. 7 Just say the word, and my boy will be healed. 8 I'm also in a chain of command, with soldiers under me. I tell one, 'Go,' and they go; I tell another, 'Come,' and they come; I tell my servant, 'Do this,' and they do it."

9 Jesus was amazed when he heard this. He told his followers, "I'm telling you the truth: I haven't found such trust even in Israel."

18 When John heard all these things, he sent his disciples 19 to ask him, "Are you the coming one, or should we look for someone else?"

22 And he replied to them, "Go and tell John what you've heard and seen. Those who:

are blind, regain their sight; have challenges of mobility, walk; have leprosy, are cured; are deaf, hear; are dead, are raised up; are poor, have good news announced to them.

23 "Blessed is the one who isn't scandalized by me."

24 And when they had left, he started to talk to the crowds about John. "What did you go out into the desert to see? A reed shaken by the wind? 25 Then what did you go out to see? A man wearing fancy clothes? Look, those who wear fancy clothes live in palaces. 26 Then what did you go out to see? A prophet? Yes, I'm telling you, and much more than a prophet, 27 because it's written about him:

Look, I'm sending my messenger ahead of you, who'll prepare your path for you.

28 "I'm telling you that John is greater than anyone who's been born, but whoever is least in God's reign is still greater than he, 29 because John came to you [...] the toll collectors and [...] 30 but [...] him.

31 "To what, then, can I compare this generation? What's it like? 32 It's like children sitting in the marketplaces calling to each other:

We played the flute for you, but you didn't dance. We mourned, But you didn't weep.

33 "John didn't come eating or drinking, and you say, 'He's demonized!' 34 The Son of Humanity has come eating and drinking, and you say, 'Look, a glutton and a drunk, a friend of toll collectors and outsiders!' 35 But Wisdom is vindicated by her children."

Chapter 9

57 And someone told him, "I'll follow you wherever you go."

58 And Jesus told him, "Foxes have holes and birds of the sky have nests, but the Son of Humanity has nowhere to rest his head."

59 But someone else told him, "Master, let me go and bury my father first."

60 But he told him, "Follow me, and let the dead bury their own dead."

Chapter 10

2 He told his disciples, "The harvest is plentiful, but the workers are few. So ask the Lord of the harvest to send workers into the fields. 3 Go! Look, I send you out like lambs among wolves. 4 Don't carry a purse, bag, sandals, or staff. Don't greet anyone on the road. 5 Whenever you enter a house, first say, 'Peace to this house.' 6 If a peaceful person is there, let your blessing rest on them; but if not, take back your blessing. 7 Stay in the same house, eating and drinking whatever they give you, because the worker is worthy of their wages. Don't move around from house to house. 8 If they welcome you in whatever town you enter, eat whatever is set before you. 9 Heal those who are sick there and tell them, 'God's reign is at hand!' 10 But if they don't welcome you in whatever town you enter, when you're leaving that town, 11 shake the dust from your feet. 12 I'm telling you that on that day, it'll be better for Sodom than for that town! 13 "Woe to you, Chorazin! Woe to you, Bethsaida! If the great deeds done in your midst had been done in Tyre and Sidon, they would have changed a long time ago in sackcloth and ashes. 14 But it will be better for Tyre and Sidon than for you in the judgment! 15 And you, Capernaum, you don't think you'll be ex-alted to heaven, do you? You'll fall down to Hades!

16 "Whoever welcomes you welcomes me, and whoever welcomes me welcomes the one who sent me."

21 Then he said, "Thank you, Father, Lord of heaven and earth, for hiding these things from the wise and learned and revealing them to children. Yes, Father, this was what you wanted. 22 My Father has given me everything. No one knows who the son is except the Father, or who the Father is except the son, and the one to whom the son wants to reveal him.

23 "Blessed are the eyes that see what you see. 24 I'm telling you that many prophets and rulers wanted to see what you see, but didn't see it; and to hear what you hear, but didn't hear it."

Chapter 11

2 "When you pray, say:
Father, We honor your holy name. Let your reign come. 3 Give us our daily bread today. 4 Forgive us our debts, because we too forgive everyone who's indebted to us. Don't put us in harm's way.

9 "I'm telling you, ask and you'll receive. Look and you'll find. Knock and it'll be opened for you, 10 because everyone who asks receives. The one who looks finds. To one who knocks it'll be opened. 11 Which of you would give your child a stone if they ask for bread? 12 Or who would give them a snake if they ask for fish? 13 So if you, evil as you are, know how to give good gifts to your children, how much more

will the heavenly Father give good things to those who ask!"

14 He was casting out a demon that couldn't speak. And when the demon came out, the person who couldn't speak started talking. And the crowds were amazed. **15** But some said, "He casts out demons with the power of Beelzebul, the ruler of the demons!"

17 Knowing what they were thinking, he told them, "Every divided empire is devastated, and a divided house will fall. **18** If the Enemy is divided, how will its empire endure? **19** But if Beelzebul gives me power to cast out demons, who gives your people power to cast them out? So they prove you wrong. **20** But if I cast out demons by the finger of God, then God's reign has come to you!

23 "Whoever isn't with me is against me, and whoever doesn't gather with me, scatters. **24** When the impure spirit leaves someone, it journeys through arid places looking for rest, but doesn't find it. Then it says, 'I'll return to the home I left'; **25** and when it comes back, it finds it swept and organized. **26** Then it goes out and brings seven other spirits that are even more evil, and they move in and live there. That person ends up even worse off than before."

16 Some demanded him to show a sign. **29** But he said, "This is an evil generation. It demands a sign, but no sign will be provided except the sign of Jonah! **30** As Jonah became a sign to the Ninevites, so the Son of Humanity will be a sign to this generation. **31** The queen of the South will rise up in the judgment with this generation and will condemn it,

because she came from the ends of the earth to hear Solomon's wisdom; and look, something greater than Solomon is here. **32** The people of Nineveh will rise up in the judgment with this generation and will condemn it, because they changed in response to Jonah's announcement, and look, something greater than Jonah is here.

33 "No one lights a lamp and hides it, but puts it on a lampstand, and it enlightens everyone in the house. **34** Your eye is the body's lamp. If your eye is single, your whole body is full of light. If your eye is evil, your whole body is dark. **35** So if the light within you is dark, how dark it is!

42 "Woe to you, Pharisees! You tithe your mint, dill, and cumin, but you ignore justice, mercy, and trust. You should've done these without ignoring the others.

39 "Woe to you, Pharisees! You clean the outside of the cup and dish, but inside they're full of greed and decadence. **41** Clean the inside of the cup, and its outside will be clean too.

43 "Woe to you, Pharisees! You love the place of honor at banquets, the front seat in the synagogues, and accolades in the marketplaces. **44** Woe to you, because you're like unmarked graves that people walk on without knowing it.

46 "And woe to you, lawyers! You load people with burdens that are hard to bear, but you yourselves won't even lift a finger to help them. **52** "Woe to you, lawyers! You shut people out of God's reign. You didn't enter, and didn't let those enter who are trying to do so.

47 "Woe to you, because you build the tombs of the prophets whom your ancestors killed. 48 You prove that you're the descendants of your ancestors. 49 So Wisdom said, 'I'll send prophets and sages. Some of them they'll kill and persecute.' 50 So this generation will be guilty of the blood of all the prophets shed from the beginning of the world, 51 from the blood of Abel to the blood of Zechariah, who died between the altar and the sanctuary. Yes, I'm telling you that this generation will be held responsible.

Chapter 12

2 "Nothing is concealed that won't be revealed, nor hidden that won't be made known. 3 Whatever I tell you in the dark, say in the light; and whatever you hear whispered in your ear, announce from the housetops.
4 "Don't be afraid of those who kill the body but can't kill the soul. 5 Instead, fear the one who can kill both the soul and the body in Gehenna.
6 "Don't five sparrows cost two pennies? Yet not one of them will fall to the ground without your Father's permission. 7 Even the hairs of your head are all numbered. Don't be afraid, because you're more valuable than many sparrows.
8 "Everyone who publicly acknowledges me, the Son of Humanity will acknowledge in front of the angels. 9 But whoever publicly denies me will be denied in front of the angels. 10 Whoever speaks out against the Son of Humanity will be forgiven, but whoever speaks out against the holy Spirit won't be forgiven. 11

When they bring you before the synagogues, don't worry about how or what you should say, 12 because the holy Spirit will teach you at that time what you should say.

33 "Don't store treasures for yourselves here on earth, where moth and rust destroy and robbers break in and steal. Instead, store treasures for yourselves in heaven, where neither moth nor rust destroy and where robbers don't break in or steal. 34 Because where your treasure is, there your heart will be too.

22 "So I'm telling you not to worry about your life, about what you'll eat; or about your body, what you'll wear. 23 Isn't life more than food, and the body more than clothes? 24 Think about how the ravens don't sow, reap, or gather into barns, yet God feeds them. Aren't you more valuable than the birds?

25 "Which of you can grow any taller by worrying? 26 And why worry about clothes? 27 Look at how the lilies grow. They don't work or spin, yet I'm telling you that even Solomon in all his glory wasn't dressed like one of these. 28 But if God clothes the grass of the field, which is here today and is thrown into the oven tomorrow, won't God clothe you even more, you who have little trust? 29 So don't worry. Don't ask, 'What are we going to eat?' or 'What are going to drink?' or 'What are we going to wear?' 30 The gentiles look for all these things, but your Father knows that you need all of them. 31 Instead, look for God's reign, and all these things will be given to you too.

39 "But know this: If the master of the house had known at what time the robber was coming, he wouldn't have let his house be broken into. 40 You too should be ready, because the Son of Humanity is coming when you don't expect it.

42 "Then who is the trustworthy and wise servant who was entrusted by their master to hand out rations to the household at the right time? 43 Blessed is that servant whose master finds them doing so when he comes. 44 I'm telling you the truth: he'll put them in charge of all that he owns. 45 But if that servant says in their heart, 'My master is late,' and starts to beat the other servants and to eat and drink with those who are addicted to alcohol, 46 the master of that servant will come when they don't expect it, at a time that they don't know, and will rip them to shreds and throw them out with those who are untrustworthy.

49 "I came to cast fire on the earth, and how I wish it were already kindled! 51 Do you think that I came to bring peace on earth? I didn't come to bring peace, but a sword! 53 Because I've come:

To pit son against father, daughter against her mother, daughter-in-law against her mother-in-law."

54 He told them, "When it's evening, you say, 'There'll be good weather, because the sky is red.' 55 In the morning, 'There'll be wintry weather today, because the sky is red and threatening.' 56 You know how to interpret the appearance of the sky. Why don't you know how to interpret the time?

58 "When you're going with your adversary, do your best to settle the case on the way there, or else your adversary may hand you over to the judge, and the judge to the officer, and the officer may throw you into prison. 59 I'm telling you that you won't get out of there until you've paid the very last penny!

Chapter 13

18 "What is God's reign like, and to what should I compare it? 19 It can be compared to a mustard seed which someone sowed in their garden. It grew and became a tree, and the birds of the sky nested in its branches."

20 "And again: To what should I compare God's reign? 21 It can be compared to yeast which a woman hid in fifty pounds of flour until it was all fermented.

24 "Enter through the narrow door, because many will try to enter, though only a few will succeed. 25 When the master of the house gets up and locks the door, you'll be standing outside and knocking on it, saying, 'Master, open up for us!'

"But he'll reply, 'I don't know you.'

26 "Then you'll start saying, 'We ate and drank with you, and you taught in our streets.'

27 "But he'll tell you, 'I don't know you. Get away from me, you criminals!'

29 "Many will come from east and west and dine 28 with Abraham, Isaac, and Jacob in God's reign, but you'll be thrown out into the outer darkness, where there'll be weeping and grinding of teeth. 30 Those who are last will be first, and those who are first will be last.

34 "Jerusalem, Jerusalem, who kills the prophets and stones those who are sent to her! How often I would've gathered your children together, like a hen gathers her chicks under her wings, but you wouldn't let me! 35 Look, your house is left abandoned. I'm telling you that you won't see me until the time comes when you say, 'Blessed is the one who comes in the name of the Lord!'

Chapter 14

11 "Whoever exalts themselves will be humbled, and whoever humbles themselves will be exalted.

16 "Someone planning a great dinner invited many guests. 17 When dinner was ready, they sent their servant to tell the invited guests, 'Come, because it's ready now!'

18 "One excused himself because of his farm. 19 Another excused himself because of his business. 21 The servant went back and told their master all this. Then the master of the house became angry and told the servant, 23 'Go out to the highways and urge people to come in so that my house may be filled.'

26 "Whoever doesn't hate father and mother can't be my disciple, and whoever doesn't hate son and daughter can't be my disciple. 27 Whoever doesn't carry their own cross and follow me can't be my disciple.

34 "Salt is good, but if it's lost its flavor, how can you get it back? 35 It's no good for the soil or the manure pile. It's thrown away.

Chapter 15

4 "Which of you, if you had a hundred sheep and lost one of them, wouldn't leave the ninety-nine in the hills and go after the one that got lost? 5 When they find it, 7 I'm telling you that they'll rejoice over it more than over the ninety-nine that didn't wander off.

8 "Or what woman with ten silver coins, if she loses one, wouldn't light a lamp, sweep the house, and look everywhere until she found it? 9 When she finds it, she calls together her friends and neighbors and says, 'Rejoice with me, because I've found the coin that I'd lost!' 10 In the same way, I'm telling you, the angels rejoice over one wrongdoer who changes.

Chapter 16

13 "No one can follow two masters, because they'll either hate one and love the other, or they'll be devoted to one and despise the other. You can't serve both God and Mammon. 16 "The Torah and the prophets were announced until John. Since then, God's reign has been violated, and the violent plunder it. 17 But it's easier for heaven and earth to disappear than for one smallest letter or one tiny pen stroke to drop out of the Torah.
18 "Everyone who divorces his wife and remarries is unfaithful to her, and whoever marries someone who's divorced is unfaithful too.

Chapter 17

1 "There's no way that people won't be tripped up, but woe to the one

who causes it! 2 It'd be better for them if a millstone were hung around their neck and they were thrown into the sea, than for them to trip up one of these little ones.

3 "If your brother offends you, correct him. If he changes, forgive him. 4 Even if he offends you seven times a day, then forgive him seven times. 5 "If you had trust as big as a mustard seed, you could tell this mulberry tree, 'Be uprooted and be planted in the sea,' and it would obey you."

20 When he was asked when God's reign would come, he replied to them, "The coming of God's reign can't be observed. 21 Nor will they say, 'Look over here!' or 'Look over there!' Because look, God's reign is among you.

23 "If they tell you, 'Look, he's in the desert!' don't go out; or 'Look, he's inside,' don't follow, 24 because as the lightning flashes in the east and is seen in the west, so will the Son of Humanity be in his day. 37 Where there's a corpse, there the vultures will gather.

26 "As it was in the days of Noah, so it will be in the day of the Son of Humanity. 27 In those days they were eating and drinking, marrying and giving in marriage, until the day that Noah entered the ark, and the flood came and swept all of them away. 30 That's what it will be like on the day the Son of Humanity is revealed.

33 "Whoever tries to find their life will lose it, but whoever loses their life for my sake will find it.

34 "I'm telling you, there'll be two men in the field; one will be taken and the other will be left. 35 There'll be two women grinding at the mill; one will be taken and the other will be left.

Chapter 19

12 "A certain person went on a trip. 13 He called ten of his servants, gave them ten minas, and told them, 'Do business with this until I return.'

15 "After a long time the master of those servants returned to settle accounts with them. 16 The first one came and said, 'Master, your mina has made ten more minas.'

17 "He told him, 'Well done, good servant! Since you've been trustworthy with a little, I'll put you in charge of much.'

18 "The second came and said, 'Master, Your mina has made five minas.'

19 "He told him, 'Well done, good servant! Since you've been trustworthy with a little, I'll put you in charge of much.'

20 "The other came and said, 'Master, 21 I know you're a strict man, reaping where you didn't sow and gathering where you didn't scatter. I went out and hid your mina in the ground. Look, here's what belongs to you!'

22 "He told him, 'You evil servant! You knew that I reap what I didn't sow and gather where I didn't scatter? 23 So why didn't you invest my money with the bankers? Then when I returned, I would've gotten it back, with interest. 24 So take the mina away from him and give it to the one who has ten minas, 26 because everyone who has will be given more, but whoever doesn't have will lose even what little they do have.'

Chapter 22

28 "You who've followed me **30** will sit on thrones, judging the twelve tribes of Israel."

Apocryphon of James

Salutation

[James writes] to [...]: Peace [to you from] peace, [love from] love, [grace] from grace, [faith] from faith, life from holy life!

Prologue

Since you asked me to send you a secret book revealed to Peter and me by the Lord, and I could neither turn you down nor talk to you (directly), [I've written] it in Hebrew letters and have sent it to you – and to you alone. But as a minister of the salvation of the saints, take care not to tell too many people about this book, which the Savior didn't want to tell all twelve of us, the disciples. But blessed are those who will be saved through the faith of this message.

Ten months ago, I sent you another secret book that the Savior revealed to me. But think of that one as revealed to me, James. And this one [...]

The Savior Appears

Now all twelve disciples [were] sitting together [at the same time] recalling what the Savior had told each of them, whether privately or publicly, and organizing it in books. [But I] was writing what went into [my book]. Look! The Savior appeared, [after] he had left [us, while we were watching] for him. Five hundred and fifty days after he had risen from the dead, we told him, "You went away and left us!"

But Jesus said, "No, but I'll return to the place from which I came. If you want to come with me, come on!"

They all replied and said, "We'll come if you tell us to."

He said, "Truly I tell you, no one will ever enter the kingdom of heaven because I ordered it, but because you yourselves are full. Leave James and Peter to me so that I may fill them."

After he called these two, he took them aside and told the rest to keep doing what they were doing.

Being Filled

The Savior said, "You've received mercy. [...] they [haven't] understood. Don't you want to be filled? Your hearts are drunk. Don't you, then, want to be sober? Then be ashamed! From now on, awake or asleep, remember that you've seen the Son of Humanity, and have talked to him in person, and have heard him in person.

Woe to those who've seen the Son of Humanity! Blessed are those who haven't seen that man, mingled with him, spoken to him, or heard a thing he's said. Yours is life! Know, then, that he healed you when you were sick, so that you might reign.

Woe to those who've found relief from their sickness, because they'll relapse into sickness. Blessed are those who haven't been sick and have found relief before getting sick. Yours is the kingdom of God! So I tell you, be full and leave no space within you empty, because the one who is coming will be able to mock you."

Then Peter replied, "Three times you've told us to be [full, but] we are full."

In [response the Savior] said, "That's why I [told] you ['be full'] – so that you won't [be lacking. Those who are lacking] won't [be saved]. It's good to be full [and] bad [to be lacking]. So just as it's good for you to be lacking and bad for you to be full, whoever is full is also lacking. One who's lacking isn't filled the same way that someone who's lacking is filled, and anyone who's full gets everything they need. So it's right to be lacking while it's possible to fill you, and to be filled while it's possible to be lacking, so that you can [fill] yourselves more. So [be] full of the Spirit but lacking in reason, because reason is of the soul – in fact, it is soul."

The Cross and Death

In response I told him, "Lord, we can obey you if you want us to, because we've abandoned our fathers, our mothers, and our villages, and have followed you. So help us not to be tempted by the devil, the evil one."

In response the Lord said, "What good is it to you if you do the will of the Father, and he doesn't give it to you as a gift when you're tempted by Satan? But if you're oppressed by Satan and persecuted and do (God's) will, I [say] that he'll love you, make you my equal, and regard [you] as having become beloved through his forethought by your own choice. So won't you stop loving the flesh and being afraid of sufferings? Or don't you know that you haven't yet been abused, unjustly accused, locked up in prison, illegally condemned, crucified by reason, nor buried in the sand as I myself was by the evil one? Do you dare to spare the flesh, you for whom the Spirit is a surrounding wall? If you consider how long the world existed <before> you, and how long it will exist after you, you'll find that your life is a single day and your sufferings a single hour. For the good won't come into the world. So scorn death and take thought for life! Remember my cross and my death, and you'll live!"

But in response I told him, "Lord, don't teach us about the cross and death, because they're far from you."

In response the Lord said, "Truly I tell you, no one will be saved unless they [believe] in my cross, [because] the kingdom of God belongs to those who've believed in my cross. So become those who seek death, like the dead who seek life; because what they seek is revealed to them. So what do they have to worry about? When you turn to the subject of death, it will teach you about election. Truly I tell you, no one who's afraid of death will be saved, because the kingdom of <God> belongs to those who are put to death. Become better than I; be like the child of the Holy Spirit."

Prophecies and Parables

Then I asked him, "Lord, how can we prophesy to those who ask us to prophesy to them? Because there are many who ask us, and who look to us to hear a message from us."

In response the Lord said, "Don't you know that the head of prophecy was cut off with John?"

But I said, "Lord, is it possible to remove the head of prophecy?

The Lord told me, "When you realize what 'head' means, and that prophecy comes from the head, understand what 'its head was removed' means. At first I spoke to you in parables, and you didn't understand. Now I speak to you openly, and you still don't perceive. But to me you were a parable among parables and something visible out in the open.

"Be eager to be saved without being urged. Rather, be ready on your own and, if possible, get there before me, because the Father will love you.

"Come to hate hypocrisy and evil intention, because intention is what produces hypocrisy, and hypocrisy is far from the truth.

"Don't let the kingdom of heaven wither, because it's like a date palm shoot whose fruit has poured down around it. It sent out some leaves, and after they sprouted, they made their productivity dry up. This is also what happened with the fruit that came from this single root; when it was picked, many acquired fruit. Wouldn't it truly be good if you could produce the new plants now? <You> would find it.

"Since I've already been glorified like this, why do you hold me back in my eagerness to go? For after the [labor], you've made me stay with you another eighteen days because of the parables. For some people, it was enough <to listen> to the teaching and understand 'The Shepherds,' 'The Seed,' 'The Building,' 'The Lamps of the Young Women,' 'The Wage of the Workers,' and 'The Silver Coins and the Woman.'

"Be eager about the message! The first stage of the message is faith, the second is love, and the third is works, because from these comes life.

"The message is like a grain of wheat. When someone sowed it, they believed in it, and when it sprouted, they loved it, because they saw many grains in place of one. And after they worked, they were saved because they prepared it as food, then kept enough left over to be sown. This is also how you yourselves can receive the kingdom of heaven. Unless you receive it through knowledge, you won't be able to find it.

Be Saved

"So I tell you, be sober! Don't be deceived. And many times I told you all together – and also to you alone, James, I've said – 'Be saved!' And I've commanded you to follow me, and I've taught you what to do in the face of the rulers.

"See that I've come down, spoken, been torn, and taken my crown when I saved you, because I came down to dwell with you so that you'll dwell with me. And when I found your houses without ceilings, I lived in the houses that could receive me at the time I came down.

"Trust me about this, my brothers (i.e., Peter and James). Understand what the great light is. The Father doesn't need me, because a father doesn't need a son, but it's the son who needs the father. I'm going to him, because the Father of the Son doesn't need you.

"Listen to the message, understand knowledge, love life, and no one will persecute or oppress you other than you yourselves.

"You wretches! You poor devils! You hypocrites of the truth! You falsifiers of knowledge! You sinners against the Spirit! Can you still bear to listen, when you should've been speaking from the beginning? Can you still bear to sleep, when you should've been awake from the beginning so that the kingdom of heaven might receive you?

"Truly I tell you, it's easier for a holy person to fall into defilement, and for an enlightened person to fall into darkness, than for you to reign – or not reign.

"I've remembered your tears, your grief, and your pain. They're far from us. But now, you who are outside of the Father's inheritance, weep where it's necessary, grieve, and proclaim what's good as the Son is ascending as he should.

"Truly I tell you, if I had been sent (only) to those who would listen to me and had spoken to them (alone), I wouldn't ever have gone up from the earth. Now, then, be ashamed for these things!

"Look, I'll leave you and go away. I don't want to continue with you anymore, just as you yourselves don't want that. Now, then, follow me eagerly. That's why I tell you that I came down for you. You're beloved; you'll bring life for many. Call on the Father. Pray to God often, and (God) will be generous with you.

"Blessed is the one who has seen you with (God) when (God) was proclaimed among the angels and given glory among the holy ones; yours is life. Rejoice and be glad as children of God. Keep (God's) will so that you may be saved. Accept my warning and save yourselves. I'm pleading for you with the Father, who will forgive you much."

Few Have Found the Kingdom

And when we heard these things, we were delighted, because we had been depressed about the things we mentioned before.

But when he saw us rejoicing, he said, "Woe to you who need an advocate! Woe to you who need grace! Blessed will be those who've spoken out and acquired grace for themselves!

"Be like foreigners. How are they viewed in your city? Why are you disturbed when you cast yourselves out on your own and separate yourselves from your city? Why do you leave your dwelling on your own and make it available for those who want to live in it? You outcasts and runaways! Woe to you, because you'll be caught!

"Or do you think that the Father is a lover of humanity, or is persuaded by prayers, or grants grace to one on behalf of another, or puts up with one who seeks?

"(God) knows about desire and what the flesh needs. It's not this (flesh) which desires the soul, because without the soul, the body doesn't sin, just as the soul isn't saved without the spirit. But if the soul is saved without evil, and the spirit is also saved, then the body becomes sinless. For it's the spirit that raises the soul, but the body that kills it; that is, (the soul) kills itself.

"Truly I tell you, (God) won't ever forgive the sin of the soul or the guilt of the flesh, because no one who's worn the flesh will be saved. Do you think that many have found the kingdom of heaven? Blessed is the one who's seen oneself (at) the fourth (stage) in heaven."

Know Yourselves

When we heard these things, we felt depressed. But when he saw that we were depressed, he said, "I'm telling you this so that you may know yourselves. For the kingdom of heaven is like an ear of grain after it had sprouted in a field. And when it had ripened, it scattered its fruit, and again it filled the field with ears of grain for another year. You, too, be eager to reap an ear of the grain of life for yourselves so that you may be filled with the kingdom!

"And as long as I'm with you, pay attention to me and trust in me, but when I leave you, remember me. And remember me because when I was with you, you didn't know me. Blessed are those who've known me. Woe to those who've heard and haven't believed! Blessed will be those who haven't seen, [but ...]!

"And once again I [appeal to] you, because I'm revealed to you building a house very valuable to you when you take shelter under it, just as it will be able to support your neighbors' house when it threatens to fall. Truly I tell you, woe to those for whom I was sent down to this place! Blessed will be those who go up to the Father. Again I warn you, you who are. Be like those who are not so that you may be with those who are not.

"Don't let the kingdom of heaven become a desert within you. Don't be haughty because of the light that enlightens, but behave toward yourselves the way that I've behaved toward you. I've put myself under the curse for you, so that you may be saved."

Final Words

But in response to these comments Peter said, "Sometimes you urge us on to the kingdom of heaven, and again at other times you turn us away, Lord. Sometimes you persuade and draw us to faith and promise us life, and again at other times you cast us out of the kingdom of heaven."

But in response the Lord told us, "I've given you faith many times. Moreover, I've revealed myself to you, James, and you haven't known me. Now again, I see you rejoicing often. And when you're delighted about the promise of life, nevertheless you're sad and depressed when you're taught about the kingdom.

"But through faith and knowledge, you've received life. Despise rejection when you hear it, but when you hear the promise, rejoice all the more. Truly I tell you, whoever will receive life and believe the kingdom will never leave it – not even if the Father wants to banish them!

"This is all I'm going to tell you up to this point, but now I'll go up to the place from which I came. But when I was eager to go, you cast me out, and instead of accompanying me, you've chased me away. But be attentive to the glory that awaits me, and when you've opened your hearts, listen to the hymns that await me up in heaven, because today I need to sit at the right hand of the Father.

"Now I've spoken (my) last word to you, and I'll leave you, because a chariot of the Spirit has taken me up, and from now on I'll strip myself so that I may clothe myself. But pay attention: Blessed are those who've proclaimed the Son before his coming down so that when I've come, I might go up. Blessed three times over are those who [were] proclaimed by the Son before they came

to be, so that you may have a portion with them."

Heavenly Ascent

When he said these things, he left. But Peter and I knelt down, gave thanks, and sent our hearts up to heaven. We heard with our ears, and saw with our eyes, the cacophony of wars and a trumpet blare and a great commotion.

And when we passed beyond that place, we sent our minds up higher and heard with our ears hymns and angelic praises and angelic rejoicing. And heavenly majesties were singing hymns, and we rejoiced too.

After this again, we wanted to send our spirit up to the Majesty. And after we went up, we weren't allowed to see or hear anything, because the other disciples called us and asked us, "What did you hear from the Teacher?" And, "What did he tell you?" And, "Where did he go?"

But we responded, "He went up." And, "He's given us his right hand and promised us all life, and he revealed to us children who are to come after us, after telling [us] to love them, as we'd be [saved] because of them."

Conclusion

And when they heard, they believed the revelation indeed, but were angry about those to be born. So, not wanting to give them a scandal, I sent each of them to a different place. But I myself went up to Jerusalem, praying to acquire a portion with the beloved ones who will be revealed.

And I pray that the beginning may come from you, because this is how I can be saved, since they'll be enlightened through me, by my faith – and through another (faith) that's even better than mine, because I want mine to be the lesser.

So do your best to be like them, and pray that you acquire a portion with them. Apart from what I've said, the Savior didn't disclose a revelation to us for them. We do indeed proclaim a portion with those for whom the proclamation was made – those whom the Lord has (accepted as) children.

INFANCY GOSPEL OF JAMES

Chapter 1: Joachim's Plight

1 In the histories of the twelve tribes of Israel, Joachim was a very rich man. And he doubled the gifts he offered to the Lord, saying to himself, "One is from my surplus for all the people, and the other is to the Lord God for forgiveness, to atone for me."

2 Now the great day of the Lord was approaching, and the people of Israel were offering their gifts. But Reubel stood before him and said, "It's not right for you to offer your gifts first, since you haven't had a child in Israel."

3 And Joachim was very grieved and went to the (history) of the twelve tribes of the people, saying to himself, "I'll look in the (history) of the twelve tribes of Israel to see whether I'm the only one who hasn't had a child in Israel." And he searched, and found that all the just people in Israel had raised children. And he remembered that in the last days of the patriarch Abraham, the Lord God gave him a son, Isaac.

4 And Joachim was very grieved, and didn't go to his wife, but gave himself to the wilderness and pitched his tent there. And Joachim fasted forty days and forty nights, saying to himself, "I won't go down for food or drink until the Lord my God considers me. Prayer will be my food and drink."

Chapter 2: Anna's Plight

1 Now his wife, Anna, mourned and lamented for two reasons. She said, "I lament that I'm a widow and that I don't have a child."

2 Now the great day of the Lord was approaching, and her servant Juthine said to her, "How long are you going to humiliate your soul? Look, the great day of the Lord has approached, and it's not right for you to grieve. But take this headband which the leader of the workplace gave me. It's not right for me to wear it, since I'm your servant, and it has a royal mark."

3 And Anna said, "Get away from me! I won't do this. The Lord God has greatly humiliated me. Maybe a trickster gave this to you, and you've come to get me to share in your sin."

And Juthine the servant said, "Why should I curse you, since you haven't heard my voice? The Lord God has made your womb infertile, to give you no fruit in Israel."

4 And Anna was very grieved, and removed her garment of mourning, washed her head, and put on her wedding garment. And at about the ninth hour she went down into her garden to walk around. She saw a laurel tree and sat down under it. And after resting, she petitioned the Lord. She said, "God of my ancestors, bless me and hear my prayer, as you blessed our mother Sarah and gave her a son, Isaac."

Chapter 3: Anna's Lament

1 Anna looked intently to heaven and saw a nest of sparrows in the laurel tree. And Anna lamented, saying to herself,

"Woe is me! Who gave birth to me? What womb bore me? I was born as a curse before the people of Israel and have been despised; they've mocked me and banished me from the Temple of the Lord my God.

2 "Woe is me! What am I like? I'm not like the birds of heaven, because even the birds of heaven are fruitful before you, Lord.

"Woe is me! What am I like? I'm not like the animals, because even the animals are fruitful before you, Lord.

"Woe is me! What am I like? I'm not like the wild beasts of the earth, because even the wild beasts of the earth are fruitful before you, Lord.

3 "Woe is me! What am I like? I'm not like these waters, because even these waters are serene yet churn, and their fish bless you, Lord.

"Woe is me! What am I like? I'm not like this earth, because the earth produces her fruits when it's time and blesses you, Lord."

Chapter 4: The Lord's Promise

1 And look! An angel of the Lord stood nearby, saying to her, "Anna, Anna, the Lord has heard your prayer. You'll conceive and give birth, and your offspring will be spoken of through the whole world." And Anna said, "As the Lord God lives, whether I give birth to a boy or a girl, I'll bring it as a gift to the Lord my God, and it will minister to him all the days of its life."

2 And look! Two angels came, saying to her, "Look, Joachim, your husband, is coming with his flocks." For an angel of the Lord had gone down to Joachim, saying, "Joachim, Joachim, the Lord God has heard your prayer. Go down from here. Look, your wife, Anna, has conceived in her womb."

3 And immediately Joachim went down and called the shepherds, saying to them, "Bring here to me ten lambs without spot or blemish, and the ten lambs will be for the Lord God. And bring me twelve tender calves for the priests and the elders. And a hundred male goats for all the people."

4 And look! Joachim came with his flocks, and Anna stood at the gate. And she saw Joachim coming with his flocks, and immediately ran and flung herself around his neck, saying, "Now I know that the Lord God has greatly blessed me. For look! The widow is no longer a widow,

and look! The one without a child in her womb has conceived."

And Joachim rested for the first day in his house.

Chapter 5: Mary's Birth

1 And the next day, he was offering his gifts, saying to himself, "If the Lord God is reconciled to me, the plate worn by the priest will make it clear to me." And Joachim offered his gifts and paid attention to the priest's plate as he went up to the altar of the Lord. And he didn't see sin in it. And Joachim said, "Now I know that the Lord God has been reconciled to me and has sent all my sins away from me." And he went down from the Temple of the Lord justified and went into his house.

2 And about six months were completed, and in the seventh month she gave birth. And Anna said to her midwife, "What is it?"

And the midwife said, "It's a girl!"

And Anna said, "My soul is magnified this day!" And she laid down her child.

And when her days were completed, Anna cleansed her flow of blood. And she gave her breast to the child, and gave her the name Mary.

Chapter 6: Mary's First Year

1 And day by day, the child grew stronger. When she was six months old, her mother stood her on the ground to test whether she could stand. And walking seven steps, she came to her mother's breast, and her mother caught her up, saying, "As the Lord my God lives, you won't walk on this ground again until I bring you into the Temple of the Lord."

And she made a sanctuary in her bedroom and didn't allow anything sacrilegious or impure to pass through it. And she called the pure daughters of the Hebrews, and they played with her.

2 And when the child grew to be a year old, Joachim made a great feast, and called the chief priests, and the priests, and the scribes, and the elders, and all the people of Israel. And Joachim brought the child to the priests, and they blessed her, saying, "God of our ancestors, bless this child and give her a name that'll be spoken forever among all generations."

And all the people said, "So be it. Amen!"

And they brought her to the chief priests, and they blessed her, saying, "Most High God, look upon this child, and bless her with a final blessing which can't be surpassed."

3 And her mother took her up to the sanctuary of her bedroom and gave her breast to the child. And Anna made a song to the Lord God, saying:

"I'll sing a holy song to the Lord my God, because God has visited me, and has removed the criticism of my enemies.

"And the Lord God has given me the fruit of God's justice, singular yet manifold before God.

"Who will report to Reubel's people that Anna nurses a child? 'Listen, listen, twelve tribes of Israel: Anna nurses a child!'"

And Anna rested in the sanctuary of her bedroom. And she went and ministered to them. When dinner was finished, they went down rejoicing and glorifying the God of Israel.

Chapter 7: Mary Goes to the Temple

1 And she cared for her child through the months. When she was two years old, Joachim said, "Let's take her to the Temple of the Lord, so that we may keep the promise we made, so that the Lord won't be angry with us and find our gift unacceptable."

But Anna said, "Let's wait until her third year, so that she won't seek her father or mother."

And Joachim said, "Let's wait."

2 And the child became three years old, and Joachim said, "Let's call the pure daughters of the Hebrews. And let them take their lamps, and let them be lit, so that the child won't turn back, and her heart won't be drawn away from the Temple of the Lord." And they did so until they went up to the Temple of the Lord. And the priest welcomed her, kissed her, and said, "The Lord God has magnified your name among all the generations. Through you, the Lord will reveal his redemption of the people of Israel in the last days."

3 And he sat her down on the third step of the altar, and the Lord God poured grace upon her. And she danced on her feet, and all the house of Israel loved her.

Chapter 8: Mary Turns Twelve

1 And her parents went down, marveling and praising and glorifying the Lord God that the child hadn't turned back. And Mary was in the Temple of the Lord. She was nurtured like a dove, and received food from the hand of an angel.

2 And when she became twelve years old, there was a council of the priests, saying, "Look, Mary has been in the Temple of the Lord twelve years. What should we do about her so that she won't pollute the sanctuary of the Lord our God?" And they said to the chief priest, "You stand at the altar of the Lord. Go in and pray about her, and if the Lord God reveals anything to you, we'll do it."

3 And the chief priest went in, taking the robe with twelve bells into the Holy of Holies, and prayed about her. And look! An angel of the Lord stood nearby, saying, "Zechariah, Zechariah, go out and assemble the widowers of the people, and let them each bear a staff. And whomever the Lord God points out with a sign, she'll be his wife."

And the heralds went down through the whole surrounding area of Judea, and sounded the trumpet of the Lord. And look! All the men rushed in.

Chapter 9: Joseph Protects Mary

1 And Joseph threw down his axe, and went to their meeting. And when they had all gathered, they went to the priest with their staffs. And having taken all their staffs, he went into the Temple and prayed. And when he had finished the prayer, he took the staffs, went out, and gave them back. But there wasn't a sign among them. And

Joseph took his staff last, and look! A dove went from the staff, and flew upon Joseph's head. And the priest said to Joseph, "You've been chosen to welcome the virgin of the Lord into your own care."

2 But Joseph refused, saying, "I have sons and am an old man, but she's young. I won't be a laughingstock among the people of Israel."

And the priest said, "Joseph, fear the Lord your God, and remember what God did to Dathan, Abiron, and Kore; how the earth opened and swallowed them all because of their rebellion. And now fear, Joseph, so that these things won't happen in your house."

3 And being afraid, Joseph welcomed her into his care, and said to her, "Mary, I've taken you from the Temple of the Lord, and now I bring you to my house. I'm going away to build houses, but I'll come back to you. The Lord will protect you."

Chapter 10: The Veil of the Temple

1 And there was a council of the priests, saying, "Let's make a veil for the Temple of the Lord."

And the priest said, "Call the pure virgins from the tribe of David to me." And the officers went out and searched and found seven. And the priest remembered that the child Mary was from the tribe of David and pure before God. And the officers went out and brought her.

2 And they brought them into the Temple of the Lord, and the priest said, "Cast lots for me to see who will spin the gold and the white and the linen and the silk and the violet and the scarlet and the true purple."

And the lot for the true purple and scarlet fell to Mary. And she took them into her house. This was the time that Zechariah fell silent, and Samuel took his place until Zechariah could speak. And Mary took the scarlet and was spinning it.

Chapter 11: The Annunciation

1 And she took the pitcher and went to fill it with water, and look! A voice was saying to her, "Rejoice, blessed one! The Lord is with you. Blessed are you among women."

And Mary looked around to the right and the left, to see where the voice might be coming from. And she became terrified and went into her house. And setting down the pitcher, she took up the purple and sat upon her throne and spun the purple.

2 And look! An angel of the Lord stood before her, saying, "Don't fear, Mary, because you've found grace before the Lord of All. You'll conceive from God's word."

And hearing this, Mary questioned herself, saying, "Will I conceive from the Lord, the living God, and give birth like all women give birth?"

3 And the angel of the Lord said to her, "Not like that, Mary, because the power of God will overshadow you, so the holy one who will be born from you will be called the Son of the Most High. And you'll call his name Jesus, because he'll save his people from their sins."

And Mary said, "Look, I'm the servant of the Lord. May it be to me according to your word."

Chapter 12: Mary Visits Elizabeth

1 And she made the purple and the scarlet, and she took it to the priest. And taking it, the priest blessed her and said, "Mary, the Lord God has magnified your name, and you'll be blessed among all the generations of the earth."

2 And Mary rejoiced and went to her cousin Elizabeth. And she knocked at the door. And Elizabeth heard, flung down the scarlet, and rushed to the door. And she opened it and blessed her and said, "How is it that the mother of my Lord should come to me? Because look, the one in me leaped and blessed you!"

But Mary forgot the mysteries which Gabriel the angel had told her. And she looked intently into heaven and said, "Lord, who am I, that all the women of the earth will bless me?"

3 And she spent three months with Elizabeth. And day by day, her womb grew larger, and Mary was afraid. She went to her house and hid herself from the people of Israel. She was sixteen years old when these mysteries happened to her.

Chapter 13: Joseph Questions Mary

1 And she was in her sixth month. And look! Joseph came from his building, and came into the house, and found her pregnant. And he struck his face and flung himself on the ground in sackcloth and wept bitterly, saying, "How can I look to the Lord God? What prayer can I say about this young girl, since I took her as a virgin from the Temple of the Lord God and didn't protect her? Who has set this trap for me? Who has done this evil thing in my house? Who has defiled the virgin? Aren't I reliving the story of Adam? For as Adam was glorifying in the hour of prayer, the serpent came, found Eve alone, and deceived her, and now it's happened to me!"

2 And Joseph stood from the sackcloth and called her and said to her, "God cared for you. Why have you done this? You've forgotten the Lord your God. Why have you humiliated your soul? You were nourished in the Holy of Holies and received food from the hand of an angel!"

3 And she wept bitterly, saying, "I'm pure, and I haven't known a man!" And Joseph said to her, "Where then did this thing in your womb come from?"

And she said, "As the Lord my God lives, I don't know where it came from!"

Chapter 14: Joseph's Dream

1 And Joseph was very afraid and kept quiet about her, considering what to do about her. And Joseph said, "If I hide her sin, I'll be found resisting the law of the Lord, but if I reveal her to the people of Israel, I'm afraid that what's inside her might be angelic, and I'll be found handing over innocent blood to the judgment of death. So what will I do about her? I'll secretly set her free from me."

And night overtook him. 2 And look! An angel of the Lord appeared to him in a dream, saying, "Don't fear this child, for the one in her is from the Holy Spirit. And she'll give birth to a son, and you'll call his name 'Jesus,' because he'll save his people from their sins."

And Joseph arose from his sleep and glorified the God of Israel, who had given grace to him. And he protected her.

Chapter 15: The Chief Priest Questions Mary and Joseph

1 And Annas the scribe came to him and said to him, "Joseph, why haven't you appeared among our traveling group?"

And he said to him, "Because I was weary from the trip and rested the first day back."

And Annas turned and saw Mary pregnant.

2 And he quickly went to the priest and said to him, "Joseph, about whom you bore witness, has acted very lawlessly."

And the priest said, "What's this?"

And he said, "The virgin that Joseph took from the Temple of the Lord, he's defiled her and has stolen her wedding and hasn't revealed it to the people of Israel."

And in response the priest said, "Has Joseph done this?"

And Annas the scribe said to him, "Send officers, and you'll find the virgin pregnant."

And the officers went and found her just as he said. And they led her together with Joseph to the court.

3 And the chief priest said to her, "Mary, why have you done this? Why have you humiliated your soul and forgotten the Lord your God? You were raised in the Holy of Holies, and received food from the hand of an angel, and you heard its hymns

and danced before it. What is this that you've done?"

And she wept bitterly, saying, "As the Lord God lives, I'm pure before God, and I haven't known a man!"

4 And the priest said, "Joseph, what is this that you've done?"

And Joseph said, "As the Lord my God lives, and the witness of God's truth, I'm pure toward her."

And the priest said, "Don't bear false witness, but tell the truth. You stole her wedding and didn't reveal it to the people of Israel, and you haven't bowed your head under the mighty hand that should bless your offspring."

And Joseph fell silent.

Chapter 16: The Test

1 And the priest said, "Return the virgin you took from the Temple of the Lord."

And Joseph was tearful.

And the chief priest said, "I'll give you the water of the Lord's rebuke to drink, and it'll reveal your sin in your eyes."

2 And taking (the water), the priest gave it to Joseph and sent him into the wilderness. And Joseph returned unharmed.

And he gave it to Mary and sent her into the wilderness. And she returned unharmed.

And all the people were amazed that their sin wasn't revealed.

3 And the priest said, "If the Lord God hasn't revealed your sin to you, neither do I judge you." And he set them free.

And Joseph took Mary and went to his house, rejoicing and glorifying the God of Israel.

Chapter 17: The Census

1 Now an order went out from Augustus the king to register how many people were in Bethlehem of Judea.

And Joseph said, "I'll register my sons. But what should I do about this child? How will I register her? As my wife? I'm ashamed. As my daughter? But the people of Israel know she's not my daughter. This is the day of the Lord; I'll do whatever the Lord wants."

2 And he saddled the donkey, and sat her on it, and his son led it, and Samuel followed.

And as they neared the third mile, Joseph turned and saw that she was sad. And he was saying, "Likely the one inside her is troubling her."

And again Joseph turned and saw her laughing, and he said to her, "Mary, why are you like this, that I see your face laughing at one time, but then sad?"

And she said to him, "It's because I see two people in my eyes. One is crying and mourning, and one is rejoicing and exulting."

3 And they came to the middle of the journey, and Mary said to him, "Joseph, take me down from the donkey, because the one who's inside me is pushing to come out."

And he took her down from the donkey and said to her, "Where will I take you and shelter you in your awkwardness? This place is a wilderness."

Chapter 18: Time Stands Still

1 And he found a cave there, brought her (to it), and stationed his sons with her and went to look for a Hebrew midwife in the region of Bethlehem.

2 Now I, Joseph, was wandering but not wandering. And I looked up to the dome of heaven and saw it standing still, and into the sky, and I was astonished to see that even the birds of heaven were still. And I looked at the ground and saw a bowl lying there, and workers reclining, and their hands were in the bowl, and they were chewing but not chewing, and they were picking up food but not picking up food, and they were bringing it to their mouths but not bringing it to their mouths. Rather, all their faces were looking up.

And I saw sheep being driven, but the sheep stood still. And the shepherd lifted his hand to strike them, but his hand was raised. And I looked into the torrent of the river and saw young goats, and their mouths were in the water but not drinking.

And suddenly, everything resumed its course.

Chapter 19: Jesus' Birth

1 And look! A woman was coming down from the mountain, and she said to me, "Man, where are you going?"

And I said, "I'm seeking a Hebrew midwife."

And in reply she said to me, "Are you from Israel?"

And I said to her, "Yes."

Then she said, "And who's the one giving birth in the cave?"

And I said, "My betrothed."

And she said to me, "She's not your wife?"

And I said to her, "Mary was nurtured in the Temple of the Lord, and it was decided by lot that she would be my wife, yet she's not my wife; but she's conceived from the Holy Spirit."

And the midwife said, "Really?"

And Joseph said to her, "Come and see."

And the midwife went with him. 2 And they stood in front of the cave, and a bright cloud overshadowed the cave. And the midwife said, "My soul is magnified today, because my eyes have seen something wonderful. Salvation has been born to Israel!"

And immediately the cloud withdrew from the cave, and a great light appeared in the cave, so that their eyes couldn't bear it. And a little later, the light withdrew until an infant appeared. And he came and took the breast of his mother, Mary. And the midwife cried out and said, "How great today is for me, that I've seen this new miracle!"

3 And the midwife went out from the cave, and Salome met her.

And she said to her, "Salome, Salome, I have to describe a new sight to you. A virgin has given birth, which is against her nature!"

And Salome said, "As the Lord my God lives, unless I examine her condition, I won't believe that the virgin has given birth."

Chapter 20: Salome's Examination

1 And the midwife went in and said, "Mary, position yourself, because there's no small test coming concerning you."

And Salome examined her. And Salome cried out and said, "Woe because of my lawlessness and my unbelief! Because I've tested the living God, and look! My hand is on fire and falling away from me!"

2 And she dropped to her knees before the Lord, saying, "God of my ancestors, remember me, that I've descended from Abraham, Isaac, and Jacob. Don't make an example of me to the people of Israel, but give me the back to the poor, because you know, Lord, that in your name I've healed people, and I've received my wages from you."

3 And look! An angel of the Lord appeared, saying to her, "Salome, Salome, the Lord of All has heard your prayer. Bring your hand to the child and lift him up, and you'll receive salvation and joy."

4 And Salome joyfully went to the child and lifted him up, saying, "I worship him, because a great king has been born to Israel." And immediately Salome was healed, and she left the cave justified.

And look! A voice was saying, "Salome, Salome, don't report the wonderful things you've seen until the child comes into Jerusalem."

Chapter 21: The Magi

1 And look! Joseph prepared to go out into Judea when a great commotion arose in Bethlehem of Judea. For magi came, saying, "Where is the king of the Jews? For we saw his star in the East and have come to worship him."

2 And when Herod heard, he was disturbed, and he sent officers to the magi, and sent for the chief priests

and questioned them in his palace, saying to them, "What has been written about the Christ? Where will he be born?"

They said to him, "In Bethlehem of Judea, for this is what's written." And he set them (the chief priests) free.

And he questioned the magi, saying to them, "What sign did you see about the one who's been born king?"

And the magi said, "We saw an immense star shining among the other stars and dimming them so much that they weren't even visible. And so we knew that a king had been born for Israel, and we came to worship him."

And Herod said to them, "Go and search, and if you find him, report to me so that I can also come and worship him."

3 And the magi went, and look! The star they had seen in the East led them until they came to the cave, and it stood over the head of the cave. And when they saw him with his mother Mary, the magi took gifts from their bags: gold, and frankincense, and myrrh.

And having been warned by the angel not to go into Judea, they returned to their country by another way.

Chapter 22: The Slaughter of the Infants

1 When Herod saw that he had been tricked by the magi, he was angry. He sent out his killers, telling them to kill all the infants two years old and younger.

2 And when Mary heard that the infants were being killed, she was afraid. She took her child, wrapped him in cloths, and put him in a manger for cows.

3 And when Elizabeth heard that John was sought, she took him up into the hills and looked around for somewhere to hide him, but there wasn't a hiding place. Then Elizabeth groaned and said, "Mountain of God, take a mother with her child," because Elizabeth was unable to go up higher. And immediately, the mountain split and took her, and a light shone through the mountain for her. For an angel of the Lord was with them, protecting them.

Chapter 23: The Murder of Zechariah

1 But Herod asked for John and sent officers to Zechariah, saying to him, "Where are you hiding your son?"

But he replied, saying to them, "I'm a minister of God, and I sit in God's Temple. How should I know where my son is?"

2 And his officers went away and reported all these things to Herod. And Herod was angry, and said, "His son is about to be king over Israel!"

And he sent his officers again, to say to him, "Tell me the truth. Where's your son? You know that your life is in my hand."

And the officers went away and reported these things to him.

3 And Zechariah said, "I'm a martyr of God if you shed my blood, because the Lord will receive my spirit, since you'll be spilling inno-

cent blood at the entrance of the Temple of the Lord."

And around daybreak, Zechariah was murdered, and the people of Israel didn't know that he was murdered.

Chapter 24: Mourning for Zechariah

1 But at the hour of greeting, the priests came, and Zechariah didn't meet them to bless them as was customary. And the priests stood around for Zechariah, waiting to greet him with a blessing and to glorify the Most High God.

2 But when he delayed, they were all afraid. But one of them gathered the courage to go into the sanctuary and saw blood clotted beside the altar of the Lord. And a voice was saying, "Zechariah has been murdered, and his blood won't be wiped away until his avenger comes!"

When he heard this saying, he was afraid, and he went and reported to the priests what he had seen and heard. 3 And they gathered their courage and went and saw what had taken place. And the panels of the Temple cried out, and they (the priests) ripped their clothes from top to bottom. And they didn't find his corpse, but they found his blood had turned to stone. And they were afraid, and they went out and reported to all the people that Zechariah had been murdered. And when all the tribes of the people heard, they mourned him and wept three days and three nights.

4 And after three days, the priests held a council about who should replace Zechariah. And the lot fell to Simeon, for he was told by the Holy Spirit that he wouldn't see death until he saw the Christ in the flesh.

Chapter 25: Conclusion

1 Now I, James, wrote this history in Jerusalem when there was a commotion over Herod's death. I went into the wilderness until the commotion in Jerusalem had died down. I was glorifying the Lord God, who gave me the wisdom to write this history. 2 And grace will be with all who fear the Lord. Amen.

Infancy Gospel of Thomas

Chapter 1: Prologue

I, Thomas the Israelite, thought it necessary to make known to all the Gentile brothers (and sisters) all the things done by our Lord Jesus Christ in the village of Nazareth, after he was born in our region of Bethlehem. This is the beginning:

Chapter 2: Jesus Makes Sparrows

1 The child Jesus was five years old. After it rained, he was playing at the ford of a flowing stream. And stirring up the dirty waters, he gathered them into pools, and he made them clean and excellent, ordering them by word alone – and not ordering them by a deed.

2 Then, having taken soft clay from the mud, he formed twelve sparrows from it. But it was the Sabbath when he did these things, and many children were with him.

3 But a certain Jew saw the child Jesus with the other children doing these things. He went to Joseph his father and slandered the child Jesus, saying that "he made clay on the Sabbath, which isn't permissible, and formed twelve sparrows."

4 And Joseph went and rebuked him (Jesus), saying, "Why are you doing these things on the Sabbath?"

But Jesus clapped his hands, ordering the birds with a shout in front of all, and said, "Go, take flight like living beings!" And the sparrows, taking flight, went away squawking.

5 And having seen this, the Pharisee was amazed, and he reported it to all his friends.

Chapter 3: Jesus Curses Annas' Son

1 And the son of Annas the high priest said to him (Jesus), "Why are you doing such a thing on the Sabbath?" And having taken a willow twig, he destroyed the pools and drained the water which Jesus had gathered, and he dried up their gatherings.

2 But having seen what had happened, Jesus said to him, "Your fruit (will have) no root, and your shoot will be withered like a scorched branch in a violent wind!"

3 And immediately that child withered away.

Chapter 4: Jesus Curses a Careless Child

1 From there he was going with his father Joseph, and someone running struck his shoulder. And Jesus said to him, "Cursed be you because of your leader!"

And immediately he died.

And the people who saw that he had died immediately cried out and said, "From where was this child born, that his word becomes deed?"

2 And when the parents of the dead child saw what had happened, they blamed Joseph his father, saying, "From wherever you have this child, you can't live with us in this village. If you want to be here, teach him to bless and not to curse, because our child has been taken away from us."

Chapter 5: Joseph Confronts Jesus

1 And Joseph said to Jesus, "Why do you say such things, and they suffer and hate us?"

And the child said to Joseph, "Since you know wise words, you're not ignorant of where they came from; /they were spoken about a five-year-old. And they won't be raised, and these will receive their punishment."

And immediately those accusing him became blind.

2 And Joseph took his (Jesus') ear and pulled hard.

3 And Jesus said to him, "It's enough for you seek and find me, and not, beyond that, to scourge me by having taken on a natural ignorance. You haven't clearly seen me, why I'm yours. Look! I've been subdued before you."

Chapter 6: First Teacher, Zacchaeus

1 A teacher named Zacchaeus (was) standing (there), hearing Jesus saying these things to his father Joseph, and he was very amazed.

2 And he said to Joseph, "Come, give him (to me), brother, so that he may be taught letters, and so that he may know all knowledge, and learn to love those his own age, and honor old age and respect elders, so that he may acquire a yearning for children, teaching them in return."

3 But Joseph said to the teacher, "And who can control this child and teach him? Don't think of him as a small person, brother."

But the teacher said, "Give him to me, brother, and don't let him concern you."

4 And the child Jesus looked at them and said to the teacher this speech: "Being a teacher comes naturally to you, but you're a stranger to the name with which you're named, because I'm outside of you and I'm within you on account of the nobility of my birth in the flesh. But you, a lawyer, don't know the law."

And he said to Joseph, "When you were born, I existed, standing beside you so that as a father you may be taught a teaching by me which no one else knows or can teach. And you will bear the name of salvation."

5 And the Jews cried out and said to him, "Oh new and incredible wonder! The child is perhaps five years old, and oh, what words he says! We've never known such words. No one – neither a lawyer nor a Pharisee – has spoken like this child."

6 The child answered them and said, "Why are you amazed? Or rather, why don't you believe the things I've said to you? The truth is that I, who was created before this world, know accurately when you were born, and your fathers, and their fathers."

7 And all the people who heard this were speechless, no longer able to talk to him. But he went up to them, skipped around, and said, "I was playing with you because I know you're small-minded, and amazed with small things."

8 Now when they seemed comforted by the child's encouragement, the teacher said to his father, "Come, bring him into the school. I'll teach him letters."

And Joseph took his hand and led him into the school. And the teacher flattered him, brought him into the school, and Zacchaeus wrote the alphabet for him and began to teach him, saying the same letter frequently. But the child didn't answer him.

And the teacher became irritated and struck him on the head.

And the child became irritated and said to him, "I want to teach you rather than be taught by you, since I know the letters you're teaching more accurately. To me these things are like a noisy gong or a clanging cymbal that don't bring out the sound, nor the glory, nor the power of understanding."

9 When the child's anger ceased, he said all the letters by himself, from the alpha to the omega, very skillfully. And looking straight at the teacher he said, "If you don't know the nature of the alpha, how can you teach another the beta? Hypocrite! If you know, first teach me the alpha, and then I will trust you to speak of the beta." Then he began to teach the teacher about the first element. And he couldn't say anything to him.

10 While many listened, he said to the teacher, "Listen, Teacher, and understand the arrangement of the first element. Now, notice how it has sharp lines and a middle stroke, which you see pointing, standing with legs apart, coming together, going out, dragging behind, lifting up, dancing around, <...>, in triple rhythm, two-cornered, of the same form, of the same thickness, of the same family, raised, balanced, isometric, of equal proportions. These are the lines of the alpha."

Chapter 7: Zacchaeus' Lament

1 When the teacher heard such good familiarity (and) such lines of the first letter Jesus talked about, he was baffled by such teaching and his defense. And the teacher said, "Woe is me! Woe is me! I've been baffled and am miserable. I've brought shame on myself, taking on this child.

2 "Take (him) away from me, brother, because I can't bear his gaze, nor the clarity of his word. This child is simply not of this earth. He can even tame fire! Perhaps this child existed before the creation of the world. What kind of womb bore him? What kind of mother raised him? I don't know. Woe is me, brother! He stupefies me. My mind can't follow him. I've deceived myself, thrice-unhappy as I am. I thought to gain a disciple, and I'm found having a teacher.

3 "Friends, I ponder my shame, old man that I am, that I've been defeated by a child. I should be cast out and die, or flee this village because of this child. I can't be seen any longer among everyone, especially those who saw that I was defeated by a very small child. But what can I say or tell anyone about the lines of the first element? The truth is that I don't know, friends, because I understand neither the beginning nor the end!

4 "Therefore, brother Joseph, lead him away with salvation into your house, because this child is a great thing – whether a god or an angel or whatever else I might say – I don't know."

Chapter 8: Jesus' Response

1 The child Jesus laughed and said, "Now may the barren bear fruit, the blind see, and the foolish in heart find understanding: that I'm here from above, so that I may deliver those below and call them up, just as the one who sent me to you has ordered me."

2 And immediately all who had fallen under his curse were saved. And no one dared to provoke him from then on.

Chapter 9: Jesus Raises Zeno

1 And again, after many days, Jesus was playing with other children on a certain roof of an upstairs room. But one of the children fell and died. And the other children saw this and went into their houses. And they left Jesus alone.

2 And the parents of the child who had died came and accused Jesus, saying, "You pushed down our child!"

But Jesus said, "I didn't push him down."

3 And they were raging and shouting. Jesus came down from the roof and stood beside the body and cried out in a loud voice, saying, "Zeno, Zeno" – because this was his name – "Rise and say whether I pushed you down."

And he rose and said, "No, sir."

And they saw and were amazed.

And again Jesus said to him, "Fall asleep!"

And the parents of the child praised God and worshipped the child Jesus.

Chapter 10: Jesus Heals a Woodcutter

1 Again, a certain young man was splitting wood into equal parts. And he split the bottom of his foot, bled out, and died.

2 A commotion arose, and Jesus ran there. Forcing his way through the crowd, he seized the stricken foot, and immediately it was healed. And he said to the young man, "Go, split your wood."

3 And the crowds saw and were amazed and said, "For he saved many souls from death, and he will continue to save all the days of his life."

Chapter 11: Jesus Carries Water in his Cloak

1 And the child Jesus was about seven years old, and his mother Mary sent him to fill up water. But

there was a great crowd at the water cistern, and the pitcher was struck and broke.

2 But Jesus spread out the cloak he was wearing, filled it with water, and carried it to his mother. And Mary saw what sign Jesus had done. She kissed him, saying, "Lord, my God, bless our child," because they were afraid lest someone bewitch him.

Chapter 12: Miracle of the Harvest

1 And at the time of the sowing, Joseph sowed seeds, and the child Jesus sowed one measure of wheat.

2 And his father reaped a hundred great measures. And he gave graciously to the poor and the orphans. But Joseph took from Jesus' seeds.

Chapter 13: Miracle of the Bed

1 Now he (Jesus) was about eight years old. And his father, being a carpenter who made ploughs and yokes, took a bed from a certain rich man so that he might make it very great and suitable. And one of the beams, called the (...), was shorter; it didn't have the (right) length. Joseph was grieved, and didn't know what to do.

The child came to his father and said, "Set down the two boards and line them up on your end."

2 And Joseph did just as he said to him. And the child Jesus stood at the other end and seized the short board and stretched it. And he made it equal with the other board.

And he said to his father, "Don't grieve, but make whatever you want to."

And Joseph embraced and kissed him, saying, "Blessed am I, that God gave this child to me."

Chapter 14: Second Teacher

1 And Joseph saw his (Jesus') wisdom and understanding. He didn't want him to be unacquainted with letters, but gave him over to another teacher.

And the teacher wrote the alphabet for him (Jesus) and said, "Say alpha."

2 And the child said, "First you tell me what the beta is, and I'll tell you what the alpha is."

And the teacher became irritated and struck him. And Jesus cursed him, and the teacher fell and died.

3 And the child went into his house to his parents, and Joseph called his (Jesus') mother and ordered her not to set him (Jesus) free from the house so that those who provoke him may not die.

Chapter 15: Third Teacher

1 And after some days, again another teacher said to his (Jesus') father Joseph: "Come, brother, give him to me in the school so that with flattery I can teach him letters."

And Joseph said to him, "If you have courage, brother, take him with salvation."

And the teacher took the child by the hand and led him away with much fear and concern. And the child went gladly.

2 And entering the school, he (Jesus) found a book lying on the lectern. And he took it, but he didn't read what was written in it, because it wasn't from God's

law. But he opened his mouth and uttered words so impressive that the teacher seated opposite heard him very gladly and encouraged him so that he might say more. And the crowd standing there was amazed at his holy words.

3 And Joseph ran quickly to the school, suspecting that this teacher was no longer inexperienced and suffered. But the teacher said to Joseph, "So that you know, brother, I indeed took your child as a disciple, but he's full of much grace and wisdom. Therefore, brother, lead him away with salvation into your house."

4 And he (Jesus) said to the teacher, "Since you spoke correctly and testified correctly, the one struck down will also be saved because of you." And immediately that teacher also was saved. And taking the child, he (Joseph) led him (Jesus) away into his house.

Chapter 16: Jesus Heals James' Snakebite

1 And James went into the grove to tie up sticks so that they might make bread. And Jesus went with him. And as they were gathering the sticks, a terrible snake bit James on his hand.

2 And he was sprawled out and dying. And the child Jesus ran to James and blew on the bite, and immediately the bite was healed. And the beast was destroyed, and James was saved.

Chapter 17: Jesus Heals a Baby

1 And after these things, in Joseph's neighborhood a certain baby was sick and died. And his mother wept very much.

But Jesus heard that there was great grief and commotion, and he ran quickly. And he found the child dead, touched his chest, and said, "I say to you, baby, don't die, but live, and be with your mother."

And he (the baby) looked up immediately and laughed. And he (Jesus) said to the mother, "Take your child, give him milk, and remember me."

2 And the crowd standing there was amazed, and said, "The truth is, this child is a god or an angel, because his every word becomes a deed!"

And Jesus went away again and played with the children.

Chapter 18: Jesus Heals a Builder

1 And after some time, a building was being constructed. There was a great commotion, and Jesus got up and went there.

And seeing a man lying dead, he (Jesus) seized his (the man's) hand and said, "I tell you, man, rise and do your work." And he (the man) immediately rose and worshipped him.

2 And the crowd saw and was amazed and said, "This child is from heaven, for he saved many souls from death, and he will continue to save all the days of his life."

Chapter 19: Jesus in the Temple

1 And when Jesus was twelve years old, his parents went, according to custom, to Jerusalem for the festival

of the Passover. But during their return, Jesus stayed behind in Jerusalem. And his parents didn't know.

2 And assuming him to be in the traveling company, they went a day's journey and searched for him among their known relatives. And not finding him, they returned to Jerusalem and searched for him.

And after three days, they found him in the temple sitting in the middle of the teachers, and listening to them and questioning them. And those hearing him were surprised how he questioned the elders and explained the main points of the law and the riddles and the parables of the prophets.

3 And his mother said to him, "Child, what have you done to us? Look, we've been searching for you in pain and grieving."

And Jesus said, "Why were you looking for me? Didn't you know that it's necessary for me to be in the place of my Father?"

4 And the scribes and the Pharisees said to Mary, "You're the mother of this child?"

She said, "I am."

And they said to her, "Blessed are you that the Lord God has blessed the fruit of your womb, because we've never seen such wisdom of praise and glory of virtue."

5 And Jesus stood up and followed his mother from there, and was obedient to his parents. And she treasured all these things, pondering them in her heart.

And Jesus advanced in wisdom and maturity and grace before God and humans. To whom be the [glory].

THE STRANGER'S BOOK

Introduction

"My [son, let's pray to God ...] to the Father of all the ages, to send us a spirit of knowledge to reveal the mysteries, so that we may know ourselves; specifically, where [we've] come from, where we're going, and what we need to do to live." And they left and went up on a mountain called 'Tabor.' And they knelt down and prayed, "O Lord God, the One above all the great realms, the One who has no beginning and no end, give us a spirit of knowledge to reveal your mysteries, so that we may know ourselves; specifically, where we've come from, where we're going, and what we need to do to live."

The Temptation of Stranger

After Stranger had said these words, [Satan] appeared [on] the earth, since he [binds the world]. He said, "[...] while you're walking up on this mountain, because although you seek, you won't find anything. But come to me, and [take for] yourself what's in my [world]. Eat my good things. Take for yourself silver, gold, and clothes."

In response Stranger said, "Depart from me, Satan, because I don't seek you but my Father, who is above all the great realms; because I've been called 'Stranger,' since I'm from another race. I'm not from your race."

Then the one who binds the [world] told him, "We ourselves [...] in my [world]."

[Then] Stranger said to him, "Depart from [me], Satan! Go away, because I don't [belong to] you."

Then Satan [departed] from him, after having angered him many times; and he wasn't able to deceive [him]. And when he had been defeated, he went away to his place in great shame.

The Transfiguration of Stranger

Then Stranger cried out in a loud voice, "O God, you who are in the great realms, hear my voice, have mercy on me, and save me from every evil! Look on me and hear me in this deserted place. Now [let your] indescribable [light] shine on me [...] your light. Yes, Lord, help me, because [I] don't know [...] forever and ever."

And while I said these things, look! A bright cloud surrounded me. Because of the way it was shining, I couldn't gaze into the light around it. And I heard something from the cloud and the light. It shone on me and said, "O Stranger, the sound of your prayer has been heard, and I've been sent here to tell you the gospel before you leave [this place], so that you may [know ...] reveal [... body] dissolve [...] the [spirit...]

The Ascent of Stranger

"[... above. But] when you go, [you'll] come to the first Power, which is the power of Desire. And it will bind you and [ask] you, 'Where are [you] going, O Stranger?' But say, 'What bound me has been killed, and I've been released. I'll go up to my Father, the One above all the great realms.' And it will release you.

"Then you'll come to the second Power, which is the power of Darkness. [And it] will bind [you and] [ask you], 'Where [are you going, O Stranger?' But say, 'What bound me has been killed, and I've been released. I'll go up to my Father, the One above all the great realms.' Then it will release you.]

"[And you'll] come to the [third] Power, which is called 'Ignorance.' It will bind you and say to you, 'Where [are you going, O] Stranger?' But say to it, 'What bound me has been killed, and I've been released. I'll go up to my Father, the One above all the great realms.' Then it will release you.

"And you'll come to the fourth Power, which [... Death. It will say to you, 'Where are you going, O Stranger?'] [But say, 'What bound me has been killed, and I've been released. I'll go up to my Father, the One above all the great realms.' And it will release you.]

"[And you'll come to the fifth] Power, [which is the] Kingdom [of the] Flesh. [And it will] say to you, '[Where are] you [going, O Stranger?' But say, 'What bound] me has been [killed], and I've [been] released. [Now] then, I'll go up to my Father, [the One] above [all the great realms.' And it will] release you.

"[And you'll come to the sixth Power, which is the Foolish] 'Wisdom' [of Flesh. And] it will say to you, 'Where [are you going,] O [Stranger]?' But say to [it, 'What] bound me [has been killed, and I've been released. I'll go up to my Father], [the One above all the great realms.' And it will release you.]

"[...] in [...] and you'll [go up] over [these] angels [...] myriads of [holy] angels [... myriads of] angels [...] Don't be faint of heart [...] Be strong [... O Stranger], because you [...] Don't be afraid [...] which was said [...]"

Conclusion

Stranger [...] he sent [...] so that they might [... the] judgment. [Peace to the one] who wrote them down [and to those who will] preserve them.

The Sophia of Jesus Christ

After he was resurrected, his twelve disciples and seven women continued to follow him and went to Galilee to a mountain named "Divination and Joy". There, they gathered, feeling uncertain about the essence of the universe, the plan, divine providence, the authority's power, and everything the Savior did with them as part of the secret holy plan. The Savior appeared to them, not looking as he did before but as an invisible spirit, resembling a magnificent angel of light, a sight too overwhelming for any mortal to withstand except for those in pure, perfect form as he had taught on the mountain known as "Of the Olives" in Galilee.

He greeted them with peace, offering his peace to them. Surprised and scared, they saw the Savior smile and ask them about their concerns and what they were seeking.

Philip responded that they were searching for the essence of the universe and the plan.

The Savior explained that from the beginning of the world, all people born into it, made of dust and seeking to understand God, have not succeeded in truly knowing Him. The wisest people have only guessed through the world's order and movements, but their guesses haven't reached the truth. He clarified that the world isn't self-directed, nor is it governed by providence or fate, contrary to what philosophers argue. He, coming from the Infinite Light, is there to share the true nature of reality. Anything that exists by itself leads a tainted life; it is self-created. Providence lacks wisdom, and fate lacks discernment. However, they have been given the opportunity to know, and those who are worthy of knowledge will receive it, provided they were born not of impure origins but sent from the First, an immortal among mortals.

Matthew said to him: "Lord, no one can find the truth except through you. Therefore, teach us the truth."

The Savior said: "The One Who Exists is beyond words. No principle knew him, no authority, no control, nor any creature from the beginning of the world until now, except he alone, and anyone to whom he chooses to reveal himself through the one who comes from the First Light. From now on,

I am the Great Savior. For he is immortal and eternal. Now he is eternal, having never been born; for everyone who is born will die. He is without origin, having no beginning; for everyone who has a beginning has an end. Since no one has authority over him, he has no name; for anyone with a name was created by someone else."

"And he possesses a unique form - not like anything you have seen or received, but a distinct form that surpasses all things and is superior to the universe. It looks in every direction and sees itself by itself. Since it is limitless, he is forever beyond understanding. He is imperishable and has no likeness to anything. He is unchanging goodness. He is flawless. He is eternal. He is blessed. While he is unknown, he always knows himself. He is immeasurable. He is beyond tracking. He is perfect, without any flaw. He is eternally blessed. He is called 'Father of the Universe'".

Philip said: "Lord, then how did he appear to those who are perfect?"

The perfect Savior said to him: "Before anything of those that are visible became apparent, his majesty and authority exist within him, since he encompasses all of totality, while nothing encompasses him. For he is all intellect. And he encompasses thought, contemplation, consideration, reasoning, and power. All of these are equal forces. They are the origins of all that exists. And their entire lineage from the first to the last was known in advance by the infinite, unbegotten Father."

Thomas said to him: "Lord, Savior, why did these things come into existence, and why were they revealed?"

The perfect Savior said: "I came from the Infinite to tell you everything. The Spirit-Who-Is was the creator, endowed with both the power to create and the nature to shape form, so that the vast riches hidden within might be revealed. Out of his mercy and love, he desired to produce offspring by himself, so he might not enjoy his goodness alone, but that other spirits of the Unwavering Generation might produce physical forms and fruits, glory, and honor, in imperishability and his boundless grace. This was so his treasures might be made known by the Self-begotten God, the father of all that is imperishable and those that came into being after them. Yet, they had not become visible. Now, there is a great distinction among those that are imperishable."

He exclaimed, saying: "Let anyone who has ears to hear about the infinite realities listen!"; and "I have spoken to those who are aware." He continued, saying: "Everything originating from what is perishable will perish since it originated from the perishable. But whatever comes from what is imperishable does not perish but remains imperishable. Thus, many people were led astray because they did not understand this distinction and they died."

Mary said to him: "Lord, how can we understand that?"

The perfect Savior said: "Proceed from the invisible aspects to the limits of what is visible, and the very essence of Thought will reveal to you how faith in the invisible was discovered within the visible, belonging to the Unbegotten Father. Let anyone who has ears to hear, listen! "The Lord of the Universe is not referred to as 'Father', but 'Forefather', the origin of those who will come to be, yet he is the beginningless Forefather. Seeing his reflection within himself like in a mirror, he appeared in a form similar to his own, but his reflection manifested as the Divine Self-Father, and as the One Who Stands before those who are faced, the First Existent Unbegotten Father. He is indeed as ancient as the Light that precedes him, but not equal in power.

"Then was revealed an entire multitude of self-originated beings, equal in age and power, glorious and beyond count, whose lineage is known as 'The Generation over Which There Is No Rulership' from whom you yourselves have emerged among these people. And this entire multitude over which there is no rulership is called 'Children of the Unbegotten Father, God, Savior, Son of God', whose image is with you. Now, he is the unknowable, filled with eternal glory and indescribable joy. They all are at peace in him, forever celebrating in indescribable joy in his unchanging glory and limitless delight; this was never heard of or understood among all the ages and their worlds up to this time."

Matthew said to him: "Lord, Savior, how was Humanity revealed?"

The perfect Savior said: "I want you to understand that the one who appeared before the universe in infinity, the Self-originated, Self-established Father, filled with shining light and beyond words, decided at the outset that his likeness should become a great power. Instantly, the essence of that Light emerged as Immortal Androgynous Humanity, so that through this Immortal Androgynous Humanity, they might find salvation and awaken from forgetfulness through the messenger who was sent, who is with you until the end of the era of deprivation.

"And his partner is the Great Sophia, who was destined in him from the beginning for union by the Self-generated Father, from Immortal Humanity, who appeared as the first in divinity and sovereignty. For the Father, known as 'Humanity, Self-Father', revealed this. And he created a vast realm named 'Ogdoad' for his own glory.

"He was granted significant authority, and he governed the creation of scarcity. He created gods, angels, and archangels, countless numbers for company, from that Light and the triple-male Spirit, which pertains to Sophia, his partner. For from this, divinity and sovereignty originated. Therefore, he was proclaimed 'God of gods' and 'King of kings'.

"The First Humanity has a distinct intellect, inner thought - just as he embodies thought - contemplation, reflection, rationality, power. All attributes that exist are perfect and immortal. In terms of imperishability, they are indeed equal. However, in terms of power, they differ, similar to the distinction between father and son, son and thought, thought and the rest. As previously mentioned, among the entities that were created, the monad is foremost.

"And subsequently, all that was revealed came forth from his power. And from what was created, all that was shaped emerged; from what was shaped, what was formed came to be; from what was formed, what was named arose. Thus, the differentiation among the unbegotten from the beginning to the end arose."

Then Bartholomew said to him: "Why is he referred to in the Gospel as 'Humanity' and 'Son of Humanity'? To which of these does this Son belong?"

The Holy One said to him: "I want you to know that the First Humanity is known as 'Begetter, Self-perfected Mind'. He, along with Great Sophia, his consort, reflected and revealed his first-born androgynous son. His male name is 'First Begetter, Son of God', and his female name, 'First Begettress Sophia, Mother of the Universe'. Some refer to her as 'Love'. Now, the First-born is called 'Christ'. Having authority from his father, he created an innumerable host of angels as companions from Spirit and Light."

His disciples said to him: "Lord, tell us about the one known as 'Humanity', that we may fully understand his glory."

The perfect Savior said: "Whoever has ears to hear, let him hear. The First Begetter Father is named 'Adam, Eye of Light,' because he originated from shining Light, and his holy angels, who are beyond description and without shadow, perpetually share in joy in their reflection, which they received from their Father. The entire Kingdom of the Son of Humanity, who is also called 'Son of God,' is filled with indescrib-

able and shadowless joy, and eternal jubilation, rejoicing in his unending glory, which has never been disclosed until now, nor has it been unveiled in the eons that followed, and their worlds. I came from the Self-generated and the First Infinite Light, to disclose everything to you."

Again, his disciples asked, "Tell us clearly how did they descend from the realms beyond, from the immortal to the mortal world?"

The perfect Savior answered, "The Son of Man agreed with Sophia, his partner, and revealed a great androgynous light. His male aspect is named 'Savior, Father of All Things'. His female aspect is named 'Mother Sophia of All'. Some refer to her as 'Faith'.

"Everyone who enters the world, like a droplet from the Light, is sent by him to the world of the Almighty, so they might be protected by him. And the chain of their forgetfulness was secured by Sophia's will, allowing the matter to be disclosed to the entire world about the arrogance and blindness of the Almighty, and his ignorance. However, I came from the higher realms by the will of the great Light, escaping from that bond. I have terminated the work of the deceivers; I have awakened the droplet sent by Sophia, so it may through me produce abundant fruit, achieve completion, and not fall short again, but be unified through me, the Great Savior, revealing his glory, thus justifying Sophia concerning that flaw, so her children may not fall short again but may attain honor and recognition, ascend to their Father, comprehend the words of the masculine Light.

And you have been sent by the Son, dispatched so you may embrace the Light, freeing yourselves from the forgetfulness imposed by the rulers, preventing it from manifesting again because of you, specifically the impure contact originating from the fearful fire that emerged from their corporeal nature. Step on their harmful plans."

Then Thomas said to him, "Lord, Savior, how many are the aeons of those who exceed the heavens?"

The perfect Savior replied, "I commend you for inquiring about the vast aeons, for your origins are in the infinite realms. Now, regarding those I mentioned before, he provided...

And he asked, "How many are the aeons of the immortals, beginning from the infinite realms?"

The perfect Savior answered, "Let those who have ears listen. The first aeon belongs to the Son of Man, who is known as 'First Born', who is also called 'Savior', having manifested himself. The second aeon belongs to Humanity, who is referred to as 'Adam, Eye of Light'. Overarching these is the aeon where no dominion presides, the realm of the Eternal Infinite God, the self-generated aeon among the aeons within it, the realm of the immortals I previously mentioned, above the Seventh, emanating from Sophia, which is the premier aeon.

"Now the Immortal Man disclosed aeons, powers, and dominions, granting authority to all who manifested within him, allowing them to fulfill their desires until the ultimate entities above chaos. For they agreed among themselves and

unveiled every splendor, including countless glorious, innumerable lights from the outset, that is, the first, second, and third aeons. The first is dubbed 'Unity and Peace'. Each has its distinct name; the third aeon was named 'Congregation' due to the vast number that emerged: within one, a multitude manifested. Since these multitudes converge and unite, we refer to them as 'The Gathering of the Eighth.' It manifested as androgynous, partly named male and partly female. The male is called 'Congregation', while the female is termed 'Life', indicating that life for all aeons originated from a female. And every name was bestowed from the start.

"For from his collaboration with his thought, powers swiftly emerged, named 'gods'; and the gods spawned gods from their wisdom; and from their insight, lords were revealed; and the lords of lords from their thoughts brought forth rulers; and from their authority, archangels were created; the archangels through their proclamations brought forth angels; from them, semblances with structure, form, and names for all aeons and their worlds were produced.

"And the immortals, whom I've just described, all received their authority from the Immortal Man, known as 'Silence', for by meditating silently, she perfected all her grandeur. Since the eternal beings held authority, each established a grand realm in the Eighth, including thrones and temples, and firmaments for their own majesty. For all these were born from the will of the Universe's Mother."

Then the Holy Apostles said to him, "Lord, Savior, tell us about those who exist in the aeons, since we need to inquire about them."

The perfect Savior responded, "If you ask about anything, I will inform you. They created countless hosts of angels for their retinue and glory, as well as virgin spirits, the indescribable and unchangeable lights. They are free from illness and weakness, driven only by will. And they came into being instantly.

"Thus, the aeons were swiftly completed in the heavens and the firmaments by the glory of Immortal Man and Sophia, his partner: the foundation from which every aeon, the world, and those that followed, drew inspiration for their creations and likenesses in the heavens of chaos and their realms. And all beings, from the unveiling of chaos, exist in the Light that shines unshadowed, and joy beyond description, and unspeakable delight. They are perpetually overjoyed due to their constant glory and the immeasurable peace, indescribable among all the aeons that were formed afterward, and all their entities. Now, all that I have just explained to you, I did so that you might shine brighter in Light than these."

Mary asked him, "Holy Lord, where did your disciples come from, where are they going, and what should their actions be here?"

The Perfect Savior told them, "I want you to understand that Sophia, the Mother of the Universe and consort, intended by herself to manifest these beings without her male counterpart. Yet, by the will of the Father of the Universe, to reveal his unfathomable kindness, he established the divide between the immortals and those that emerged later, ensuring that consequences would ensue across every aeon and chaos - to expose the flaw of the female, allowing for Error to challenge her. This led to the creation of the veil of spirit. From the aeons above, the emanations of Light, as previously mentioned, a droplet of Light and Spirit descended to the lower realms of the Almighty in chaos, so that their formed bodies might emerge from that droplet, serving as a judgment against him, the Arch-Creator, known as 'Yaldabaoth'. That droplet unveiled their formed bodies through breath, as a living soul. It withered and lay dormant in the ignorance of the soul. When heated by the breath of the Great Light of the Male, taking thought, names were assigned to all existing within the world of chaos and everything within it by that Immortal One, when the breath was breathed into him. But this occurred by the will of Mother Sophia - so that the Immortal Man might gather the garments there as a judgment on the deceivers - <he> then accepted the breath; however, being soul-like, he could not claim that power for himself until the count of chaos was complete, i.e., when the period set by the great angel concluded.

"Now, I have instructed you about the Immortal Man and have released the ties of the deceivers from him. I have shattered the gates of the merciless in their view. I have diminished their harmful intent, and they have all been humbled and lifted from their ignorance. For this reason, I came here, so they might merge with that Spirit and Breath, and from two become one, just as from the beginning, that you might bear abundant fruit and ascend to Him Who Is from the Start, into unspeakable joy, glory, honor, and the grace of the Father of the Universe. "Thus, whoever truly knows the Father will proceed to the Father and rest in the Unbegotten Father. However, those who know him inadequately will go to the deficiency and the remainder of the Eighth. Now, anyone who knows the Immortal Spirit of Light in silence, through contemplation and agreement in truth, let them show me signs of the Invisible One, and they will become a light in the Spirit of Silence. Whoever understands the Son of Man in knowledge and love, let them present me a sign of the Son of Man, that they may proceed to the places of those in the Eighth. "See, I have disclosed to you the name of the Perfect One, the entire intent of the Mother of the Holy Angels, so that the masculine multi-tude may be fulfilled here, enabling their presence in the aeons, the infinite realms, and those that manifested in the boundless wealth of the Great Invisible Spirit, so all might partake of his goodness, even the wealth of their peace that reigns without dominion over it. I emerged from the First Who Was Sent, to unveil to you Him Who Is from the Beginning, due to the pride of the Arch-Creator and his angels, since they claim to be gods. And I arrived to free them from their blindness, that I might inform everyone about the God above all universes. Therefore, tread upon their graves, diminish their harmful intent, and break their chains, while stirring my own. I have endowed you with authority over all things as Children of Light, that you might trample their powers beneath your feet."

These are the words the blessed Savior spoke, and then he vanished from their sight. From that moment, all the disciples were filled with great, indescribable joy in spirit. And they began to spread the Gospel of the eternal, imperishable Spirit of God. Amen.

THE SAYINGS OF JESUS FROM OXYRHYNCHUS

Prologue

"These are the words which Jesus, the Living One, spoke to [his disciples] and to Thomas. And he declared, 'Whoever hears these words shall not taste death.'"

Saying I

"Let not the seeker stop until they find. Upon finding, they will be astonished, and in their astonishment, they will reign supreme, and having reigned, they shall find rest."

Saying II

"[Judas asked] 'Who then are those that draw us, and when shall the kingdom that is in heaven come?' Jesus answered, 'The birds of the air and all creatures under the earth or upon the earth, and the fishes of the sea, these are what draw you. And the kingdom of heaven is within you. Whoever knows themselves shall find it. And having found it, you will know that you are sons and heirs of the Almighty Father, and you will know that you are in God and God in you. And you are the City of God.'"

Saying III

"A man should not hesitate to ask concerning the place [of the kingdom], for 'many who are first shall be last, and the last, first.'"

Saying IV

"What is in front of your face, and what is hidden from you, will be disclosed. For nothing concealed will remain unexposed, and nothing buried will not be unearthed."

Saying V

"His disciples questioned him, asking, 'How shall we fast, and how shall we pray, and how shall we give alms, and what diet shall we observe?' Jesus replied, 'Do not lie, and do not do what you hate, for all things are plain in the sight of truth. Blessed is the one who...'"

Saying VI

"And then you will see clearly enough to remove the speck from your brother's eye."

Saying VII

"Jesus declared, 'Unless you abstain from the world, you will not find the kingdom of God. And if you do not observe the Sabbath for the entire week, you will not see the Father.'"

Saying VIII

"I stood in the midst of the world, and in flesh, I appeared to them. I found all men intoxicated, none thirsting for truth. My soul grieves for the children of men, for they are blind in their hearts and do not see."

Saying IX

Only the word "poverty" has been preserved from this saying.

Saying X

"Jesus says, 'Wherever there are two, they are not without God; and where there is one alone, I say I am with him. Lift up the stone, and there you shall find me; cleave the wood, and I am there.'"

Saying XI

"Jesus says, 'A prophet is not accepted in his own country, nor does a physician heal those who know him.'"

Saying XII

"Jesus says, 'A city built upon the top of a high mountain and established cannot fall, nor can it be hidden.'"

Saying XIII

The content is largely lost; only a fragment remains suggesting listening or hearing, symbolized by the reference to one ear being open and the other closed.

Gospel of the Egyptians

The Inquiry of Salome

It makes sense that after the Word spoke of the End, Salome asked, "How long will people continue to die?" Scripture discusses humanity in two aspects: the physical form we see and the soul; it also differentiates between those who are saved and those who are not, labeling sin as the soul's demise. The Lord thoughtfully replied, "Death will persist as long as women give birth".

Reflections on Childbearing

Why do those who deviate from the true essence of the Gospel fail to mention the rest of the conversation with Salome? When she pondered, "Have I then done well in not bearing children?" (implying that perhaps avoiding childbirth was advisable), the Lord responded, "Consume every plant, but steer clear of any that are bitter".

The Revelation to Salome

Upon Salome's questioning of when the knowledge she sought would be revealed, the Lord said, "When you have overcome the garment of shame, and when unity is achieved, with no distinction between male and female".

THE EPISTLE OF THE APOSTLES

1 The book that Jesus Christ disclosed to His disciples: and how Jesus Christ made this revelation to the group of apostles, the followers of Jesus Christ, a book intended for all humanity. Simon and Cerinthus, identified as deceitful apostles, about whom it is noted that no one should adhere to them due to their deceit leading individuals to ruin. This book was composed so that you may remain firm, not waiver, nor be distressed, and not stray from the Gospel message you have received. As we have heard it, we remember and have documented it for the entirety of mankind. We express our joy for you, our sons and daughters, in the name of God the Father, the Lord of the universe, and of Jesus Christ. May grace be abundantly bestowed upon you.

2 We, John, Thomas, Peter, Andrew, James, Philip, Bartholomew, Matthew, Nathanael, Judas Zelotes, and Cephas, write to the churches in the east and west, in the north and south, to announce and share with you matters regarding our Lord Jesus Christ: we write based on what we have personally seen, heard, and touched of Him, after He was resurrected from the dead; and how He unveiled to us truths both mighty and marvelous.

3 We understand this truth: that our Lord and Redeemer, Jesus Christ, is the Son of God, sent by God, the Lord of the entire world, its maker and creator. He is known by all names, supreme over all entities, Lord of lords, King of kings, Sovereign of sovereigns, the celestial one, seated above the cherubim and seraphim at the right hand of the Father's throne. It was through His word that the heavens were made, the earth and all within it were formed, and the seas were given their boundaries to not overflow. He commanded the springs and deeps to gush forth, covering the earth; He established day and night, the sun and the moon, and the stars in the heavens. He separated light from darkness, summoned the underworld, and instantly brought forth winter rains, snow, hail, and frost, setting the days in their seasons. He causes the earth to tremble and then stabilizes it again, created humanity in His own image and likeness, as proclaimed by the ancient fathers and prophets, preached

by the apostles, and touched by His disciples. We believe in God, the Lord, the Son of God, the Word made flesh, born of the Holy Virgin Mary by the Holy Spirit, not from human desire but by God's will. He was swaddled in Bethlehem, revealed to the world, grew, and matured, all of which we witnessed.

4 Jesus Christ, under the care of Joseph and Mary, was sent to learn. When His teacher asked Him to say 'Alpha', He replied, asking instead about 'Beta'. This event is acknowledged as a genuine truth.

5 Subsequently, at a wedding in Cana of Galilee, where He, His mother, and His brothers were invited, He transformed water into wine. He resurrected the dead, made the lame walk, healed a man with a withered hand, and a woman who had bled for twelve years was healed by touching His garment. Amazed by this miracle, when He inquired, "Who touched me?" we thought it was the crowd. But He knew power had left Him. The woman confessed, and He declared her faith had healed her. He gave hearing to the deaf, sight to the blind, expelled demons, and cleansed lepers. A possessed man, known as Legion, protested His presence, but Jesus commanded the spirits to leave without harm, driving them into swine, which then drowned.

Afterwards, He walked on the sea, calmed the stormy winds, and when questioned about tax, instructed catching a fish containing a coin for payment. With only five loaves and two fishes and a multitude to feed, over five thousand were satiated, leaving surplus that filled twelve baskets, symbolizing our faith in the Christian doctrine: in the Father, the Almighty Lord, in Jesus Christ our Redeemer, in the Holy Spirit the Comforter, in the holy church, and in the forgiveness of sins.

6 These are the teachings and revelations our Lord and Savior imparted to us. We follow in His footsteps so you too can share in the grace of our Lord, our ministry, and our gratitude, contemplating eternal life. Remain firm and unswerving in your faith and confidence in our Lord Jesus Christ, and He will show mercy and grant you salvation that lasts forever, without end.

7 Cerinthus and Simon wander the world as adversaries of our Lord Jesus Christ, twisting His words and the truth about faith in Jesus Christ. Stay well clear of them, for they are bearers of death, contamination, and corruption, destined for judgment, ending, and eternal damnation.

8 Thus, we have not hesitated to write to you about the testimony of Christ our Savior, about His deeds when we were His followers, and how He opened our minds...

9 We bear witness that the Lord was the one crucified by Pontius Pilate and Archelaus among two thieves, and was interred at a site known as the place of a skull. Three women, Mary related to Martha, Mary Magdalene, and another, went to the tomb with ointments to anoint His body, crying and lamenting what had happened. Approaching the sepulchre, they peered inside and discovered the body was gone.

10 As they grieved and cried, the Lord appeared to them, asking: For

whom do you weep? Do not weep, for I am He whom you seek. He instructed one of them to inform the brethren: Come, for the Master has risen from the dead. Martha came and told us. We questioned her incredulously: What does this concern us, woman? Can the dead and buried live again? We did not believe her claim that the Savior had risen. She returned to the Lord, reporting our disbelief. He then said: Let another go and tell them once more. Mary came and informed us again; still, we did not believe, and she went back to tell the Lord.

11 The Lord then said to Mary and her sisters, "Let us go to them". Upon arriving, He found us indoors and called us out, but we suspected He was a ghost and did not believe it was truly the Lord. He reassured us, "Come, do not be afraid. I am your master, yes, Peter, the one you denied three times; do you deny me yet again?" We approached Him, still doubting in our hearts whether it was Him. He then questioned us, "Why do you still doubt and disbelieve? I am the one who told you about my flesh, my death, and my resurrection. But for you to know it is I, Peter, place your finger in the holes of the nails in my hands, and you, Thomas, place your finger in the wound from the spear in my side; and you, Andrew, observe my feet to see if they leave impressions on the ground; for as it is written by the prophet: A specter or a demon leaves no footprints".

12 We touched Him to confirm for ourselves whether He had indeed risen in the flesh, and overwhelmed, we fell to our faces, confessing our sin of disbelief. Then our Lord and Savior encouraged us, "Stand, for I will reveal to you what is above and in heaven, and the rest that awaits you in the kingdom of heaven. My Father has granted me the power to elevate you and all who believe in me to there".

13 What He disclosed to us was this: "When I was to come here from the Father of all, passing through the heavens, I donned the wisdom of the Father and His mighty power. In heaven, I moved past the archangels and angels, appearing as one of them, through the dominions and authorities, because I held the wisdom of Him who sent me. The archangel Michael, along with Gabriel, Uriel, and Raphael, accompanied me to the fifth heaven, thinking I was one of them, such power had my Father bestowed upon me. On that day, I graced the archangels with a splendid voice, commanding them to approach the altar of the Father, to serve and execute their duties until my return to Him. Through my wisdom, I enacted all forms; I became everything to everyone, to extol the Father's plan and glorify Him who sent me and then to return to Him".

14 "You are aware that the angel Gabriel announced the news to Mary", He continued. We confirmed, "Yes, Lord". He then asked, "Do you not recall that I told you I became an angel among angels, and became all things in all?" We affirmed, "Yes, Lord". He elaborated, "On the day I assumed the form of the angel Gabriel, I appeared to Mary and spoke with her. Her heart accepted me, she believed, and I conceived my-

self and entered her body. I became flesh through my own ministration concerning Mary, appearing in the guise of an angel. This was necessary for me to do. Afterwards, I returned to my Father".

15 Remember to commemorate my death. As Easter approaches, one among you will be imprisoned for my name's sake, feeling sorrow and distress for celebrating Easter while separated from you, lamenting the inability to observe it together. My power, in the guise of the angel Gabriel, will open the prison doors, allowing him to join you for the night vigil until dawn. After commemorating me and sharing in the Agape feast, he will be imprisoned again as a testament, until released to preach the teachings I have entrusted to you.

And we asked Him, "Lord, must we continue to take the cup and drink?" He replied, "Yes, until the day I return with those who have died for my cause".

16 We inquired further, "Lord, will Your return be in the form of any creature or appearance?" He assured us, "Truly, I tell you, I shall come like the sunrise, with my brightness outshining it sevenfold. Clouds shall carry me in splendor, with the cross's sign leading, as I descend to judge both the living and the dead".

17 "Lord, when will this occur?" we asked. He told us, "When the time from Pentecost to the Feast of Unleavened Bread completes its hundred and twentieth cycle, then will my Father's arrival be imminent".

Confused, we questioned, "You say 'I will come,' yet also speak of 'He who sent me.' How so?" He clarified, "I am in the Father, and the Father in me". Worried about His departure, we asked where we could find another teacher. He comforted us, "Have I not been with you as I am with Him who sent me?" Puzzled, we wondered, "Can you be both here and there?" He affirmed, "I am fully in the Father and He in me, in our shared form, power, completeness, light, measure, and voice. I am the Word, the manifestation of His thought, present in the Ogdoad, the Lord's day".

18 After His crucifixion, resurrection, and the fulfillment of His mission in flesh, ascending as the days concluded, He declared, "...But the full realization will be evident after the redemption I have brought. You will witness my ascent to my Father in heaven. Now, I leave you with a new commandment: Love and obey one another, ensuring peace always prevails among you. Love your enemies and do not do to others what you would not have them do to you".

19 Proclaim this message and teach those who believe in me to preach about the kingdom of heaven of my Father, highlighting how my Father has granted me the authority to draw my heavenly Father's children closer. Preach, and they will find faith, making you the ones destined to guide His children to heaven.

We questioned Him, "Lord, you can surely achieve what you describe, but how can we?" He assured us, "Truly, I tell you, preach and announce as I have instructed you, for I will be with you. It is my desire to accompany you, so you may share in the inheritance of the kingdom of heaven, the kingdom of Him who sent me. Truly, I tell you, you will be my brothers and my friends, for my Father delights in you, and through you, those who believe in me will also be delighted. Truly, I tell you, my Father has prepared such immense joy for you that even the angels and powers long to witness it, yet they are not permitted to see my Father's glory". We asked, "Lord, what is this marvel you speak of?"

He responded, "You will witness a light superior to any other, outshining all brightness, and surpassing perfection. Through the Father, who is Light and the epitome of perfection, the Son will be made perfect, embodying a perfection beyond perfection. I am fully united with the Father, at His right hand, the source of all that is made perfect".

We expressed to Him, "Lord, you have become our salvation and life, offering us such hope". He encouraged us, "Be strong and find peace in me. Truly, I say, your rest will be transcendent, in a place devoid of hunger, thirst, worry, or sorrow, and without the fading of its inhabitants. You will share in my Father's eternity just as I am in Him, you will be in me".

Curious, we inquired further, "In what form will this be? As angels, or in flesh?" He clarified, "Behold, I have assumed your flesh, in which I was born, crucified, and resurrected through my Father in heaven, fulfilling David the prophet's prophecy about my death and resurrection:

'Lord, they are increased that fight against me, and many rise up against me. Many say of my soul: He has no salvation in God. But you, O Lord, are my shield, my glory, and the lifter of my head. I cried to the Lord with my voice, and He heard me. I laid down and slept; I awoke, for the Lord sustains me. I will not fear the tens of thousands set against me. Arise, O Lord; save me, O my God! For you strike all my enemies on the cheek; you break the teeth of the wicked. Salvation belongs to the Lord; your blessing is upon your people.'

If all words spoken by the prophets were fulfilled in me (for I was present in them), how much more will what I say to you indeed come to pass, glorifying Him who sent me through you and those who believe in me?"

20 After He shared these words with us, we expressed our gratitude, acknowledging His mercy and revelations. Curious, we sought His permission to inquire further. He welcomed our questions, recognizing our eager attentiveness and pleasure in His teachings, and promised to respond kindly to our desires.

21 He assured us, "Truly, just as my Father resurrected me, so shall you also rise and ascend to the highest heaven, to the place I've mentioned since the beginning, prepared by Him who sent me. In this way, all divine plans will be fulfilled by me, who, though not begotten by human means, came in the flesh for your resurrection in a second birth into an imperishable form, alongside all who hope and believe in Him who sent me. This is my Father's will, to grant you and those I choose the promise of His kingdom".

Upon hearing this, we were amazed by the hope He offered. He questioned our faith in His words, and we affirmed our belief. He then declared, "I have received all authority from my Father to bring those in darkness to light, from corruption to incorruption, from death to life, and to free the bound. What is impossible for humans is possible for the Father. I am the hope for the hopeless, aid for the unaided, wealth for the impoverished, health for the ill, and the resurrection for the dead".

22 Intrigued, we asked if the flesh would be judged alongside the soul and spirit, with parts destined for heaven and others for eternal punishment while still alive. He implored us to question less and have more faith.

23 Yet, we felt compelled to seek His guidance further, as He commanded us to preach and we wished to gain certainty from Him to be effective messengers. Our inquiries aimed to ensure that those taught by us would believe in Him confidently.

24 He explained that the resurrection would indeed involve the body, soul, and spirit together. We pondered the feasibility of restoring what has decayed and vanished. Our questions were not from disbelief in His power but from a place of faith in His words. Nevertheless, He rebuked our lack of faith and urged us to ask freely, promising to answer openly. He emphasized the importance of adhering to His commandments, serving others without bias, fear, or avoidance, to ensure

His continued favor and make the Father rejoice in us.

25 Once more we approached Him, feeling somewhat embarrassed for repeatedly questioning Him. He reassured us, "I understand your questions come from a place of faith and wholeheartedness; thus, I am delighted by them. Indeed, I say to you, both my Father within me and I rejoice when you inquire, for your eagerness brings me joy and grants you life". Encouraged by His words, we felt heartened to ask further. "Lord, you enliven us in every way and show us mercy. Will you then answer what we now ask of you?" He posed to us, "What is transient, the flesh or the spirit?" We responded, "The flesh is transient". To this, He declared, "What has fallen will rise, what was lost shall be rediscovered, and what was frail will be strengthened, so that in these acts the glory of my Father may manifest. As He has done for me, so shall I do for all who believe in me".

26 "Truly, I tell you, the flesh will resurrect, and the soul will live, so that on that day, each may be judged for their deeds, whether good or evil. This will distinguish the faithful who have adhered to my Father's commandments from the rest. The judgment shall be executed with rigor. For my Father advised me, 'My Son, in the day of judgment show no favor to the wealthy nor sympathy for the impoverished; but judge each solely by their sins to assign eternal punishment. Yet, to my cherished ones who have observed my Father's decrees, I will grant eternal life in the kingdom of heaven, where they will witness the

bounty He has bestowed upon me. I have been given the authority to act as I wish, to bestow what I have promised and decided to those who believe".

27 "For this purpose, I descended to Lazarus's place to preach to the righteous and prophets, leading them from the lower rest to the higher; I bestowed upon them the baptism of life, forgiveness, and salvation from all harm, just as I have for you and those who believe in me. However, anyone who believes in me but fails to follow my commands, despite confessing my name, gains nothing and follows a fruitless path, ending in ruin and despair for neglecting my instructions".

28 "Yet, I have saved you, the children of light, from all evil and the dominion of rulers, and all who believe in me through you. The promises made to you shall also be granted to them, to liberate them from the bondage and shackles of rulers. You asked, 'Lord, having bestowed upon us the promise of life and confirmed our faith with wonders, will you not also preach to us as you did to the righteous and the prophets?' To this, I affirm, 'Truly, I say to you, I will elevate all who have faith in me and in Him who sent me to heaven, to the place prepared by my Father for the chosen, where I will grant you the kingdom, the chosen kingdom, in peace, and everlasting life.'"

29 Anyone who transgresses my commandments, distorts Scripture for their own gain, and leads astray those who sincerely believe in me, will face eternal damnation. We asked, "Lord, will there be teachings contrary to yours?" He explained that such divergence is necessary to distinguish between good and evil, ensuring that judgment is rightfully passed based on their actions, resulting in their condemnation to death. We expressed gratitude for witnessing and hearing His words, acknowledging the miracles He performed. He emphasized, "Indeed, those who believe without seeing are even more blessed and will be deemed perfect in the kingdom".

Questioning how people would accept His departure, He reassured us, "A time will come when I ascend to my Father, but your faith will sustain you".

30 But he spoke unto us, saying: Venture forth and proclaim to the twelve tribes, and likewise unto the gentiles, across all the lands of Israel, from the east unto the west, from the south to the north, and many shall place their faith in me, the Son of God. Yet, we questioned him, saying: Lord, who shall place faith in our words, or listen to us, or learn of the might, signs, and wonders that you hast wrought? He then replied, saying: Venture forth and proclaim the compassion of my Father, and through me what he has accomplished, I will enact through you, for I dwell within you. I shall bestow upon you my peace and endow you with the might of my spirit, so that you may prophesy unto them for eternal life. And unto others, I shall also grant my might, so they may teach the remnants of the nations.

31 And lo, a man named Saul, also known as Paul upon interpretation—a Jew, circumcised as per the law—shall encounter you. He shall hear my voice from the

heavens with fear, terror, and trembling. His sight shall be obscured, but through your hands and by the sign of the cross, protection shall be his. Do unto him as I have done unto you. Pass on the Word of God to others. And in that moment, his eyes shall be opened, and he shall exalt the Lord, my Father in heaven. He shall gain influence among the people, preaching and teaching; and many who hear him shall attain glory and redemption. Yet, thereafter, men shall turn against him, delivering him into the hands of his foes. He shall bear testimony before mortal kings, and his destiny shall be to turn towards me, despite his initial persecution. He shall preach, instruct, and dwell among the chosen, as a vessel selected and a steadfast wall, the last to become a preacher to the Gentiles, perfected through my Father's will. As the Scripture foretold through your ancestors, the prophets, about me, so it has been fulfilled. He charged us, saying: Therefore, be ye also guides unto them; recount all that I have spoken unto you about myself, that I am the Word of the Father, and the Father is in me. Thus shall you be unto this man, as is fitting. Instruct him and remind him of what the Scriptures say of me and its fulfillment, and he shall be the salvation of the Gentiles.

32 We inquired of him: Lord, do we and they share the same expectation of inheritance? He answered, saying: Are the fingers of one hand identical, or the ears of corn in a field, or do all fruit trees bear the same fruit? Does not each yield according to its nature? We asked him again: Lord, will you once more speak to us in parables? He replied: Do not mourn. Truly, I say unto you, you are my brethren and my companions in the kingdom of heaven unto my Father, for this is his will. Truly, I tell you, to those also whom you teach and who believe in me, I will grant that expectation.

33 Once more we asked him: When shall we meet this man, and when will you ascend to your Father, our God and Lord? He answered: The man shall come from the land of Cilicia to Damascus in Syria, to uproot the church you shall establish there. It is I who speak through you, and he shall arrive swiftly: he shall grow steadfast in faith, so that the word of the prophet may be fulfilled, which states: Behold, from Syria I shall start to gather a new Jerusalem, and Zion shall I bring under my dominion, and it shall be taken, and the place which is barren shall be known as the son and daughter of my Father, and my bride. For such is the pleasure of Him who sent me. Yet, this man I will turn away from his malicious intent, and through him, the glory of my Father shall be fully realized. And after I return to my Father, I shall speak to him from heaven, and all that I have foretold you regarding him shall come to pass.

34 Again, we spoke unto Him, saying: Lord, You hast shared with us such profound revelations and wisdom as have never before been uttered, granting us peace and showing us favor. After Thy resurrection, You unveiled all things that we might truly be saved; yet, You mentioned only of signs and won-

ders to occur in the heavens and upon the earth before the world's end. How shall we recognize these times? He replied: I shall instruct you; not only you but also those whom you teach and who believe, as well as those who shall hear that man and believe in Me. In those years and days, it shall come to pass. We questioned Him further: Lord, what events are to transpire? And He said unto us: Then, both believers and non-believers shall hear a trumpet in the heavens, witness great stars visible by day, marvelous visions in the sky reaching down to earth; stars plummeting to the ground like flames, and a massive, fiery hail. The sun and the moon shall clash, accompanied by endless roars and flashes of thunder and lightning, along with earthquakes; cities shall crumble, and people perish in their ruin, a relentless famine from lack of rain, a dreadful plague causing vast death, so severe that the dead shall go unburied: and the carrying of brothers, sisters, and relatives shall be upon a single bier. Kin shall show no mercy to kin, nor any man to his neighbor. And those overthrown shall rise to see their conquerors unburied, for the plague will breed hatred, pain, and jealousy: and people will steal from one another, only for conditions to deteriorate further.

35 Then, My Father will display His wrath due to mankind's wickedness, for their sins are numerous, and the abomination of their impurities weighs heavily upon them, corrupting their lives.

We inquired: And what of those who trust in Thee? He responded:

You are still not fully understanding; how much longer must this be? Verily, I say unto you, as the prophet David spoke concerning Me and My people, so shall it be for those also who believe in Me. But for the deceivers and adversaries of righteousness in this world, David's prophecy shall befall them: "Their feet rush into sin; they speak lies; venom like that of serpents lies under their lips". You associate with thieves and partake with adulterers, you speak ill of your brother and place stumbling blocks before your own mother's son. Do you think I am akin to you? Behold, how the prophet of God has spoken of all, that everything he foretold may come to pass.

36 Again, we asked Him: Lord, will then the nations inquire: Where is their God? And He responded: This will distinguish the chosen, that despite such trials, they will emerge. We asked: Will their departure from this world be due to a pestilence that causes them suffering? He answered: No, should they endure such trials, it shall test their faith and remembrance of My teachings, and their adherence to My commands. These shall rise, and their wait shall be brief, that He who sent Me may be glorified, and I along with Him. For He sent Me to you to declare these things; that you may share them with Israel and the Gentiles so they might listen, be redeemed, believe in Me, and avoid the anguish of destruction. Yet, those who escape death's devastation will be seized and confined in torment akin to that of a thief. We then asked Him: Lord, will believers be treated as non-believers,

and will You punish those who have escaped the pestilence? And He said unto us: If those who believe in My name act as sinners, then it is as though they had never believed. We inquired further: Lord, is there no life for those upon whom this fate has befallen? He answered: Whoever has fulfilled My Father's praise shall dwell in My Father's place of rest.

37 We then said unto Him: Lord, instruct us on what shall happen next? And He answered: In those years and days, wars will ignite upon wars; the world's four corners shall clash and combat each other. Then shall arise swarms of locusts or clouds, darkness, famine, and persecution against those who believe in Me and the chosen ones. Thereafter, doubt, discord, and violations against one another shall arise. Many will claim belief in My name yet pursue evil and propagate false teachings. People will follow them for their wealth, succumb to their arrogance, crave indulgence, accept bribes, and show partiality among them.

38 But those who yearn to see God's face, who disregard the rich sinners and are unashamed before the misled masses, yet confront them, shall be crowned by the Father. And those who admonish their neighbors, for they are sons of wisdom and faith. However, if they do not become children of wisdom, anyone who hates his brother, persecutes him, and shows no kindness, will be despised and rejected by God.

Yet, those who pursue truth and knowledge in faith, and love towards Me, enduring insults—they have remained steadfast despite poverty, enduring hatred and disgrace. They have been stripped bare, despised for enduring hunger and thirst, but after their patient endurance, they shall know the bliss of heaven and dwell with Me eternally. But woe to those who walk in arrogance and vanity, for their end is destruction.

39 We asked Him: Lord, is it your intention, as you leave us, to let such hardships happen to them? He answered: How will judgment be made? Will it be fair or unfair?

We questioned Him: Lord, on that day, might they not accuse you, saying: Have you not differentiated between righteousness and wickedness, light and darkness, evil and good? Then He declared: I will answer them, saying: Adam was given the choice between two paths: he chose the light, embracing it, while he rejected the darkness, casting it aside. Thus, all people have the ability to believe in the light, which is life and the Father who sent me. Anyone who believes and lives by the light will reside in it; however, if someone claims to be of the light while practicing deeds of darkness, such a person has no defense, nor can he look upon the Son of God, which I am. For to him I will say: As you have sought, so have you found; as you have asked, so have you received. Why do you judge me, O man? Why have you abandoned and denied me? And why do you acknowledge me yet deny me? Does not every person have the choice of life and death? Those who follow my commands will be children of the light, that is, of the Father within me. But for those who twist my words, I came down from heaven. I am the Word; I became flesh, faced hardships, and proclaimed: Those burdened shall find salvation, while those who stray shall be lost forever. They will face punishment and torment in both body and soul.

40 We said to Him: O Lord, we truly grieve for their situation. And He told us: You are right to do so, for the righteous grieve for the sinners and intercede for them, praying to my Father. We then asked Him: Lord, is there no one who intercedes for them before you? And He replied: Yes, and I will listen to the prayers of the righteous on their behalf.

After He had said this, we told Him: Lord, you have enlightened us and shown mercy, saving us so we can preach to those who are deemed worthy of salvation, and that we might be rewarded in your presence.

41 He replied: Go and preach, and you will be laborers, fathers, and teachers. We said to Him: You are the one who will preach through us. Then He replied: Aren't you all to be fathers or teachers? We reminded Him: Lord, you told us: Call no one your father on earth, for you have one Father, who is in heaven, and one teacher. Why then do you now tell us: You will be fathers to many, and servants and masters? He answered: As you have understood correctly. For truly, I tell you: whoever listens to you and believes in me will receive through you the light of the seal and baptism through me: you will be fathers, servants, and masters.

42 But we questioned Him: Lord, how can each of us fulfill these three roles? He replied: Truly, I tell you: You will be called fathers, for with hearts full of praise and love, you have revealed to them the mysteries of the kingdom of heaven. You will be known as servants, for through you, they will receive the baptism of life and the forgiveness of their sins by my hand. And you will be called masters, for you have generously shared the word, advised them, and through your guidance, they have been converted. You did not desire their wealth, nor were you intimidated by their presence, but you kept my Father's commandments and fulfilled them. Thus, a great reward awaits you with my Father in heaven, and they will receive forgiveness for their sins and eternal life, becoming partakers in the kingdom of heaven.

We then said to Him: Lord, even if we had ten thousand tongues each, we couldn't fully express our gratitude for the promises you have made to us. He responded: Just do as I have instructed you, just as I have done myself.

43 And you shall be akin to the prudent virgins who stayed vigilant and did not sleep but proceeded to meet the lord in the bridal chamber: whereas the foolish virgins failed to keep watch, succumbing to slumber. We asked Him: Lord, who are the prudent and who are the foolish? He told us: Five are wise and five are foolish; these are the ones the prophet spoke of: They are the children of God. Now hear their names. Yet we wept and were distressed for those who slept. He said to us:

The five wise represent Faith, Love, Grace, Peace, and Hope. Those among the faithful possessing these virtues shall lead those who have believed in Me and in He who sent Me. For I am the Lord, and I am the bridegroom they have welcomed; they have entered the bridegroom's abode and lie with Me in the bridal chamber, rejoicing. However, the five foolish, upon waking from their slumber and finding the bridal chamber's doors closed, approached and knocked, to no avail. They then wept and lamented, for none would open the door to them. We inquired of Him: Lord, did their prudent sisters within the bridegroom's residence not relent and open to them, feeling no sorrow for their plight nor plead with the bridegroom on their behalf? He answered: They were not yet in a position to secure favor for them. We asked Him: Lord, when then will they be allowed entry for the sake of their sisters? He replied: He who is excluded, remains excluded. We questioned Him further: Lord, is this decree final? Who, then, are the foolish? He informed us: Listen to their names. They are Knowledge, Understanding, Obedience, Patience, and Compassion. These attributes were dormant in those who believed and professed Me but did not adhere to My commandments.

44 Because of those who were negligent, they shall be barred from the kingdom and the shepherd's fold and his sheep. But whoever remains outside the fold, the wolves will devour, and he shall be tormented and perish amidst severe suffering: he will find neither solace nor resilience, and even though subjected to harsh punishment, torn asunder, and tormented with prolonged and grievous agony, he shall not swiftly find death.

45 We expressed to Him: Lord, You have indeed made all things clear to us. He then inquired: Do you not comprehend these teachings? We affirmed: Yes, Lord. By the grace of five virtues, shall men enter into Your kingdom: nonetheless, those vigilant were with You, the Lord and bridegroom, albeit saddened for their slumbering counterparts. He explained: Indeed, they shall rejoice for being admitted alongside the bridegroom, the Lord; yet, they grieve for their slumbering sisters, for all ten are daughters of God, the Father. We then asked: Lord, is it then Your responsibility to grant them favor on account of their sisters? He responded: It falls not upon Me, but upon Him who sent Me, and I am in agreement with Him.

46 Be steadfast, preach accurately, teach, and be neither dismayed nor fearful of any man, especially the wealthy, for they do not adhere to My commandments but take pride in their riches. We queried: Lord, is it solely the affluent? He clarified: Should any person of modest means give to the poor and needy, he shall be deemed a benefactor.

47 If someone falters under the weight of sin, his neighbor shall reprimand him for the good previously done. Should the errant neighbor repent and amend, he will be saved, and the one who corrected him shall be rewarded and live eternally. For a needy individual who, upon witnessing his benefactor sinning and

fails to admonish him, shall face stern judgment. If a blind man leads another blind, both shall fall into a pit: and anyone showing partiality shall be likened to the blind, as the prophet declared: Woe to those who show partiality and vindicate the wicked for gain, for whom their appetite is their god. Their fate shall be judgment. Truly, I say to you: On that day, I will neither favor the rich nor pity the poor.

48 If you observe a sinner, counsel him privately: (if he listens, you have reclaimed your brother); if he disregards, involve one to three others, and guide your brother: still, if he resists, let him be unto you as an outsider or a tax collector.

49 Should you hear anything against your brother, lend it no belief; do not slander, nor take pleasure in slander. For it is written: Let not your ear entertain accusations against your brother: but if you witness anything amiss, correct, admonish, and guide him back.

We addressed Him: Lord, You have instructed and cautioned us in all respects. But, Lord, regarding the faithful, specifically those destined to believe in Your gospel: is division, skepticism, jealousy, confusion, animosity, and envy predetermined to arise among them? For You stated: They shall criticize one another, favor the sinful, and despise those who reprimand them. He replied: How then shall the judgment proceed, that the wheat might be stored in the barn and its chaff burnt in the fire?

50 Those who despise such actions, yet love me and reprimand those not obeying my commandments, will be scorned, persecuted, ridiculed, and mocked. People will intentionally spread falsehoods about them and conspire against those who love me. But these faithful will correct them, aiming for their salvation. However, those willing to admonish, discipline, and warn will be detested, pushed away, scorned, and kept at a distance by those wishing to harm them. Yet, those who withstand such trials will be akin to the martyrs in the presence of the Father, for they have fought for righteousness and not corruption.

We questioned Him: Lord, will such events occur among us? He reassured us: Do not fear; it will happen to only a few, not many. We asked for more details: How will this come about? He explained: A new, confusing doctrine will emerge, driven by self-promotion, leading to the propagation of harmful teachings. This will introduce a lethal impurity, turning those who believe in me away from my teachings and severing them from eternal life. But woe to those who distort my words and commands, leading astray those who listen to them from the true path and isolating themselves from the commandments of life: they will face eternal judgment alongside their followers.

51 After saying this and concluding His talk with us, He spoke again: Behold, at the third hour on the third day, the one who sent me will arrive, and I shall depart with Him. As He spoke, thunder roared, lightning flashed, the earth shook, the heavens split open, and a bright cloud appeared, lifting Him upwards. Many

angels' voices were heard, celebrating and praising, chanting: Gather us, O Priest, into the light of the majesty. As they approached the firmament, we heard His voice bidding us: Depart in peace.

The Apocalypse of Peter

The Akhnim fragment

1 Many among them will be false prophets, teaching divergent paths and doctrines leading to destruction. 2 They will become children of doom themselves. 3 Then, God will approach my faithful ones who in this life have endured hunger, thirst, and affliction, and have tested their souls, to judge the wicked.

4 The Lord then suggested, "Let's ascend the mountain to pray". 5 Accompanying Him, we, the twelve disciples, implored Him to reveal to us one of our virtuous brethren who had departed from the world, so we might see their form, be encouraged, and likewise encourage those who would hear us.

6 As we prayed, suddenly, two men appeared before the Lord, radiating a brightness that was difficult to gaze upon. 7 They emitted a brilliance like the sun, their garments shimmering in a way no human eye has seen before, beyond any earthly comparison. Their appearance was such that no words could fully capture their glory and the beauty of their faces. 8 They were whiter than any snow and redder than any rose, 9 the red and white blending in such a manner that their beauty was indescribable. Their hair, curly and lush, framed their faces and shoulders like garlands made of various flowers, or like a rainbow in the sky, such was their allure.

11 Astonished by their beauty, which appeared suddenly, 12 I approached the Lord to inquire, "Who are these?" 13 He explained, "These are your righteous brethren, whose appearance you wished to see". 14 I further questioned, "And where are all the righteous, or what is the nature of the world they inhabit that they possess such splendor?" 15 The Lord revealed to me a vast, luminous realm beyond our world, filled with light and an atmosphere brightened by the sun's rays, where the ground itself bloomed with everlasting blossoms and was laden with fragrant spices and plants, yielding undying, blessed fruit. The fragrance from this bloom was so potent that it reached us.

17 The inhabitants wore garments as radiant as those of angels, matching the splendor of their environment.

18 Angels surrounded them, bustling with activity. 19 Everyone

there shared the same glory, unanimously praising the Lord God, filled with joy in that realm.

20 The Lord informed us, "This is the abode of your patriarchs and the righteous leaders".

21 I then observed another, far less pleasant area, a place of punishment where both the suffering souls and their tormenting angels were cloaked in darkness, mirroring the gloom of their surroundings. 22 Some were suspended by their tongues, suffering for blaspheming the path of righteousness, with flames beneath them.

23 A vast lake of burning sludge was visible, the abode of those who turned from righteousness, overseen by tormenting angels.

24 Women hung by their hair over this seething mire, punished for adorning themselves for adultery, while men complicit in these acts, dangling by their feet with their heads submerged, lamented their disbelief in facing such a fate.

25 Murderers and their accomplices were thrown into a confined space filled with vile creatures, tormented by the beasts and enveloped in darkness by swarming worms. The spirits of their victims stood by, witnessing the torment, affirming the justice of God's judgement.

26 Nearby, another grim location featured a stream where discharged filth and stench accumulated, resembling a foul lake where women, up to their necks in the mire, faced the cries of prematurely born children, their aborted offspring, whose fiery glares punished the mothers.

27 Further on, men and women were half-burned, thrown into darkness, lashed by demons, their insides consumed by relentless worms—these were persecutors of the righteous, now facing divine retribution.

28 Close by, individuals gnawed their lips in agony, with heated iron applied to their eyes for blaspheming and maligning the path of righteousness.

29 Opposite them, more individuals suffered, their tongues afflicted, mouths filled with fire—these were the false witnesses.

30 Another area featured razor-sharp, heated stones, over which men and women in filthy garments were rolled, punished for their wealth and indifference to the needy, ignoring God's commands.

31 In a vast, repugnant lake filled with pus and blood, stood individuals implicated in usury, enduring their sentence.

32 Others were repeatedly cast down from a high cliff, compelled to climb back up, only to be thrown down again, suffering endlessly—these were individuals guilty of sexual immorality, defiling their bodies.

33 Near this cliff, a fiery domain was reserved for idolaters, who crafted images as substitutes for God, now tormented by their creations.

34 Adjacent to them, individuals were scorched, endlessly rotating as if on a spit—these were those who abandoned God's way.

The Ethiopic Text

The Second Coming of Christ and the Resurrection of the Dead, as revealed by Christ to Peter, concern those who perished due to their transgressions, for they did not adhere to the commandments of God, their Creator.

In the moments of quiet reflection, Peter sought understanding of the profound mystery embodied by the Son of God, the embodiment of compassion and love for mercy.

As the Lord sat upon the Mount of Olives, His disciples gathered around Him. Each of us, in turn, fervently beseeched and pleaded with Him, imploring, "Reveal to us the signs of Your imminent return and the conclusion of this age, so we may discern and recognize the timing of Your coming. This knowledge will enable us to guide those who succeed us—those to whom we preach Your Gospel and appoint as stewards over Your Church—so they, upon hearing, might prepare themselves and be vigilant for Your arrival".

The Lord, in His response, counseled us with solemnity, "Be vigilant, lest anyone mislead you. Do not be swayed by doubt or turn to other deities. Many shall claim my title, proclaiming, 'I am the Christ.' Do not believe them, nor approach them. For my return, the advent of the Son of God, will not be a hidden event but will illuminate the entire sky from east to west, as lightning flashes across the heavens. I shall descend upon the clouds with grandeur, surrounded by a mighty host, my cross leading the way. My arrival will be marked by a brilliance surpassing the sun sevenfold, accompanied by all my saints and celestial beings. My Father will place a crown upon my head, empowering me to judge both the living and the dead, rewarding each according to his deeds.

"Let the fig tree teach you a lesson: when its branch becomes tender and sprouts leaves, you know that summer is near. Likewise, when you observe these signs, know that the end is imminent".

I, Peter, prompted by curiosity, inquired further, "Lord, explain the parable of the fig tree so we might fully grasp its significance. The fig tree annually sprouts and yields fruit for its owner. What, then, does the fig tree symbolize in this parable? This remains unclear to us".

And the Lord responded to me, saying: Do you not comprehend that the fig tree symbolizes the house of Israel? Just as a man plants a fig tree in his garden, expecting fruit from it, but finds none. For many years he seeks its fruit, but to no avail, and he tells his gardener: Remove this fig tree, lest it render our soil barren. The gardener pleads with God: Allow us to clear the weeds, to till the soil around it, and to water it. If it still bears no fruit, we shall uproot it from the garden and replace it with another. Have you not grasped that the fig tree represents the house of Israel? Truly, I tell you, when its branches bud in the final days, false Christs shall emerge, stirring hope by claiming: I am the Christ, who has now come into the world. When Israel recognizes the evil of their deeds, they shall follow these deceivers and deny the true Christ, whom their ancestors praised yet crucified, committing a grave sin. But these deceivers are not the Christ. And upon their rejection, he will slay many, creating numerous martyrs. Then, the branches of the fig tree, the house of Israel, will flourish: many will be martyred by his hand. Enoch and Elijah will be sent to instruct them that this is the deceiver who will come into the world, performing signs and wonders to mislead. Those who die by his hand will be martyrs and counted among the virtuous and righteous martyrs who have found favor with God in their lives.

He revealed to me in his right hand the souls of all humanity, and on his right palm, the image of the final day's events: how the righteous and sinners will be divided, the fate of those upright in heart, and the eternal eradication of wrongdoers. We saw how sinners, in profound distress and sorrow, cried so bitterly that all who saw, be they righteous or angels, and even He Himself, wept.

I implored Him, saying: Lord, allow me to express my thoughts concerning the sinners: It would have been better for them had they never been born. The Savior replied: Peter, why do you say that non-existence would have been preferable for them? You oppose God. You cannot presume to have greater compassion than He has for His creation; He created them from nothing. Your heart is troubled because you have witnessed the future lamentation of sinners. But I will show you their deeds, by which they have offended the Most High.

Behold what awaits them in the last days, when the day of God's judgement arrives. From east to west, all humanity will be assembled before my eternal Father. He will order hell to relinquish all within its adamantine gates.

He will command the wild beasts and birds to return all flesh they have consumed, for He intends for mankind to reappear; before God, nothing is lost, and nothing is impossible, for all things belong to Him.

For everything will occur on the day of judgement, at God's command, just as everything came into being at His word during creation—so it will be in the end; with God, all things are possible. Hence, the scripture says: "Son of man, prophesy to the bones, and say: 'Bones, join together with sinews, nerves, flesh, skin, hair, [soul, and spirit].'"

And the great Uriel shall bestow upon them soul and spirit at the command of God; for God has appointed him over the resurrection of the dead at the day of judgment.

Behold and consider the grains of wheat sown into the earth. Like lifeless things, devoid of soul, they are planted in the soil: yet they revive, produce fruit, and the earth returns them, as a trust it has been charged with.

How much more, then, shall God resurrect those who believe in Him and are chosen by Him, for whom He created the world, on the day of decision? The earth shall return all things on that day of judgment, for it too shall face judgment alongside them, and so shall the heavens.

This will occur on the day of judgment for those who have forsaken their faith in God and have sinned: Torrents of fire shall be unleashed; darkness and gloom shall rise, enveloping and veiling the entire world, the waters transformed into burning coals, consuming all within them, and the sea shall turn to fire. Beneath the heavens, an unrelenting fire will rage, flowing to fulfill the judgment of wrath. The stars shall dissolve in flames as if they never existed, and the firmaments of heaven shall vanish, parched for lack of water, as if they had never been. Lightning shall cease, their once-terrifying flashes now only serving to alarm the world.

When creation itself dissolves, people from the east shall flee westward, those from the south to the north, in all directions they shall run, but the wrath of a fearsome fire shall pursue them. An unstoppable flame shall herd them towards the judgment of wrath, into the streams of an inextinguishable fire, blazing fiercely. As its waves part, a great gnashing of teeth will rise among humanity.

Then, all shall witness my arrival on an eternal cloud of brilliance. The angels of God accompanying me shall sit upon the throne of my glory at the right hand of my Heavenly Father, and He shall crown me. Upon seeing this, every nation shall mourn separately.

He shall then command them to enter the river of fire, where the deeds of each shall be laid bare before them, rewarding or punishing each according to their actions. The elect, who have committed good deeds, shall draw near to me and not witness death by the consuming fire. However, the wicked, sinners, and hypocrites shall dwell in the depths of darkness that shall not dissipate, their punishment being the fire, where angels shall reveal their sins and fashion a place for their eternal punishment (each according to his transgression).

Uriel, the angel of God, shall bring forth the souls of those sinners (each according to his transgression), who perished in the flood and all who dwelled in idols, every cast image, every object of affection, and images, and those who resided on all hills and in stones and by the wayside, whom men deemed gods: they shall be incinerated along with them (the objects they inhabited, or their worshippers?) in everlasting fire; and once all of them and their abodes are annihilated, they shall endure eternal punishment.

Then, men and women shall be led to the place prepared for them. By their tongues, with which they blasphemed the path of righteousness, they shall be suspended. Beneath them burns unquenchable fire, from which there is no escape.

Behold, yet another place: a vast, deep pit. Within it are those who denied righteousness, tormented by angels of punishment who ignite the flames of their torment.

And again, behold two women: they are hung by their necks and their hair; they shall be thrown into the pit. These are the ones who braided their hair not for goodness or beauty but to lure men into fornication, thereby ensnaring their souls into damnation. The men who engaged with them in fornication will be hung by their loins in that fiery place; they shall admit to one another: We did not realize we would face eternal punishment.

Murderers and their accomplices will be thrown into the fire, in a place filled with venomous creatures, tormented incessantly, acutely aware of their agony; their worms will be as numerous as a dark cloud. The angel Ezrael will bring forth the souls of those who have been slain, and they will witness the torment of their killers, saying to one another: Righteous and just is God's judgment. We heard but did not believe we would come to this place of eternal judgment.

Near this flame, there will be a great and very deep pit, into which all manner of torment, filth, and corruption flows from above. Women will be submerged up to their necks and suffer intense pain. These are the ones who caused their children to be born prematurely, corrupting the work of God who created them. Opposite them will be another place where their children sit alive, crying out to God. Lightning bolts emanate from these children, striking the eyes of the women who, for the sake of fornication, caused their demise.

Other men and women will stand above them, naked; their children, positioned in a place of joy, will sigh and cry to God about their parents, saying: These are they who despised and cursed, transgressing Your commandments and consigning us to death; they cursed the angel who formed us, hung us up, and denied us the light You granted to all creatures. The milk from their mothers' breasts will curdle, giving rise to flesh-devouring beasts that emerge, tormenting them and their partners forever, for they aban-doned God's commandments and killed their children. Their children, however, will be entrusted to the angel Temlakos. Those who killed them will suffer eternal torment, as God has decreed.

Ezrael, the angel of wrath, will bring forth men and women with half of their bodies burning, casting them into a realm of darkness, the hell of humanity; a spirit of wrath will punish them with diverse torments, and a ceaseless worm will consume their insides. These are the persecutors and betrayers of the righteous.

Adjacent, men and women gnaw their tongues; they will be tortured with red-hot iron and their eyes burned. These are the ones who slandered and doubted righteousness. Other men and women, whose deeds were cloaked in deceit, will have their lips removed, and fire will fill their mouths and innards. These are the false witnesses.

Nearby, upon a sharpened pillar of fire, more pointed than swords, men and women clad in tattered and filthy garments will suffer unending judgment. These are the wealthy who scorned widows and orphans, disregarding God's commandments.

Close by, in a filthy abyss, men and women stand knee-deep. These are the usurers.

Other men and women throw themselves from heights, pursued by demons. These are idol worshipers, driven to despair, continually casting themselves down, enduring endless torment. These are men who mutilated themselves to resemble women, and the women who were with them, all defiled themselves.

Beside them, the angel Ezrael prepares a place of intense fire for all idols made of gold and silver, the handiwork of humans, and the likenesses of creatures. Those who crafted and worshiped these images will be bound in chains of fire, punished for their folly before idols, enduring eternal judgment.

Next to them, men and women endure the burning fire of judgment, suffering eternally. These are those who abandoned God's commandment, succumbing to demonic persuasions.

In another elevated place, those who dishonored their parents will face unceasing torment, slipping and falling in a cycle of agony, a fitting punishment for their disregard and withdrawal from parental care, chastised forevermore.

Moreover, the angel Ezrael will guide children and maidens to witness the suffering of those tormented. They will be subjected to agony, suspended, and suffer numerous wounds inflicted by birds that consume flesh. These are individuals who pridefully indulged in their sins, disobeyed their parents, disregarded their fathers' teachings, and failed to respect their elders.

Adjacent to them will be girls cloaked in darkness as if it were their attire, enduring severe punishment, their flesh torn asunder. These are the ones who did not preserve their virginity until marriage, and for such actions, they will endure these torments and deeply feel their consequences.

Moreover, other men and women will incessantly gnaw their tongues, enduring eternal flames. These are the servants who failed to heed their masters; this will be their perpetual judgment.

Near this place of torment, there will be men and women, both mute and blind, dressed in white, who will cluster together and fall upon burning coals that never extinguish. These are individuals who boasted of their righteousness before God through almsgiving, yet did not truly pursue righteousness.

Ezrael, the angel of God, will extract them from this fire to conduct a decisive judgment. This will be their fate: a river of fire will surge, drawing all under judgment into its midst, and Uriel will position them there.

Surrounding them will be wheels of fire, with men and women suspended by the force of their rotation. Those within the pit will be consumed by flames; these are the sorcerers and witches. These wheels will enact judgment through fire unceasingly.

Subsequently, the angels will escort the chosen and righteous, who are impeccable in their integrity, carrying them in their arms, dressing them in garments of eternal life. They will witness the retribution meted out on their adversaries, and each individual's torment will be eternal, proportionate to their actions.

All those enduring torment will unanimously plead for mercy, acknowledging God's judgment, which was foretold to them, yet they did not believe. The angel Tartaruchus will then inflict even greater torment upon them, admonishing them for repenting when it is too late for repentance and no life remains. They will concede: God's judgment is righteous, as we now understand and acknowledge that His judgment is just; we are recompensed according to our deeds.

Subsequently, I will grant my chosen and righteous the cleansing and salvation they have sought, in the field of Akrosja, known as Elysium. They will decorate the righteous' domain with flowers, and I will revel with them. I will usher the nations into my everlasting kingdom, revealing to them the eternal life they have hoped for, as promised by me and my Father in heaven.

I have disclosed this to you, Peter. Proceed, therefore, to the land or city of the west.

And my Lord Jesus Christ, our King, instructed me: Let us ascend the holy mountain. Accompanied by his disciples, we prayed. Suddenly, two men appeared, their faces radiating light brighter than the sun, their garments indescribably luminous, unmatched by anything in this world. Their beauty was beyond words, their presence awe-inspiring. Another's appearance shone brighter than crystal, their appearance as vibrant as rose blossoms, their hair like rainbows in water, their beauty adorned with every ornament. Astonished by their sudden appearance, I approached Lord Jesus Christ and inquired: "O my Lord, who are these?" He informed me: "They are Moses and Elijah". I questioned him further about Abraham, Isaac, Jacob, and the rest of the righteous forefathers. He then revealed to us a vast, open garden filled with beauti-

ful trees, blessed fruits, and the fragrance of perfumes, pleasing to our senses, abundant in fruit. My Lord and God Jesus Christ then asked me if I had observed the assembly of the forefathers.

In the tranquility of their rest lies equally the honor and splendor for those persecuted for my righteousness. I rejoiced, affirmed, and grasped the truth inscribed in the gospel of my Lord Jesus Christ. I inquired of Him, "O my Lord, do you desire that I erect here three shelters, one for You, one for Moses, and one for Elijah?" In His ire, He responded, "Satan wages war against you, clouding your discernment; the material pleasures of this world overcome you. Thus, your eyes must be opened, and your ears cleared to perceive a sanctuary, not crafted by human hands, but by my Heavenly Father for me and the chosen ones". We saw it and were overwhelmed with joy.

Suddenly, a divine voice proclaimed from the heavens, "This is my beloved Son, with whom I am well pleased: adhere to His commandments". Then, a magnificent, exceedingly bright cloud enveloped us, lifting our Lord, Moses, and Elijah away. Trembling and filled with fear, we gazed upwards as the heavens unfolded, revealing men in the flesh, who approached to greet our Lord, Moses, and Elijah, before ascending into another realm. This event fulfilled the scripture, "This is the generation that seeks Him, that seeks the face of the God of Jacob". A profound awe and turmoil ensued in the heavens, as angels crowded,

ensuring the prophecy was realized: "Open the gates, O princes".
Subsequently, the heavens closed, once open.

We prayed and descended the mountain, exalting God, who inscribed the names of the virtuous in the celestial book of life.

Peter began, addressing me, "Listen, my son Clement, God fashioned all creation for His glory", elaborating on this concept. The glory of those who rightly extol God is depicted using imagery from the Revelation: "At His arrival, the Son will resurrect the dead...and will illuminate my faithful more brightly than the sun sevenfold, their crowns glistening like crystal and rainbows during rainfall, adorned with the scent of nard and beyond visual comparison, embellished with rubies, with the gleam of emeralds, with topazes, jewels, and golden pearls radiating like stars in the sky, and like sunbeams, too dazzling to behold". Regarding the angels: "Their faces beam brighter than the sun; their crowns resemble rainbows after rainfall, fragranced with nard. Their eyes sparkle like the morning star. The splendor of their visage is beyond words... Their garments, unspun, are as white as the fuller's cloth, as I witnessed on the mount where Moses and Elijah stood. Our Lord revealed the attire of the end times, of the resurrection day, to Peter, James, and John, sons of Zebedee, and a luminous cloud enshrouded us. We heard the Father's voice declare, 'This is my Son, whom I adore and with whom I am well pleased: heed Him.' Overawed, we forgot earthly matters and speech, bewildered by the grandeur of that day and the mountain that unveiled the second coming in the everlasting kingdom".

Next: "The Father has entrusted all judgment to the Son". The fate of the wicked—their eternal condemnation—is more than Peter can bear; he implores Christ for mercy on them.

My Lord replied, "Have you grasped what I previously conveyed? You are allowed knowledge of your inquiry: yet, do not divulge what you learn to the sinners, lest they further transgress and sin". Peter wept for many hours, ultimately finding solace in a response that, albeit extensive and ambiguous, hinted at eventual forgiveness for all: "My Father will grant them life, glory, and an enduring kingdom", (...) "It is for those who have believed in me that I have come. It is also for them, at their behest, that I will show mercy towards humanity".

THE APOCALYPSE OF PAUL

Here begins the vision of Saint Paul the Apostle.

Yet, I shall speak of visions and divine revelations bestowed by the Lord. Fourteen years past, I came to know a man in Christ—whether in the flesh or apart from it, remains unknown to me, God alone is aware—that he was taken up to the third realm of heaven. Of such a man, whether in corporeal form or not, I cannot say—God is the witness—that he was elevated into paradise and was privy to unspeakable truths, which man is not permitted to convey. For this individual, I will take pride, yet for myself, I will not boast, except in my frailties.

1 The revelation came to light during the consulship of Theodosius Augustus the Younger and Cynegius. In Tarsus, a man of distinction residing in the house once inhabited by Saint Paul received a nocturnal visit from an angel. This divine messenger instructed him to dismantle the home's foundation and reveal what he found. Initially, the man deemed this vision fallacious. 2 However, upon the angel's third visit, which included chastisement and compulsion to dig, he complied.

His excavation uncovered a marble box, etched with inscriptions, containing the revelation of Saint Paul, along with the shoes Paul had worn while preaching the word of God. Hesitant to open it, he brought it to the local magistrate, who then forwarded it, still lead-sealed, to Emperor Theodosius, fearing its contents might be malevolent. The Emperor, upon receiving it, broke the seal, unveiling Saint Paul's revelation. A copy was sent to Jerusalem, while the original was kept with him.

3 While I was yet in the flesh and ascended to the third heaven, the Lord's word came to me, commanding, "Speak to this people: How long will you persist in your rebellion, stacking sin upon sin, challenging the Lord who made you? You claim lineage from Abraham yet follow the path of the adversary. You profess to be God's children while serving the devil, boasting of God's protection in name only, yet destitute due to your transgressions. Be mindful and recognize that all of creation submits to God's will, except humanity, which alone sins. It dom-

inates all creation yet surpasses all in sinfulness.

4 Frequently, the sun, the great luminary, has petitioned the Lord, lamenting, "O Lord God Almighty, I behold the iniquity and injustice of humans. Grant me permission, and within my power, I will demonstrate that You are the only God". A voice responded, "I am well aware of these matters; My eyes observe, and My ears hear everything. Yet, My patience with them persists until they repent and turn back to Me. Should they fail to do so, I will judge them accordingly".

5 Occasionally, the moon and the stars have pleaded with the Lord, "O Lord God Almighty, You have entrusted us with the governance of the night; how much longer must we witness the evil deeds, the licentiousness, and the murders committed by humans? Allow us to exercise our power, that they might recognize You as the sole deity". A voice replied to them, "I am fully cognizant of all these occurrences; My sight is upon them, and My hearing catches every sound, yet My forbearance with them will continue until they repent and return to Me. However, if they do not turn back to Me, I will enact judgment upon them".

6 Often, the sea too has cried out, saying: "O Lord God Almighty, humans have desecrated Your holy name in me: allow me and I will rise and cover every forest and tree and all the earth, until I erase all humanity from Your presence, that they may recognize You are God alone". And again, a voice came, saying: "I know all, for My eyes see everything, and My ears hear, but My patience endures with them until they turn and repent. But if they do not return, I will judge them".

Sometimes, the waters also have lodged a complaint against humans, saying: "O Lord God Almighty, humans have defiled Your holy name". And a voice came, saying: "I know all things before they come to pass, for My eyes see and My ears hear everything; but My patience endures with them until they turn. And if not, I will judge". Often, the earth too has cried out to the Lord against humans, saying: "O Lord God Almighty, I endure harm more than all Your creation, bearing the fornications, adulteries, murders, thefts, false oaths, sorceries, and witchcrafts of humans, and all the evils that they commit, so that father rises against son, and son against father, stranger against stranger, each one to defile his neighbour's wife. The father ascends upon his son's bed, and the son likewise upon his father's couch; and with all these evils, those who offer sacrifices unto Your name have defiled Your holy place. Therefore, I endure harm more than the whole creation, and I would not yield my excellence and my fruits unto humans. Allow me and I will destroy the excellence of my fruits". And a voice said: "I know all things, and none can hide from his sin. And their wickedness I know; but My holiness endures them until they turn and repent. But if they do not return unto Me, I will judge them".

7 Behold then, you children of humans. The creation is subject unto God; but humankind alone sins.

Therefore, you children of humans, bless the Lord God unceasingly at all times and on all days; but especially when the sun sets. For in that hour, all the angels proceed unto the Lord to worship Him and to present the deeds of humans which every person does from morning until evening, whether they be good or evil. And there is an angel that departs rejoicing from the person in whom he dwells.

When therefore the sun sets, at the first hour of the night, in that same hour goes the angel of every people and of every man and woman, who protect and keep them, because human is the image of God: and likewise at the hour of morning, which is the twelfth hour of the night, do all the angels of men and women proceed to meet God and present all the work which every person has wrought, whether good or evil. And every day and night, the angels present unto God the account of all the deeds of humankind. Unto you, therefore, I say, O children of humans, bless the Lord God unceasingly all the days of your life.

8 At the appointed hour, therefore, all the angels, each one rejoicing, come forth before God together to meet Him and worship Him at the set hour; and behold, suddenly at the designated time there was a gathering, and the angels came to worship in the presence of God, and the spirit came forth to meet them, with a voice asking: "From where do you come, our angels, bringing tidings?" 9 They answered and said: "We come from those who have renounced the world for the sake of Your holy name, wandering as strangers in the caves of the rocks, weeping every hour they spend on earth, hungering and thirsting for the sake of Your name; with their waists girded, holding the incense of their hearts in their hands, praying and blessing at every hour, enduring hardship and disciplining themselves, weeping and mourning more than all who dwell on the earth. And we, their angels, do mourn with them; therefore, wherever it pleases You, command us to go and serve, especially the poor, more than all who dwell on the earth".

And the voice of God came unto them, saying: "Know that henceforth my grace shall be established with you, and my help, which is my dearly beloved Son, shall be with them, ruling them at all times; and He shall serve them and never forsake them, for their place is His dwelling".

10 When, then, these angels departed, behold, there came other angels to worship in the presence of the majesty, to meet therewith, and they were weeping. And the spirit of God went forth to meet them, and the voice of God asked: "From where have you come, our angels, bearing burdens, ministers of the news of the world?" They answered and said in the presence of God: "We come from those who have called upon Your name; and the snares of the world have made them wretched, devising many excuses at all times, and not offering even one pure prayer from their whole heart throughout their lives. Why then must we be with humans who are sinners?" And the voice of God came unto them: "You must

serve them until they turn and repent; but if they do not return to me, I will judge them".

Know therefore, O children of humans, that whatever you do, the angels report it unto God, whether it be good or evil.

11 After these events, I saw one of the spiritual beings coming towards me, and he lifted me in the spirit, transporting me to the third heaven.

The angel spoke to me, saying: "Follow me, and I will show you the place of the righteous where they are taken after death. Then, I will take you to the bottomless pit to show you the souls of the sinners and the type of place they are taken to after death".

I followed the angel, and he led me into heaven. There, I observed the firmament and saw the powers residing below it; forgetfulness that deceives and draws the hearts of men, the spirit of slander, the spirit of fornication, the spirit of anger, and the spirit of arrogance, along with the princes of wickedness. These things I saw beneath the firmament of heaven.

Looking further, I saw angels without mercy, showing no pity, their faces full of rage, teeth protruding from their mouths, their eyes glowing like the morning star of the east, and from the hairs of their head and their mouths, sparks of fire emerged. I asked the angel, "Who are these, Lord?" The angel replied, "These are the angels present in the hour of need, for those who did not believe they had the Lord as their helper and did not trust in Him".

12 Then, I looked higher and saw other angels whose faces shone like the sun, their loins girded with golden belts, holding palms in their hands, and wearing garments inscribed with the name of the Son of God, embodying all gentleness and mercy. I asked the angel, "Who are these, Lord, of such great beauty and compassion?" The angel responded, "These are the angels of righteousness sent to accompany the souls of the righteous in their time of need, those who believed they had the Lord as their helper". I inquired, "Do the righteous and sinners encounter each other after death?" The angel explained, "All pass unto God through the same path, but the righteous, having a holy helper, are not troubled as they appear in the presence of God".

13 I said to the angel, "I wish to see the souls of the righteous and sinners as they leave the world". The angel directed me, "Look down upon the earth". From heaven, I looked down at the earth and beheld the entire world, which appeared insignificant in my eyes; I saw humanity as though they were nothing, utterly vanishing. I was astonished and said to the angel, "Is this the magnitude of humans?" The angel replied, "Indeed, these are they who cause harm from morning until evening". I observed a vast cloud of fire covering the entire world and asked the angel, "What is this, Lord?" He explained, "This is the unrighteousness mixed by the princes of sinners".

14 When I heard this, I sighed and wept, then said to the angel: "I want to wait for the souls of the right-

eous and the sinners, and see how they depart from the body". The angel replied, "Look again upon the earth". I looked and saw the entire world: people appeared insignificant, utterly diminished. I observed a man on the verge of death; the angel informed me, "The man you see is righteous". I then saw all his deeds done in the name of God, all his desires, both remembered and forgotten, presented before him in his time of need. I noticed the righteous man had grown in righteousness, finding rest and confidence. Before he left the world, holy angels, as well as evil ones, stood by him. I saw them all; the evil ones found no place in him, but the holy ones took charge of his soul, guiding it until it left the body. They encouraged the soul, saying, "O soul, acknowledge your body from which you have come; for you must return to it on the day of resurrection to receive what is promised to all the righteous". They then took the soul from the body, kissed it as if it was a long-known friend, and said, "Be brave, for you have done God's will on earth". The guardian angel that watched over it daily came forward, saying, "Be brave, O soul, for I am joyful in you because you have fulfilled God's will on earth; I have reported all your deeds to God". Likewise, the spirit came forth to greet it, saying, "O soul, do not fear or be troubled until you reach a place you never knew; but I will be your helper, for I found in you a place of rest while I was with you on earth". The spirit strengthened it, and its angel carried it into heaven.

The angel continued, "Evil powers under heaven came out to meet it, including the spirit of error, which said, 'Where are you running, O soul, thinking to enter heaven? Stop and let us see if you carry anything of ours.' But we found nothing in you. I see also God's help and your angel; the spirit rejoices with you because you did God's will on earth". A conflict between good and evil angels ensued. The spirit of error first expressed regret, then the spirit of temptation and fornication approached it but the soul escaped, and they lamented. All principalities and evil spirits confronted it, found nothing, and gnashed their teeth. The guardian angel instructed them to retreat, "You tempted this soul, and it did not listen to you but worshipped in God's presence". After they retreated, Michael and all the angelic hosts fell and worshipped at God's footstool, saying to the soul, "This is the God of all, who made you in His image and likeness". The angel reported back, saying, "Lord, remember his deeds; this is the soul whose works I reported to you. Lord, act according to your judgment". Similarly, the spirit declared, "I am the quickening spirit that breathed upon it; I found rest in it when I dwelled within, acting according to your judgment". Then God's voice proclaimed, "As this soul has not grieved me, neither will I grieve it. Since it showed mercy, I too will show mercy. Let it be entrusted to Michael, the angel of the covenant, to lead it into the paradise of joy, to become co-heir with all the saints". I then heard the voices of thousands of angels, archangels, cherubim, and the twenty-four elders, singing hymns, glorifying the Lord, and proclaiming, "Righteous are You, O Lord, just are Your judgments, and You show no partiality, but reward each according to their deeds". The angel asked me, "Do you believe and understand that what each one of you has done is seen by God at the time of need?" And I replied, "Yes, Lord".

15 The angel said to me, "Look down again upon the earth and wait for the soul of a wicked man leaving the body, one who has defied the Lord day and night, proclaiming: 'In this world, I know nothing else but to eat, drink, and enjoy worldly pleasures. For who has descended into hell and returned to tell us of judgment there?' Then I looked and saw the disdain of the sinner and all his deeds, presented before him in his time of need. At the moment he was led from his body towards judgment, he exclaimed, 'It would have been better for me had I never been born.' The holy angels and the evil ones, along with the soul of the sinner, gathered, but the holy angels found no place in it. Instead, the evil angels dominated it, and as they took it from the body, they warned it thrice, 'O wretched soul, behold your flesh from which you have emerged; for you must return to your flesh on the day of resurrection to receive the just reward for your sins and wickedness.'

16 As they led it forth, the guardian angel went before it, saying, 'O miserable soul, I am the angel who accompanied you, reporting your evil deeds to the Lord daily. I ministered to you, hoping for even a single day of repentance; yet, I could achieve nothing, for God is merciful and a just judge. He commanded us to continue ministering to your soul until you might repent, but you wasted the opportunity for repentance. I am now a stranger to you, and you to me. Let us proceed to the just judge. I will not leave you until I ensure that from this day forward, I am a stranger to you.'

The spirit confused it, and the angel disturbed it. As they approached the principalities, and it attempted to enter heaven, it was burdened one after another: met by error, forgetfulness, whispering, the spirit of fornication, and the rest of the powers, which said, 'Where are you going, wretched soul, daring to advance into heaven? Halt, so we may see if you carry any of our properties, for we do not see a holy helper with you.'

Then, I heard voices from the heights of the heavens, declaring, 'Present this miserable soul before God, that it may recognize there is a God, whom it has scorned.' Upon its entry into heaven, seen by thousands upon thousands of angels, all exclaimed in unison, 'Woe to you, miserable soul, for the deeds you committed on earth. How will you answer God when you come near to worship Him?' The accompanying angel said, 'Weep with me, my dearly beloved, for I have found no peace in this soul.' The angels responded, 'Remove this soul from our midst, for its stench afflicts us since its arrival.' Subsequently, it was presented to worship in God's presence, and its angel revealed the Lord God who created it in His image and likeness, proclaiming, 'O Lord God Almighty, I am this soul's angel, whose deeds I reported to you day and night, not acting according to Your judgment.' Likewise, the spirit declared, 'I am the spirit that dwelled within it since its creation, aware of its nature, which did not follow my guidance. Judge it, Lord, according to Your judgment.' God's voice then addressed it, 'Where are the fruits worthy of the blessings you received? Did I differentiate you from the righteous, not allowing the sun to rise on you as it does on them?' The soul remained silent, with no response; and God declared, 'The judgment of God is just, showing no favoritism. Those who show mercy will receive mercy, and those who do not will not find mercy from God. Let it be handed over to the angel Tartaruchus, overseer of torments, cast into the outer darkness where there is weeping and gnashing of teeth, to remain until the great day of judgment.' Afterward, I heard the angels and archangels proclaiming, 'Righteous are You, O Lord, and just is Your judgment.'"

17 I observed again, and behold, a soul was escorted by two angels, who wept and pleaded: "Have mercy on me, O righteous God, O Judge; for today marks seven days since I departed my body. I was entrusted to these two angels, and they have led me to places I had never seen before". The righteous Judge, God, inquired: "What have you done? You never showed mercy; hence you were handed over to such merciless angels. Since you did not act justly, they too showed you no compassion in your time of need. Confess

the sins you committed while you were in the world". The soul responded: "Lord, I have not sinned". God was greatly angered by its claim of sinlessness, as it was a lie. God declared: "Do you think you are still in the world? While people may hide their sins from others there, nothing is concealed here. Upon arriving to worship before the throne, the deeds and sins of each soul are fully revealed". Hearing this, the soul was silent, with no reply to offer.

The righteous Lord God then commanded: "Come forth, angel of this soul, and stand in the center". The angel of the sinful soul approached, holding a document detailing all the sins of the soul from its youth to that day, from the age of ten. The angel mentioned, "Lord, if you command, I can also recount its deeds starting from when it was fifteen years old". The righteous Judge, God, clarified: "I do not request an account starting from its fifteenth year. Instead, reveal its sins from the five years preceding its death". God then swore by Himself, His holy angels, and His power, proclaiming: "Had it repented in the five years before its death, even for just a year, all its previous misdeeds would have been forgotten, granting it pardon and forgiveness. But now, let it be destroyed". The angel of the sinful soul requested, "Lord, command the specific angels to bring forth certain souls".

18 In that instant, the souls were brought forth, and the sinner's soul recognized them. God then addressed the sinner's soul: "Confess your actions against these souls you see here, from when you were in the world". The soul confessed: "Lord,

it has not been a full year since I murdered one of them, spilling their blood upon the earth, and with another, I committed fornication; not only that, but I also wronged them by taking their possessions". The righteous Judge, God, inquired: "Did you not know that one who harms another, if the victim dies first, is held in this place until the perpetrator also dies, and then both appear before the judge? And now, each has received according to their deeds".

A voice then decreed: "Let this soul be handed over to Tartaruchus, to be taken down into hell, placed in the lower prison, cast into torments, and left there until the great day of judgment". Following this, I heard thousands upon thousands of angels singing a hymn to the Lord, proclaiming: "Righteous are You, O Lord, and just are Your judgments".

19 The angel asked me, "Have you understood all these things?" I replied, "Yes, Lord". He then said, "Follow me once more, and I will take you to show the places of the righteous". I followed the angel, and he took me up to the third heaven, positioning me in front of a gate's door. Observing it, I noticed the gate was made of gold, with two pillars of gold adorned with golden letters. The angel turned to me and said, "Blessed are you if you enter through these gates, for entry is granted only to those who have preserved the goodness and purity of their bodies in all respects". Curious, I asked the angel, "Why are these letters inscribed on these panels?" He explained, "These are the names of the righteous who wholeheartedly

serve God and dwell on the earth". I further inquired, "Are their names inscribed here while they are still on earth?" He elaborated, "Not only their names but also their faces and likenesses of those who serve God are known in heaven, recognizable to the angels; for they identify those who serve God with all their heart before they leave the world".

20 Upon entering the gates of paradise, an old man whose face shone like the sun greeted me, embracing me, saying, "Hail, Paul, dearly loved by God". He kissed me joyfully yet wept. Puzzled, I asked, "Father (Brother), why do you weep?" With a sigh and tears, he expressed, "Because we are troubled by humans, deeply saddened; for the Lord has prepared many blessings and great are His promises, yet many fail to accept them". I turned to the angel, inquiring, "Who is this, Lord?" He revealed, "This is Enoch, the scribe of righteousness".

I proceeded inside and immediately saw Elijah, who greeted me warmly. Upon seeing me, he turned away, wept, and said, "Paul, may you receive the reward for your labor among humankind. I have witnessed vast and varied blessings God has prepared for all the righteous, and immense are God's promises. Yet, the majority do not accept them; indeed, only a few, through significant effort, enter these places".

21 The angel responded and said to me, "Have you fully grasped all that I have shown you here, and everything you have heard? Do not reveal them to anyone on the earth". He then led me forward and showed me more; I heard words there that are not lawful for a man to speak. And he said again, "Follow me once more, and I will show you things that you must share and proclaim openly".

He took me down from the third heaven and led me into the second heaven, and from there he led me to the firmament, and from the firmament, he led me to the gates of heaven. The foundation of it began at the river that waters the entire earth. I asked the angel, "Lord, what is this river of water?" He said to me, "This is the Ocean". Suddenly, I was taken out of heaven, and I realized it is the light from heaven that shines upon the whole earth. And there, the earth was seven times brighter than silver. I asked, "Lord, what is this place?" He said to me, "This is the land of promise. Have you not heard what is written: 'Blessed are the meek, for they shall inherit the earth'? Therefore, the souls of the righteous, when they depart from the body, are sent temporarily to this place". I asked the angel, "Will this land then be revealed in time?" The angel answered me, "When Christ, whom you preach, comes to reign, then by the decree of God, the first earth will be dissolved, and this land of promise will be revealed and become like dew or a cloud; and then the Lord Jesus Christ, the eternal king, will be revealed and will come with all His saints to dwell therein. He will reign over them for a thousand years, and they will eat of the good things which I will now show you".

22 And I looked around that land and saw a river flowing with milk and honey. And there were trees planted at the brink of the river, full of fruits. Each tree bore twelve fruits in a year, providing a variety of fruits. And I observed the creation of that place and all the works of God. There, I saw palm trees of twenty cubits and others of ten cubits height. And that land was seven times brighter than silver. The trees were full of fruits from the roots to the uppermost branches. I asked the angel, "Why does each tree produce thousands of fruits?" The angel answered and said to me, "Because the Lord God, in His bounty, gives abundantly to the worthy. They also, of their own will, afflicted themselves while they were in the world, doing everything for His holy name's sake".

23 The angel continued, saying to me, "Follow me, and I will bring you into the city of Christ". He stood upon the lake Acherusa, placed me in a golden ship, and three thousand angels sang a hymn before me until I arrived at the city of Christ. Those dwelling in the city rejoiced greatly as I approached, and I entered and saw the city of Christ, which was entirely made of gold. Twelve walls surrounded it, and within were twelve towers, with a furlong between each wall encircling it. I asked the angel, "Lord, how much is a furlong?" The angel answered, saying, "It is as much as the distance between the Lord God and the men on the earth, for the great city of Christ stands alone". There were twelve gates around the city of great beauty, and four rivers that encircled it: a river of honey, a river of milk, a river of wine, and a

river of oil. I asked the angel, "What are these rivers that surround this city?" He said to me, "These are the four rivers which flow abundantly for those in this promised land. Their names are Phison for the river of honey, Euphrates for the river of milk, Geon for the river of oil, and Tigris for the river of wine. Since the righteous did not exercise their dominion over these things in the world but hungered and afflicted themselves for the sake of the Lord God, therefore, when they enter this city, the Lord will give them these things in abundance, without measure".

24 As I entered through the gate, I saw before the doors of the city trees tall and majestic, bearing no fruits but only leaves. I saw a few men scattered among the trees, mourning deeply as they saw anyone enter the city. These trees performed penance for them, humbling and bowing down, then raising themselves up again.

I observed and wept with them, asking the angel, "Lord, who are these not permitted to enter the city of Christ?" He replied, "These are they who earnestly renounced the world day and night through fasting but had hearts prouder than others, glorifying and praising themselves, doing nothing for their neighbors. They greeted some warmly but ignored others completely, showing kindness selectively and boasting about any small act of neighborliness. I then asked, "So their pride has prevented them from entering the city of Christ?" The angel answered, "Pride is the root of all evil. Are they better than the Son of God, who came to the Jews in great humility?" I inquired further, "Why then do the trees humble and raise themselves?" The angel explained, "While they served God on Earth, they were momentarily ashamed by men's shame and reproach, humbling themselves; but they were not truly grieved nor repented, failing to abandon the pride within them. This is why the trees humble themselves and are then raised up again". I asked, "Why are they allowed near the city's gates?" The angel responded, "Because of God's great kindness, and because this is the entrance for all His saints entering the city. They are left here so that when Christ, the eternal king, enters with His saints, the righteous will intercede for them, allowing them to enter the city alongside them, though they cannot possess the confidence of those who have humbled themselves, serving the Lord God all their life".

25 I proceeded, and the angel led me to the river of honey, where I encountered Isaiah, Jeremiah, Ezekiel, Amos, Micah, and Zechariah, among other greater and lesser prophets, who greeted me within the city. I asked the angel, "What is this path?" He told me, "This is the path of the prophets: everyone who has grieved his soul and not pursued his own will for the sake of God, upon departing from the world and being brought before the Lord God to worship Him, is then, by God's command, delivered to Michael. He brings them into this city, to this place of the prophets, and they are greeted as friends

and neighbors because they have fulfilled the will of God".

26 Once more, he led me to the river of milk, and there I saw all the children whom King Herod had slain for the sake of Christ's name. They greeted me, and the angel explained, "All those who maintain purity and chastity, upon leaving their bodies and after worshiping the Lord God, are entrusted to Michael and brought to these children. They welcome them, declaring, 'These are our brothers, friends, and fellow members. Among them, they shall inherit the promises of God.'"

27 He then guided me to the northern side of the city, leading me to the river of wine. There, I encountered Abraham, Isaac, Jacob, Lot, Job, and other saints, who greeted me. Inquiring about this place, the angel informed me, "All who have shown hospitality, upon departing the world and first worshiping the Lord God, are delivered to Michael and brought through this path into the city. All the righteous welcome them as sons and brothers, saying, 'Because you have practiced kindness and hospitality, come and inherit a place in our Lord God's city.' Each righteous individual will receive rewards from God in the city according to their deeds".

28 Next, he brought me to the river of oil on the city's east side. I observed men rejoicing and singing psalms. Curious, I asked, "Who are these, Lord?" The angel replied, "These are they who devoted themselves to God with all their heart and harbored no pride. All who rejoice in the Lord God and sing praises to Him with their entire heart are brought here into this city".

29 Leading me into the city's midst, near the twelve walls, I saw a higher wall. I questioned if there was a wall in Christ's city more honored than this. The angel clarified, "Each wall surpasses the previous in glory, up to the twelfth. One excels another in splendor". Wondering why, I asked for an explanation. The angel said, "Any trace of slander, envy, or pride diminishes one's glory, even within Christ's city. Look behind you".

Turning, I beheld golden thrones at the gates, with men adorned in golden crowns and jewels. Within the twelve, I saw thrones of greater glory, beyond description. I asked, "Lord, who occupies these thrones?" The angel told me, "These thrones belong to those who, out of simplicity and heartfelt understanding, might have seemed foolish to the world for God's sake. Knowing little of Scripture or psalms but earnestly following a single chapter of God's commandments, they acted with great diligence and pure intention before the Lord. Such innocence earns them immense admiration and glory among all saints before God, who marvel at the unlearned, acknowledging the grandeur of their rewards due to their purity".

In the city center, I saw an exceedingly high altar. Standing beside it was one whose appearance shone like the sun, holding a psaltery and a harp, and singing praises, "Alleluia". His voice filled the city, and as all those on the towers and gates heard him, they echoed, "Alleluia", causing the city's foundations to tremble. I asked, "Who is this of such great power?" The angel informed me, "This is David. This city is Jerusalem; when Christ, the eternal king, fully establishes His reign, David will lead in praising Him, and all the righteous will join in chanting, 'Alleluia.'" Curious, I asked why David uniquely initiates the praises. The angel explained, "As Christ sits at His Father's right hand in the heavens, David will praise Him in the seventh heaven. This practice is mirrored on earth, where David's psalms are essential for offering sacrifices to God. Just as in heaven, so it is on earth, where David's praises accompany the offering of Christ's body and blood".

30 And I asked the angel, "Lord, what does Alleluia mean?" The angel replied, "You seek understanding in all things". He explained, "Alleluia is a word in Hebrew, the language of God and the angels, meaning 'Let us bless Him all together.'" Intrigued, I further inquired, "Lord, do all who say Alleluia bless God?" The angel confirmed, "Indeed, they do. Moreover, if someone sings Alleluia and those present do not join in, they sin by not participating. However, this does not apply to those who are unable or elderly". Clarifying, the angel added, "Only those who are capable but choose not to join in are considered to scorn the word, as it shows pride and disrespect not to bless the Lord, their Creator".

31 After explaining, the angel led me outside the city, through the trees, back from the land of blessings, to the river of milk and honey, and then to the ocean that supports heaven's foundation. "Do you realize that you are leaving this place?" he asked. "Yes, Lord", I answered. The angel then said, "Come, follow me, and I will show you the place of the ungodly and sinners, so you may understand their fate". We traveled westward, to the beginning of heaven, founded upon a vast river. Curious, I asked about the river, and he told me, "This is the ocean that encircles the earth". Beyond the ocean, I found darkness, sorrow, and gloom, which made me sigh.

32 I then saw a river of fire, with countless men and women submerged at various depths, some up to their knees, others to their navel, some to their lips, and others to their hair. I asked, "Lord, who are these in the river of fire?" The angel explained, "These are the lukewarm, neither counted among the righteous nor the wicked, as they lived lives mixing prayer with sin and fornication until death. Those up to their knees are those who left the church to engage in futile discussions. Those submerged to their navel are those who partook of Christ's body and blood only to commit sins of fornication without repentance. Those up to their lips are the slanderers within God's church, and those up to their eyebrows are those who secretly plotted against their neighbors".

33 On the north side, I observed a place of varied and severe torments, filled with souls and a river of fire pouring over them. I saw deep pits, where many souls were piled upon one another, their depths seemingly

bottomless. Hearing their pleas for mercy, unanswered, I asked, "Who are these, Lord?" The angel responded, "These are they who lacked faith in the Lord as their helper". Wondering about the capacity of these pits to hold generations of souls, the angel taught me about the abyss's boundlessness, illustrating its depth and the lengthy descent of the souls. Mourning for humanity, the angel consoled me, reminding me of God's patience and goodness, emphasizing that God's mercy surpasses our understanding, allowing all to exercise free will during their earthly lives.

34 Once more, my gaze fell upon the river of fire, where I beheld a man seized by the throat by the hell's guardians, the Tartaruchi, holding a three-pronged iron instrument with which they pierced the entrails of the elderly man. I questioned the angel, "Lord, who is this elder subjected to such torment?" The angel disclosed, "The man you see was a priest who failed to honor his sacred duties; indulging in eating, drinking, and lechery, he performed the Lord's sacrifice at His holy altar without reverence".

35 Not far from there, I witnessed another elder being forcefully brought by four malevolent angels. They submerged him to his knees in the river of fire, assaulting him with stones, marring his visage as if by a storm, and denied him the chance to plead, "Have mercy on me". Inquiring about his identity, the angel informed me, "This man was a bishop who fell short of embodying the sanctity expected of his high calling. Granted a revered title, he neither practiced righteousness nor showed compassion towards widows and orphans throughout his life; now, he faces retribution for his sins and actions".

36 Additionally, I observed another man in the river of fire, submerged up to his knees, his outstretched hands bloodied, worms emerging from his mouth and nostrils. He groaned, lamented, and cried out for mercy, claiming to endure greater agony than others in similar plight. I asked, "Who is this, Lord?" The angel replied, "This is a deacon who misappropriated offerings and engaged in fornication, failing to act righteously in God's sight. Thus, he eternally suffers for his transgressions".

Beside him, another man was hurriedly thrown into the river of fire, submerged up to his knees. An angel responsible for meting out punishments approached with a glowing hot razor, with which he severed the man's lips and tongue. Distressed and tearful, I questioned, "Who is this man, Lord?" The angel answered, "He was a reader who proclaimed the word to the people but failed to heed God's commandments. He now endures the consequences of his disobedience".

37 I saw yet another multitude of pits in that place, with a central river filled with countless men and women being devoured by worms. I wept and sighed, asking the angel, "Lord, who are these?" He explained, "These are individuals who amassed wealth through usury, placing their trust in their riches rather than in God as their protector".

Looking further, I noticed an exceedingly narrow area, surrounded by a wall of fire. Inside, men and women gnawed at their tongues. Curious, I inquired, "Who are these, Lord?" The angel revealed, "They are those who scoffed at God's word within the church, paying no heed, effectively scorning God and His angels. Thus, they now endure appropriate punishment".

38 Peering deeper, I beheld another pit with a surface resembling blood. I queried, "Lord, what is this place?" He informed me, "This pit is where all torments converge". Observing men and women submerged up to their lips, I asked, "Who are these, Lord?" The angel replied, "These are sorcerers who led men and women astray with magical spells, finding no peace till their demise".

Moreover, I saw individuals with darkened complexions in a fiery pit, causing me to sigh and weep. I questioned, "Who are these, Lord?" He explained, "These are fornicators and adulterers who, despite having their own spouses, pursued illicit relationships. Similarly, the women engaged in adultery. As a result, they incessantly bear the consequences of their actions".

39 I saw there girls clad in black raiment, and four dreadful angels holding in their hands red-hot chains, which they placed upon their necks and led them away into darkness. And again, I wept and inquired of the angel, "Who are these, Lord?" He responded, "These are the girls who, while virgins, defiled their virginity, unbeknownst to their parents. As a consequence, they perpetually endure their punishment".

Further, I beheld men and women with their hands and feet severed, standing naked amidst ice and snow, while worms consumed them. Upon witnessing this, I wept and questioned, "Who are these individuals, Lord?" He elucidated, "These are those who oppressed orphans, widows, and the destitute, not placing their trust in the Lord. Thus, they are subjected to unending punishment".

Additionally, I observed individuals hanging over a channel of water, their tongues extremely parched, with various fruits positioned before their eyes, yet they were not permitted to partake of them. I questioned, "Who are these people, Lord?" He explained, "These are the ones who broke their fast prior to the designated time, and for this reason, they endlessly suffer this penalty".

Moreover, I saw other men and women suspended by their eyebrows and hair, being pulled by a river of fire. I inquired, "Who are these individuals, Lord?" He disclosed, "These are those who did not dedicate themselves to their own spouses but instead to adulterers, and hence, they face ceaseless punishment".

I also noticed individuals covered in dust, their appearance resembling blood, trapped in a pit of pitch and brimstone, sinking into a river of fire. I asked, "Who are these, Lord?" He stated, "These are the ones who engaged in the egregious acts of Sodom and Gomorrah, men with men, and as a result, they undergo never-ending torment".

40 I looked and observed men and women dressed in bright attire, yet their eyes were blind, and they were positioned in a pit. I queried, "Who are these, Lord?" He revealed, "These are the pagans who performed acts of charity but did not recognize the Lord God; therefore, they are subject to ceaseless punishment".

Next, I saw additional men and women on a spit of fire, being torn apart by beasts, and they were not allowed to utter, "Lord, have mercy on us". I witnessed the angel of torments inflicting severe punishments upon them, commanding them to acknowledge the Son of God. He elaborated that these individuals had disregarded God's scriptures when presented to them, justifying the divine judgment upon them for their misdeeds. Overwhelmed with sorrow, I wept and inquired about these individuals' identities. He clarified that they were women who tainted God's creation through childbirth resulting from sinful unions and men who participated in these acts. Their offspring, however, sought justice from God and the angels presiding over torments, leading to their parents' eternal suffering while the offspring found themselves in a place of mercy.

I also saw individuals clad in tattered garments, coated with pitch, engulfed in flames, with dragons entwined around their necks and shoulders, as angels with fiery horns restrained them, chastising them for failing to repent in time. He identified these individuals as those who outwardly renounced worldly temptations yet fell short in acts of charity, hospitality, and adherence to God's commandments, consequently enduring endless torment alongside those who overtly neglected God.

Deeply mourning, I lamented the fate of all sinners, questioning the purpose of their existence. The angel reminded me of God's mercy and the choice given to each individual to select between good and evil, yet underscored the importance of repentance and righteousness. He then hinted at more severe torments yet unseen, promising to reveal the deeper realms of hellish punishment.

41 The angel then led me from the north side to the west and positioned me above a well that was sealed with seven seals. The angel accompanying me spoke to the guardian of that place, saying, "Open the mouth of the well, so that Paul, dearly beloved of God, may look upon it; for he has been granted the power to see all the torments of Hell". The angel then cautioned me, "Stand back, so you may endure the stench that emanates from this place". When the well was opened, immediately an extremely foul and unbearable stench arose, surpassing all other torments. Peering into the well, I observed masses of fire burning from every direction, filled with anguish, and the entrance so narrow, it seemed only one person could pass through at a time. The angel explained to me, "Anyone who is cast into this abyssal well and then sealed over will never be remembered before the Father, the Son, and the Holy Ghost, nor before the holy angels".

Intrigued, I inquired, "Lord, who are those cast into this well?" He responded, "Those are the individuals who refuse to confess that Christ has come in the flesh, that the Virgin Mary bore Him, and those who deny the bread and the cup of the Eucharist as the body and blood of Christ".

42 Turning my gaze from the north to the west, I witnessed the unceasing worm and heard the gnashing of teeth. The worms there measured about one cubit and bore two heads. I saw both men and women enduring the cold, shivering and grinding their teeth in agony. Curiously, I asked, "Lord, who are the souls enduring this place?" He informed me, "These are the ones who denied that Christ has risen from the dead and that the flesh shall rise again". Further questioning the absence of fire or warmth, He clarified, "This place harbors only biting cold and snow. Despite this, even if the sun—or seven suns, according to some texts—were to shine upon them, it would not bring them warmth, due to the extreme cold and snow here". Hearing this, I was moved to tears and lamented, expressing a wish that we, sinners, had never been born.

43 As those within this cold domain witnessed my weeping, accompanied by the angel, they too began to cry out and weep, pleading for mercy from the Lord God. Shortly thereafter, the heavens opened, revealing Michael the Archangel descending from heaven, accompanied by all the heavenly host. They approached those tormented souls, who upon seeing them, wept anew and implored for mercy, acknowledging the judgment of God and the Son of God they had now recognized. They lamented their inability to pray for this recognition before their damnation, attributing their failure to repent to the distractions and temptations of worldly life. Michael, addressing all present, proclaimed his unwavering stance before God, advocating for humanity both day and night, lamenting their ceaseless engagement in sin and failure to produce goodness on earth. He vowed to continue interceding for the Earth's fertility and to advocate for any who commit even the slightest act of goodness, striving to protect them from the judgment of torment. He then urged those tormented to weep, promising to join their lamentations in hopes of eliciting God's mercy. Upon hearing these words, they cried out and wept bitterly, collectively beseeching the Son of God for mercy. I, Paul, overwhelmed by the scene, also sighed and prayed for God's mercy on His creation, the children of men, and His own image.

44 I witnessed heaven tremble as if it were a tree shaken by the wind. Suddenly, all present prostrated themselves before the throne. I observed the twenty-four elders and the four living creatures worshipping God. I saw the altar, the veil, and the throne, all rejoicing, with the smoke of a sweet fragrance rising beside the altar of God's throne. I heard a voice inquire, "Why do you beseech me, our angels and ministers?" They responded, "We appeal to you, witnessing your immense kindness towards humanity". Then, I saw the

Son of God descending from heaven, crowned. Upon seeing Him, those enduring torments cried out in unison, "Have mercy on us, O exalted Son of God. You, who have provided relief to all in heaven and on earth, extend your mercy to us as well; for having seen you, we have found solace". A voice from the Son of God echoed through all the places of torment, questioning, "What righteous deeds have you done to merit asking for my solace? My blood was shed for you, yet you did not repent. For your sake, I wore a crown of thorns, endured blows on my face, yet you remained unrepentant. When I was crucified, I thirsted, and they gave me vinegar mixed with gall; they pierced my side with a spear. For my name's sake, they killed my prophets and the righteous. Despite all this, I offered you a chance for repentance, which you rejected. Yet now, because of Michael, the archangel of my covenant, the angels with him, and Paul, my dearly beloved, whom I do not wish to distress, and because of your brethren who make offerings, your sons who keep my commandments, and my own benevolence, I grant all of you in torment a day and a night of reprieve forever, on the day I rose from the dead". Overjoyed, they all exclaimed, "We praise you, Son of God, for granting us respite for a day and a night. This brief relief is more precious to us than our entire earthly existence. Had we truly understood that this place was reserved for sinners, we would have refrained from all worldly endeavors, abstaining from trade and sin. What value did

our arrogance bring in the world? Now, our pride entraps us, and our anguish, tears, and the worms beneath us inflict greater suffering than the torments we endure". As they lamented, the angels of torment and the demonic angels rebuked them, "How long will you weep and moan? You showed no mercy, and thus, you face God's judgment. Nevertheless, you've received this significant grace, a respite on the Lord's Day, thanks to Paul, the dearly beloved of God, who descended to you".

45 After witnessing these events, the angel inquired of me, "Have you seen all these things?" To which I affirmed, "Yes, Lord". He then directed me, "Follow me, and I will take you to Paradise, so the righteous there may behold you. They eagerly anticipate your arrival, ready to greet you with joy and celebration". Following the angel with the swiftness imparted by the Holy Spirit, he placed me in Paradise, proclaiming, "This is Paradise, where Adam and his wife transgressed". Entering Paradise, I observed the source of the waters. The angel pointed out, "Behold these waters. This is the river Phison, encircling the land of Evila; and this, Geon, circumnavigating the land of Egypt and Ethiopia; this other is Tigris, opposite the Assyrians; and this, Euphrates, watering the land of Mesopotamia". Venturing further, I encountered a tree from whose roots flowed waters, marking the origin of the four rivers. The Spirit of God dwelled upon this tree, and the waters surged forth with its breath. I queried, "Lord, is this the tree that causes the waters

to flow?" He explained, "Before the manifestation of heaven and earth, when all was void, the Spirit of God hovered over the waters. Since creation, the Spirit has rested upon this tree, prompting the waters to flow whenever it breathes". He guided me to the tree of the knowledge of good and evil, stating, "This tree introduced death into the world when Adam, upon his wife's urging, partook of it, bringing death among us". He then revealed another tree at Paradise's heart, declaring, "This is the tree of life".

46 As I continued to gaze upon the tree, a virgin approached from afar, preceded by two hundred angels singing hymns. Curious, I asked, "Lord, who is this, arrayed in such splendor?" He informed me, "This is Mary, the virgin, mother of the Lord". Approaching, she greeted me, "Hail, Paul, dearly beloved by God, angels, and humans. All the saints have implored my son Jesus, my Lord, for your presence here in the flesh, that they might see you before your departure from the world". The Lord reassured them, "Be patient a little longer, and you shall see him, and he shall abide with you forever". Unitedly, they entreated Him, expressing a deep desire to witness you in the flesh, for your ministry has immensely glorified His name on earth, surpassing all deeds, both minor and major. They questioned newcomers, 'Who guided you in the world?' The answer was unanimously 'Paul'; through his proclamation of Christ and the persuasive eloquence of his words, many were led into the kingdom. "Behold, all the righteous eagerly advance to greet

you. I, Paul, assure you, it is for this reason I precede them, to welcome those who have fulfilled the will of my son and Lord Jesus Christ. I approach them first, ensuring they are not left as strangers until they peacefully reunite with Him".

47 While she was still speaking, I beheld three men of surpassing beauty, resembling the visage of Christ, accompanied by their shining forms and angels. Curious, I inquired, "Who are these, Lord?" He revealed, "These are the patriarchs of the people: Abraham, Isaac, and Jacob". Approaching, they greeted me warmly, proclaiming, "Hail, Paul, dearly beloved by God and men. Blessed is the one who suffers for the Lord's sake". Abraham then spoke, introducing Isaac as his son and Jacob as his most cherished, stating, "We recognized the Lord and followed Him. Blessed are those who, believing in your teachings, shall inherit God's kingdom through labor, self-sacrifice, sanctification, humility, charity, meekness, and true faith in the Lord. We, too, were devoted to the Lord you preach, pledging to visit every believer's soul, serving them as fathers do their sons".

As they spoke, I noticed twelve men of distinction approaching from afar. Inquiring about their identity, the Lord informed me, "These are the patriarchs". They, too, extended their salutations, expressing joy at seeing me in the flesh before my departure from this world. Each patriarch introduced himself, from Reuben to Benjamin, with Joseph adding, "I am the one who was sold. Yet, for all the hardships my brothers imposed upon me, I bore them no ill will, from dawn till dusk. Blessed is he who endures suffering for the Lord's cause, for he shall receive greater rewards upon leaving this world".

48 While Joseph spoke, another figure of striking beauty approached, surrounded by angels chanting hymns. Puzzled, I asked, "Lord, who is this fair-faced individual?" He inquired if I did not recognize him, to which I confessed ignorance. He then disclosed, "This is Moses, the lawgiver, to whom God delivered the law". As Moses drew near and wept before greeting me, I questioned the reason for his tears, given his unparalleled meekness. He lamented the fruitlessness of his labor with the Israelites, who strayed like sheep without a shepherd, neglecting the wonders he performed and failing to grasp the essence of his teachings. He marveled at how foreigners, the uncircumcised, and idol worshippers have embraced the faith and entered into God's promises, whereas Israel has not. Moses then recounted the sorrow of God the Father, Michael, all angels, Abraham, Isaac, Jacob, and the righteous over the crucifixion of Jesus, the Son of God, lamenting the actions of his people. He concluded by blessing me and the generations who have accepted my teachings.

49 As he was speaking, another group of twelve approached and recognized me, asking, "Are you Paul, who is celebrated in heaven and upon earth?" I replied, inquiring who they were. The first declared, "I am Isaiah, whom Manasseh sawed in two with a wooden saw". Similarly, the second revealed, "I am Jeremiah, who was stoned and killed by the children of Israel". The third proclaimed, "I am Ezekiel, dragged by the children of Israel by my feet over the mountain stones until my brains were scattered. All of us endured these hardships, hoping to save the children of Israel. I tell you, despite the trials they inflicted upon me, I would prostrate myself before the Lord, praying for them and kneeling until the second hour of the Lord's day, until Michael lifted me from the ground. Blessed are you, Paul, and blessed are those who have believed through you".

As they moved on, I noticed another, radiantly beautiful, and inquired, "Who is this, Lord?" [Seeing me, he was joyful] and said to me, "This is Lot, found righteous in Sodom". Approaching, he greeted me, saying, "Blessed are you, Paul, and blessed is the generation you have served". I asked him, "Are you Lot, who was deemed righteous in Sodom?" He responded, "I hosted angels in my home as strangers. When the city's people sought to harm them, I offered my two virgin daughters, who had not known any man, allowing them to use them as they pleased, only asking that no harm come to these men, for they were under my roof. Hence, we should be assured that God rewards manifold more for any deed done when one comes to Him. Blessed are you, Paul, and blessed is the generation that has believed your word".

After he finished speaking, I saw another coming from afar, with a very beautiful countenance, smiling, accompanied by angels singing hymns. I asked the angel beside me, "Does each righteous individual have an angel companion?" He explained, "Each of the saints has their own angel who stands by them, sings hymns, and never departs from their side". Curious, I asked, "Who is this, Lord?" He informed me, "This is Job". Approaching, Job greeted me, saying, "Brother Paul, you are highly esteemed by God and men. I am Job, who endured great suffering for thirty years due to a plague. Initially, the blisters that emerged on my body were the size of wheat grains, but by the third day, they grew to the size of a donkey's hoof, and the worms falling from them were four fingers in length. Three times the devil appeared to me, tempting me to curse God and die. Yet, I refused, declaring if it were God's will for me to endure this affliction for the rest of my life, I would not cease blessing the Lord, for I knew the sufferings of this world are insignificant compared to the refreshment that follows. Therefore, blessed are you, Paul, and blessed are the people who have believed because of you".

50 As he spoke, another voice called out from a distance, proclaiming, "Blessed are you, Paul, and blessed am I to have beheld you, the beloved of the Lord". I inquired of the angel, "Who is this, Lord?" He informed me, "This is Noah, from the time of the flood". We immediately exchanged greetings, and he, filled with joy, questioned me, "Are you Paul, the one most beloved by God?" Curious, I asked him to identify himself. He responded, "I am Noah, who

lived during the flood. But let me tell you, Paul, I spent a hundred years building the ark, never changing the tunic I wore, nor did I shave the hair of my head. Moreover, I abstained from approaching my wife, and throughout those hundred years, the hair on my head did not grow longer, nor did my clothes become soiled. During that time, I implored people, warning, 'Repent, for a deluge is coming upon you.' However, they mocked and scorned my words, claiming it was a time for unrestrained play and sin, believing God was indifferent to their actions and that no flood would befall the world. Their transgressions persisted until God eradicated all life that breathed. Know this, Paul, God cherishes one righteous individual more than the entire realm of the wicked. Thus, you are blessed, O Paul, and so is the generation that has come to believe through you".

51 Turning, I observed other righteous figures approaching from the distance. I questioned the angel, "Who are these, Lord?" He replied, "These are Elijah and Elisha". Upon their greeting, I asked them to identify themselves. One answered, "I am Elijah, the prophet of God. I am the Elijah who prayed, and by my word, the heavens withheld rain for three and a half years due to mankind's iniquities. Righteous and true is God, fulfilling the desires of His servants. Often, angels petitioned the Lord for rain, but He would reply, 'Be patient until my servant Elijah prays for it, and then I will send rain upon the earth.'" It was not until my subsequent prayer that He provided them with rain. "But you,

O Paul, are blessed, for your teachings have made your followers heirs to the kingdom. Know, O Paul, that anyone who believes through you is greatly blessed, with a special blessing reserved for them". Then, he departed from my presence.

The accompanying angel then guided me forward, saying, "Behold, this mystery and revelation are granted to you: as you wish, make it known to humankind".

And I, Paul, was brought back to my senses, fully aware of all that I had seen. In life, I found no peace until I could reveal this mystery, which I wrote down and hid beneath the ground and the foundations of the house of a trustworthy man in Tarsus, a city in Cilicia, where I frequently stayed. Upon my release from this temporal life and my standing before the Lord, He questioned me, "Paul, did we reveal all these things to you for them to be hidden beneath a house's foundations?" He then commanded me to share this revelation, allowing people to read it and turn towards the path of truth, to spare them from enduring these severe torments.

And so, this revelation was uncovered. (...)

THE APOCALYPSE OF THOMAS

Here begins the letter from the Lord to Thomas regarding what is to transpire in the latter days.

Listen, Thomas, to the events that must occur in the last days: there will be famine, war, and earthquakes in various places, along with snow, ice, and severe drought. There will also be many disagreements among people, blasphemy, wickedness, envy, evil deeds, laziness, pride, and excessive indulgence, so that everyone will say whatever they please. My priests will not have peace among themselves but will offer sacrifices to me with deceitful hearts: therefore, I will not regard them. Then the priests will see the people leaving the house of the Lord and turning to the world, and establishing (or violating) sacred boundaries in the house of God. They will claim for themselves many things and places that were lost, which will be under Caesar's control (?) as they were before, imposing taxes on the cities, including gold and silver. The leading figures of the cities will be judged, and their wealth taken to† the treasury of the kings, and it will be filled.

There will be a great unrest among all the people, leading to death. The house of the Lord will become desolate, and its altars despised, so that spiders will weave their webs there. The sacred places will be defiled, the priesthood will be corrupted, distress will increase, virtue will be defeated, joy will disappear, and happiness will fade. In those days, evil will flourish: there will be favoritism, songs of praise in the house of the Lord will stop, truth will vanish, and greed will be rampant among the priests; an honest man (or an honest priesthood) will not be found.

Suddenly, near the end of times, a king who loves the law will rise to power, but his reign will be short: he will leave behind two sons. The elder is named after the first letter (A, Arcadius), and the younger after the eighth (H, Honorius). The elder will die before the younger (Arcadius died in 408; Honorius in 423).

After this, two rulers will rise to oppress the nations, under whom there will be a severe famine in the eastern part, causing nations to fight against each other and be expelled from their own lands.

Another king will then rise, a deceitful man, who will order a golden statue of Caesar to be made (or worshipped in the house of God), which will lead to an increase in martyrdoms. Then faith will return to the servants of the Lord, holiness will grow, and distress will increase. The mountains will be comforted and will drip with the sweetness of fire, so that the number of saints may be fulfilled.

After a short while, a king from the east, a lover of the law, will come to power, ensuring that all necessary goods abound in the house of the Lord. He will show mercy to widows and the needy, and order a royal donation for the priests: in his time, there will be an abundance of everything.

Then, a king will rise in the southern part of the world, reigning for a short period: during his time, the treasury will be depleted due to the salaries of the Roman soldiers, †forcing the wealth of the elderly to be taken and given to the king to distribute†.

After that, there will be plenty of grain, wine, and oil, but money will be extremely scarce, so much so that gold and silver will be exchanged for grain, leading to a great scarcity.

At that time, the sea will rise tremendously, making it impossible for anyone to communicate news to another. The kings of the earth, along with princes and captains, will be anxious, and no one will speak openly. Grey hair will be seen on young boys, and the young will not show respect to the elderly.

After this, another king will arise, a deceitful man, who will rule for a brief period. During his reign, every kind of evil will occur, including the death of the human race from the east to Babylon. And then, death, famine, and war will spread from the land of Canaan to Rome. All water sources and wells will boil over and turn into dust and blood. The sky will shake, stars will fall to the earth, the sun will be split in half like the moon, and the moon will not give its light. There will be significant signs and wonders in those days as the Antichrist approaches. These are the signs for those living on the earth. In those days, the agony of great distress will come upon them. Woe to those who build, for they will not live in their buildings. Woe to those who till the soil, for they will work in vain. Woe to those who marry, for they will have children in times of famine and need. Woe to those who consolidate houses or lands, for everything will be consumed by fire. Woe to those who do not care for themselves while they have the chance, for later they will be condemned forever. Woe to those who ignore the poor when asked for help.

These are the seven signs before the end of the world. There will be famine, great diseases, and distress across the earth: then all people will be taken captive among all nations and fall by the sword.

On the first day of judgment, a great wonder will occur. At the third hour of the day, a loud and powerful voice will be heard in the sky, and a great cloud of blood will descend from the north, followed by loud thunders and intense lightning, resulting in a rain of blood over the entire earth. These are the signs of the first day.

On the second day, a great voice will be heard in the sky, and the earth will shift out of its place. The gates of heaven will open in the eastern sky, and a tremendous force will be emitted from the gates of heaven, covering the sky until evening. These are the signs of the second day.

On the third day, around the second hour, a voice will be heard from heaven, and the depths of the earth will make their sound from the four corners of the world. The first heaven will roll up like a scroll and immediately disappear. Due to the smoke and smell of sulfur from the abyss, the days will darken until the tenth hour. Then all people will say, "I think the end is near, that we are about to perish." These are the signs of the third day.

On the fourth day, at the first hour, the land of the east and the abyss will make noise: then the entire earth will shake from a powerful earthquake. On that day, all the idols of the pagans and all the structures of the earth will fall. These are the signs of the fourth day.

On the fifth day, at the sixth hour, there will be sudden great thunderings in the sky, and the forces of light and the sun's orbit will be taken away, leading to great darkness over the world until evening, and the stars will be removed from their functions. On that day, all nations will hate the world and despise the life of this world. These are the signs of the fifth day.

On the sixth day, there will be signs in the sky. At the fourth hour, the sky will split from the east to the west. The angels of heaven will look down upon the earth through the opening in the sky. And all people will see the host of angels looking out from heaven. Then all people will flee.

GOSPEL OF NICODEMUS OR ACTS OF PILATE

Prologue

I, Ananias, the Protector, of Praetorian rank, knowledgeable in the law, have recognized our Lord Jesus Christ through the divine scriptures and came closer to him through faith. I was deemed worthy of holy baptism. I sought out the historical records from the time of our master Jesus Christ, which were stored by the Jews with Pontius Pilate. I discovered these records in Hebrew and, by God's favor, I translated them into Greek to share the knowledge with all who call upon the name of our Lord Jesus Christ. This happened during the reign of our Lord Flavius Theodosius, in his seventeenth year, and Flavius Valentinianus, in his sixth year, during the ninth indiction.

Therefore, all of you who read this and decide to translate it into other books, remember me and pray for me, that God may show grace and mercy towards me for the sins I have committed against him.

May peace be upon those who read and listen to these things and upon their servants. Amen.

In the fifteenth year of the rule of Tiberius Caesar, emperor of the Romans, and of Herod, king of Galilee, in the nineteenth year of his reign, on the eighth day before the Calends of April, which is the 25th of March, during the consulate of Rufus and Rubellio, in the fourth year of the two hundred and second Olympiad, Joseph, who is Caiaphas, being the high priest of the Jews:

These are the events that Nicodemus recorded and handed over to the high priest and the rest of the Jews after the crucifixion and passion of the Lord. Nicodemus compiled these accounts in Hebrew.

Chapter 1

1 The chief priests and scribes, including Annas, Caiaphas, Somne, Dothaim, Gamaliel, Judas, Levi, Nepthalim, Alexander, Jairus, and other Jews, gathered in council and approached Pilate to accuse Jesus of various acts. They stated, "We

recognize this man as the son of Joseph the carpenter, born of Mary. He claims to be the Son of God and a king; furthermore, he violates the sabbaths and intends to abolish our ancestors' law."

Pilate asked, "What has he done that he would abolish the law?"

The Jews replied, "Our law forbids healing anyone on the sabbath. Yet, this man, through his actions, has healed the lame, the bent, the withered, the blind, the paralytic, the mute, and those possessed, on the sabbath day!"

Pilate inquired, "Through what actions?"

They told him, "He is a magician, and by Beelzebub, the prince of demons, he expels demons, all of whom obey him."

Pilate responded, "Exorcising demons does not come from an unclean spirit, but by the god Asclepius."

2 The Jews appealed to Pilate, "We ask your excellency to have him appear before your tribunal for judgment." Pilate summoned them and questioned, "How can I, a governor, judge a king?" They answered, "We are not claiming he is a king; he says so himself."

Pilate then summoned the messenger and directed, "Bring Jesus here, but gently." The messenger, upon finding Jesus, showed him reverence, spread the kerchief he was holding on the ground, and said, "Lord, walk on this and enter, for the governor summons you." When the Jews saw what the messenger had done, they protested to Pilate, "Why didn't you command him to be summoned by a herald rather than a messenger? The messenger, upon seeing him, showed him reverence, spread his kerchief on the ground, and made him walk on it as if he were a king!"

3 Pilate then questioned the messenger, "Why did you do this, spreading your kerchief on the ground and making Jesus walk upon it?" The messenger answered, "Governor, when you sent me to Jerusalem to Alexander, I saw Jesus riding on a donkey, and the Hebrew children were holding branches and shouting, while others spread their garments under him, saying: 'Save now, you who are in the highest: blessed is he who comes in the name of the Lord.'"

4 The Jews loudly objected to the messenger, "The Hebrew children shouted in Hebrew; how then do you recount it in Greek?" The messenger replied, "I asked one of the Jews, 'What are they shouting in Hebrew?' and he explained it to me." Pilate asked them, "And how did they shout in Hebrew?" The Jews answered, "Hosanna membrome barouchamma adonai." Pilate inquired, "And the Hosanna and the rest, what does it mean?" The Jews explained, "Save now, you who are in the highest: blessed is he who comes in the name of the Lord." Pilate said, "If you yourselves confirm the words said by the children, how has the messenger erred?" And they fell silent.

The governor instructed the messenger, "Go and bring him in however you see fit." The messenger went and did as before, telling Jesus, "Lord, enter, the governor summons you."

5 When Jesus entered, and the ensigns were holding the standards, the images on the standards bowed and showed reverence to Jesus. Seeing how the standards bowed and showed reverence, the Jews vehemently protested against the ensigns. Pilate asked the Jews, "Are you not amazed that the images showed reverence to Jesus?" The Jews accused the ensigns of manipulating the standards. The governor questioned the ensigns, who replied, "We are Greeks and temple servants; how could we have done this? The images bowed and showed reverence on their own while we were holding them."

6 Pilate then told the synagogue leaders and elders, "Select strong and capable men to hold the standards, and let's see if they bow on their own." The Jewish elders chose twelve strong men to hold the standards in front of the governor's seat. Pilate said to the messenger, "Take him out of the hall and bring him in again as you did before." Jesus and the messenger exited. Pilate warned those who had held the standards, "I swear by Caesar's safety, if the standards do not bow when Jesus reenters, I will have your heads."

Pilate ordered Jesus to be brought in again. The messenger did as before, urging Jesus to walk on his kerchief. Jesus did so and entered. Upon his entry, the standards bowed again and showed reverence to Jesus.

Chapter 2

1 Pilate, upon witnessing these events, became fearful and tried to rise from his judgement seat. Before he could stand, his wife sent a message to him, saying, "Stay away from this innocent man, for I have suffered a great deal because of him in my dreams tonight." Pilate then summoned all the Jews and said to them, "You are aware that my wife is a God-fearing woman who respects Jewish customs, aren't you?" They confirmed, "Yes, we know." Pilate continued, "Look, my wife has sent me a message advising me to have nothing to do with this just man because she has suffered a lot due to him tonight." However, the Jews replied to Pilate, insisting, "Didn't we tell you that he is a sorcerer? Look, he has even caused your wife to have a disturbing dream."

2 Pilate called Jesus to him and asked, "What do these people accuse you of? Won't you respond?" Jesus answered, "If they had no power, they would say nothing. Everyone has control over their own mouth to choose to speak good or evil. They will deal with the consequences."

3 The Jewish elders retorted to Jesus, "What will we see then? First, that you were born out of wedlock; second, that your birth in Bethlehem resulted in the massacre of infants; third, that your father Joseph and your mother Mary had to flee to Egypt because they couldn't face the people."

4 Some bystanders, devout Jews, spoke up, "We do not claim he was born out of wedlock. We know that Joseph was pledged to marry Mary, and he was not born out of wedlock." Pilate addressed the Jews who accused Jesus of being born out of wedlock, "Your claim is false

because there was a betrothal, as these others from your community affirm." Annas and Caiaphas contested to Pilate, "The majority of us insist he was born out of wedlock, and yet we are not believed. However, these are converts and followers of his." Pilate inquired from Annas and Caiaphas about converts, to which they explained, "They were born from Greek families and later adopted Judaism." Those defending Jesus, including Lazarus, Asterius, Antonius, and others, stated, "We are not converts but born Jews, and we are telling the truth. We were actually present at Joseph and Mary's betrothal."

5 Pilate summoned the twelve men who claimed Jesus was not born out of wedlock and asked them under the solemn oath of Caesar's safety, "Is it true that he was not born out of wedlock?" They answered Pilate, "Our law forbids us to swear as it is a sin. But if those accusers swear by Caesar's safety that our statement is false, and it proves to be true, let us be subject to death." Pilate turned to Annas and Caiaphas, "Do you have any response to this?" Annas and Caiaphas said to Pilate, "We believe these twelve men who claim he was not born out of wedlock, but the vast majority of us insist he was born out of wedlock, is a sorcerer, claims to be the Son of God and a king, yet we are not believed."

6 Pilate then ordered the entire crowd to leave, except for the twelve men who said Jesus was not born out of wedlock. With Jesus set aside, Pilate asked them, "Why do they want to kill him?" They explained to Pilate, "They are envious because he

heals on the sabbath." Pilate was astonished, "They want to kill him for doing good deeds?" They confirmed, "Yes."

Chapter 3

1 Pilate was overtaken by frustration and stepped outside the judgement hall, declaring to those present, "I swear by the Sun that I find no fault in this man." The Jews retorted to the governor, "If he were not a criminal, we would not have handed him over to you." Pilate responded, "Then take him and judge him according to your law." The Jews informed Pilate, "We are not permitted to put anyone to death." Pilate questioned, "Has God forbidden you to kill but allowed me?"

2 Pilate returned inside the judgement hall and privately questioned Jesus, asking, "Are you the King of the Jews?" Jesus replied to Pilate, "Are you asking this on your own, or did others talk to you about me?" Pilate responded, "Am I a Jew? Your own nation and the chief priests have brought you to me. What have you done?" Jesus stated, "My kingdom does not belong to this world. If it did, my followers would fight to prevent me from being handed over to the Jews. But my kingdom is from another place." Pilate inquired, "So you are a king, then?" Jesus answered, "You say that I am a king. I was born and came into this world to testify to the truth. Everyone on the side of truth listens to me." Pilate asked, "What is truth?" Jesus told him, "Truth comes from heaven." Pilate wondered, "Isn't there truth on earth?" Jesus responded, "You see

how those who speak the truth are judged by those with authority on earth."

Chapter 4

1 Pilate left Jesus in the judgement hall and went out to the Jews, stating, "I find no fault in him." The Jews argued, "This man claimed, 'I can destroy this temple and rebuild it in three days.'" Pilate asked, "Which temple?" The Jews replied, "The one that Solomon built in forty-six years, but this man claims he will destroy and rebuild it in three days." Pilate declared, "I am innocent of this man's blood. It's your responsibility." The Jews exclaimed, "Let his blood be on us and our children!"

2 Pilate summoned the elders, priests, and Levites, advising them in secret, "Don't proceed with this; there's nothing he's done that deserves death, as your accusations involve healing and breaking the Sabbath." The elders, priests, and Levites asked, "If a man blasphemes against Caesar, does he deserve death?" Pilate affirmed, "He does deserve death." The Jews then said to Pilate, "If someone deserves death for blaspheming against Caesar, this man has blasphemed against God."

3 Pilate ordered all the Jews out of the judgement hall and asked Jesus privately, "What should I do with you?" Jesus answered Pilate, "Do as it has been decreed for you." Pilate inquired, "And what has been decreed?" Jesus mentioned, "Moses and the prophets foretold of my death and resurrection." The Jews eavesdropped on this conversation and then said to Pilate, "Why do you need to hear more of this blasphemy?" Pilate told the Jews, "If this statement is blasphemous, then take him for his blasphemy, bring him to your synagogue, and judge him according to your law." The Jews informed Pilate, "Our law dictates that if someone sins against another, they may receive up to thirty-nine lashes; but one who blasphemes against God should be stoned."

4 Pilate told them, "Take him and deal with him as you see fit." The Jews insisted to Pilate, "We want him to be crucified." Pilate objected, "He does not deserve crucifixion."

5 Observing the crowd of Jews around him, Pilate noticed many were crying and said, "Not everyone here wants him to die." An elder of the Jews claimed, "The entire crowd of us came here for him to be put to death." Pilate asked the Jews, "Why should he die?" The Jews answered, "Because he claimed to be the Son of God and a king."

Chapter 4

1 And Pilate left Jesus in the judgement hall and went out to the Jews and said to them: I find no fault in him. The Jews said to him: This man claimed: I can destroy this temple and rebuild it in three days. Pilate asked: Which temple? The Jews replied: The one that Solomon built in forty-six years, but this man claims he will destroy and rebuild it in three days. Pilate said to them: I am innocent of this just man's blood: see to it yourselves. The Jews said: His blood be on us and on our children.

2 And Pilate called the elders, priests, and Levites to him and said to them privately: Do not do this, for there is nothing deserving death in what you have accused him of, since your accusation is about healing and breaking the Sabbath. The elders, priests, and Levites said: If a man blasphemes against Caesar, does he deserve death or not? Pilate said: He deserves death. The Jews said to Pilate: If a man deserves death for blaspheming against Caesar, this man has blasphemed against God.

3 Then the governor ordered all the Jews to leave the judgement hall, and he called Jesus to him and said to him: What should I do with you? Jesus said to Pilate: Do what has been determined. Pilate asked: How has it been determined? Jesus said: Moses and the prophets have foretold about my death and resurrection. The Jews listened secretly and heard this, and they said to Pilate: Why do you need to hear more of this blasphemy? Pilate said to the Jews: If this statement is blasphemous, take him for his blasphemy, and judge him according to your law in your synagogue. The Jews said to Pilate: It is written in our law, that if a man sins against another man, he can receive up to forty lashes minus one; but whoever blasphemes against God should be stoned.

4 Pilate said to them: Take him and judge him however you see fit. The Jews said to Pilate: We want him to be crucified. Pilate said: He does not deserve to be crucified.

5 As the governor looked around at the crowd of Jews standing by, he saw many of them weeping and said:

Not all the people wish for him to be put to death. An elder of the Jews said: We all have come here for the sole purpose of having him put to death. Pilate asked the Jews: Why should he die? The Jews said: Because he claimed to be the Son of God and a king.

Chapter 5

1 But a certain man, Nicodemus, a Jew, came and stood before the governor and said: I beg you, honorable sir, allow me to say a few words. Pilate said: Speak. Nicodemus said: I said to the elders, priests, Levites, and to all the crowd of Jews in the synagogue: Why are you contending with this man? This man performs many and wonderful signs, which no one has ever done before, nor will anyone be able to do. Leave him alone and do not devise any harm against him: if the signs he performs are from God, they will endure; but if they are from men, they will come to nothing. Indeed, Moses, when sent by God to Egypt, performed many signs that God commanded him before Pharaoh, king of Egypt; and there were men, Pharaoh's servants, Jannes and Jambres, who also performed several signs like those of Moses, and the Egyptians considered them gods, Jannes and Jambres. However, since the signs they performed were not from God, they perished, and so did those who believed in them. And now, let this man go, for he is not deserving of death.

2 The Jews said to Nicodemus: You have become his disciple and are speaking in his defense. Nicodemus

said to them: Has the governor also become his disciple that he speaks in his defense? Wasn't he appointed to his position by Caesar? And the Jews were furious and gnashed their teeth at Nicodemus. Pilate said to them: Why do you gnash your teeth at him when you've heard the truth? The Jews said to Nicodemus: May you accept his truth and share his fate. Nicodemus said: Amen, Amen: may I receive it as you have said.

Chapter 6

1 Now, one of the Jews stepped forward and asked the governor if he could say something. The governor said: If you have something to say, go ahead. And the Jew said: For thirty-eight years, I was confined to my bed, suffering in pain, and when Jesus came, many who were possessed or afflicted with various diseases were healed by him. Some young men took pity on me, carried me with my bed, and brought me to him; and when Jesus saw me, he felt compassion, and said to me: Take up your bed and walk. And I took up my bed and walked. The Jews said to Pilate: Ask him on which day he was healed? The healed man said: On the Sabbath. The Jews said: Didn't we tell you so, that he heals and casts out devils on the Sabbath?

2 And another Jew came forward and said: I was born blind: I could hear words but saw no one's face: and as Jesus passed by, I cried out loudly: Have mercy on me, O son of David. He took pity on me, placed his hands on my eyes, and I immediately regained my sight.

Another Jew came forward and said: I was hunched over, and he straightened me with a word. And another said: I was a leper, and he healed me with a word.

Chapter 7

And a certain woman named Bernice, shouting from a distance, said: I had been suffering from bleeding for twelve years and touched the hem of his garment, and immediately my bleeding stopped. The Jews said: We have a law that forbids a woman from giving testimony.

Chapter 8

And many others, both men and women, cried out, saying: This man is a prophet, and demons are subject to him. Pilate asked those who said the demons are subject to him: Why then are not your teachers subject to him? They said to Pilate: We don't know. Others also said: He raised Lazarus from the dead, who had been in his tomb for four days. The governor became afraid and said to all the crowd of Jews: Why do you want to spill innocent blood?

Chapter 9

1 Pilate summoned Nicodemus and the twelve men who had testified that Jesus was not born of fornication, questioning them on how to handle the escalating unrest among the people. They replied that they were unsure and suggested letting the people decide. Pilate then addressed the Jewish crowd, reminding them of their custom to release

a prisoner during the feast of unleavened bread. He presented them with a choice between Barabbas, a condemned murderer, and Jesus, in whom Pilate found no fault. The crowd chose Barabbas. When Pilate asked what should be done with Jesus, called the Christ, the response was a demand for crucifixion. Some Jews warned Pilate that releasing Jesus would be an act against Caesar, as Jesus had claimed to be the Son of God and a king, suggesting a preference for Jesus over Caesar as king.

2 Pilate expressed frustration with the Jews, accusing them of constant sedition and ingratitude towards their benefactors. The Jews questioned which benefactors he referred to, and Pilate listed the many ways their God had aided them, from the Exodus from Egypt to providing sustenance in the wilderness, despite their provocations and idolatry. Pilate refuted their accusation of him being disloyal to the emperor.

3 Attempting to leave, Pilate was stopped by the Jews proclaiming their loyalty to Caesar over Jesus, recounting how wise men had once brought gifts to Jesus as to a king, leading Herod to seek to kill him, which resulted in the massacre of the infants of Bethlehem.

4 These statements alarmed Pilate. He attempted to calm the increasingly vocal crowd, inquiring if Jesus was the one Herod had sought. The Jews confirmed this. Pilate then publicly washed his hands, declaring his innocence in Jesus' fate, while the Jews declared themselves and their descendants responsible for Jesus' blood.

5 Pilate, behind a veil at his judgment seat, informed Jesus that he had been condemned by his own people as a king. Therefore, Pilate decreed that Jesus would be scourged according to the law and then crucified in the garden where he was arrested, along with the malefactors Dysmas and Gestas.

Chapter 10

1 Jesus, along with the two malefactors, was led out of the judgment hall to the crucifixion site. There, Jesus was stripped, dressed in a linen cloth, crowned with thorns, and crucified alongside Dysmas and Gestas. Jesus asked for forgiveness for those crucifying him, stating their ignorance. The gathered crowd, including chief priests and rulers, mocked Jesus, challenging him to save himself and come down from the cross if he truly was the Son of God. Soldiers also mocked him, offering him vinegar mixed with gall, and challenged his claim as the King of the Jews. Pilate ordered that a sign in Greek, Latin, and Hebrew be placed above Jesus, declaring him the King of the Jews.

2 One of the crucified malefactors, named Gestas, taunted Jesus, urging him to save himself and them if he was the Christ. However, the other malefactor, Dysmas, rebuked Gestas, acknowledging their just punishment and Jesus' innocence. Dysmas asked Jesus to remember him in his kingdom, to which Jesus assured him that he would be with him in paradise that very day.

Chapter 11

1 Darkness enveloped the land from the sixth hour until the ninth because the sun lost its light. Simultaneously, the temple's veil tore in half. Jesus then loudly entrusted his spirit to the Father's care and died. This sight led the centurion to honor God, acknowledging Jesus' righteousness, while the witnessing crowds, stricken by what they saw, lamented and departed.

2 The centurion relayed the day's events to the governor, deeply troubling him and his wife, to the point of forgoing food and drink. Pilate, in turn, sought the Jews' perspective, who dismissed the day's darkness as a common solar eclipse.

3 Onlookers from Galilee and Jesus' acquaintances watched from a distance. Joseph of Arimathaea, a council member and follower of Jesus, requested and was granted Jesus' body by Pilate, which he then respectfully enshrouded and placed in a new, unused tomb.

Chapter 12

1 News of Joseph's actions prompted the Jews to pursue him, the twelve defenders of Jesus' legitimacy, Nicodemus, and others who had publicly supported Jesus. While most went into hiding, Nicodemus faced the Jews. In this confrontation, Nicodemus, and later Joseph, affirmed their allegiance to Jesus amidst threats from the Jews. The Jews responded by confining Joseph, intending to deny him a proper burial, threatening to expose his body to scavengers. Joseph countered by invoking divine retribution, reminding them of their self-imposed curse related to Jesus' blood.

2 The Sabbath saw the Jewish authorities decreeing a congregation in the synagogue to deliberate on Joseph's punishment. However, their plans were thwarted when they found Joseph's prison sealed yet empty upon their return, causing dismay and preventing further harm to Jesus' defenders.

Chapter 13

1 While they were still sitting in the synagogue, amazed by Joseph, some guards whom the Jews had asked Pilate to station at Jesus' tomb came forward. They feared that his disciples might come and steal his body. These guards reported to the synagogue leaders, priests, and Levites what had happened: there was a great earthquake, and they saw an angel descend from heaven, roll the stone away from the entrance of the tomb, and sit on it. The angel shone like snow and lightning, causing them great fear, and they lay on the ground as if they were dead. They heard the angel tell the women at the tomb not to be afraid because Jesus, who was crucified, had risen as he said. The angel invited them to see where Jesus had been laid and then quickly go and tell his disciples that he had risen from the dead and was in Galilee.

2 The Jews asked which women the angel spoke to, but the guards admitted they didn't know. When asked about the time, the guards said it

happened at midnight. The Jews questioned why the guards hadn't detained the women, to which the guards responded they were paralyzed with fear and didn't expect to live to see the daylight, so how could they have detained them? The Jews expressed disbelief, but the guards countered by pointing out that the Jews had witnessed many signs from Jesus and yet did not believe, so why would they believe the guards now? Indeed, they said, "as the Lord lives," because he truly lives. The guards also mentioned hearing about the Jews detaining the man who requested Jesus' body and sealing the tomb, only to find it empty when opened. They proposed that if the Jews handed over Joseph, they would return Jesus. The Jews replied that Joseph had gone to his own city. The guards then reiterated that Jesus had risen, as the angel said, and was in Galilee.

3 Hearing this, the Jews became very afraid and worried that if this news spread, everyone would believe in Jesus. They decided to bribe the soldiers, telling them to claim that while they slept, Jesus' disciples came and stole his body. They assured the soldiers that if the governor heard about this, they would convince him and protect the soldiers. The soldiers took the money and did as instructed. This fabricated story was widely disseminated.

Chapter 14

1 A priest named Phinees, a teacher named Addas, and a Levite named Aggaeus, who had come from Galilee to Jerusalem, reported to the synagogue leaders, priests, and Levites that they saw Jesus and his disciples on the mountain called Mamilch. Jesus told his disciples to preach to all creation that those who believe and are baptized will be saved, while those who do not believe will be condemned. He added that believers would cast out demons, speak new languages, handle serpents safely, not be harmed by poison, and heal the sick by laying hands on them. While Jesus was still speaking, they saw him ascend into heaven.

2 The elders, priests, and Levites asked them to give glory to the God of Israel and confess if they truly heard and saw these things. The witnesses swore by the God of Abraham, Isaac, and Jacob that they did hear and see these events and saw Jesus ascend into heaven. Questioned about their purpose, whether to report these events or fulfill vows to God, they said it was to fulfill their vows. The religious leaders then questioned the relevance of their story, considering it idle talk in front of the people. Phineës, Addas, and Aggaeus responded that if their testimony was considered sinful, they were ready to face the consequences. The leaders then made them swear not to spread this story, provided them with food and drink, sent them away with money and three men to escort them as far as Galilee, ensuring their peaceful departure.

3 After their departure to Galilee, the chief priests, synagogue leaders, and elders gathered, lamenting over the events and fearing their implications for Israel. Amlas

and Caiaphas attempted to reassure them by suggesting that the disciples had bribed the tomb guards to spread the story of the angel and the rolling away of the stone. However, the question of how Jesus could physically be in Galilee if his disciples had merely stolen his body remained unanswered. In the end, they resolved that as Jews, they could not accept the testimony of the non-Jewish guards, maintaining the stance that the disciples had fabricated the story of the resurrection, despite the difficult questions that remained.

Chapter 15

1 And Nicodemus stood up before the council, saying, "You are right. Do you not know, O people of the Lord, about the men from Galilee, who fear God and are men of means, who despise lies and are peacemakers? They have sworn to you, saying: 'We saw Jesus on Mount Mamilch with his disciples, teaching them everything you have heard from them, and we saw him ascend into heaven.' And no one asked them how he ascended. Just as the holy scriptures have taught us that Elijah was taken up into heaven, and Elisha cried out loudly, and Elijah threw his cloak to Elisha, who then threw the cloak over the Jordan, crossed over, and went to Jericho. And the sons of the prophets met him, asking, 'Elisha, where is your master Elijah?' and he replied that he was taken up into heaven. They suggested to Elisha that perhaps a spirit had taken him and thrown him onto a mountain, but let us take our servants and search for him. They convinced Elisha, and he went with them, but after searching for three days, they did not find him and realized he had been taken up. Now, listen to me, let's send messengers throughout Israel to see if Christ was taken up by a spirit and left on a mountain." This idea pleased everyone, and they searched throughout the regions for Jesus but did not find him. However, they found Joseph of Arimathea, and no one dared lay hands on him.

2 And they reported to the elders, priests, and Levites, saying, "We searched all over Israel and did not find Jesus; only Joseph we found in Arimathea."

Hearing about Joseph, they were glad and praised the God of Israel. The synagogue leaders, priests, and Levites planned how to approach Joseph, writing him a letter:

"Peace be with you. We acknowledge our sins against God and against you, and we have prayed to the God of Israel, hoping you would join your ancestors and your family, for we are distressed, having not found you when we looked: and we understand our plans against you were evil, but God has thwarted them, O honorable Joseph, revered by all."

3 They chose seven men, friends of Joseph, who he also considered friends, and the synagogue leaders, priests, and Levites told them, "If he reads our letter and accepts it, he will come with you to us; but if he does not, it means he holds a grudge against us. Wish him peace and return to us." They

blessed the men, who then went to Joseph, greeted him with reverence, and said, "Peace be with you." He replied, "Peace to you and all Israel." They handed him the letter; Joseph read it, embraced it, praised God, saying, "Blessed be the Lord, who saved Israel from shedding innocent blood; blessed is He who sent His angel to protect me." He hosted them, offering food and drink, and they stayed the night.

4 Rising early, they prayed, and Joseph, riding his donkey, accompanied the men to Jerusalem. The people welcomed him, wishing peace upon his arrival. He greeted them back, and everyone embraced him. People prayed with Joseph, amazed by his presence.

Nicodemus welcomed him home, hosting a great feast for Annas, Caiaphas, elders, priests, and Levites. They celebrated, praising God, and each returned home, but Joseph stayed with Nicodemus.

5 The next day, synagogue leaders, priests, and Levites visited Nicodemus's home early. Nicodemus greeted them with peace, which they returned, extending it to Joseph and their households. They convened, placing Joseph between Annas and Caiaphas, but none dared speak directly to him. Joseph asked why they summoned him. Nicodemus was prompted to explain that the esteemed doctors, priests, and Levites wished to learn from him. Joseph agreed to answer their questions. Annas and Caiaphas, using the law book, asked him to honor God and confess, reminding him of Achar's truthfulness to the prophet

Joshua, urging Joseph to be equally forthcoming. They expressed their dismay over Joseph's actions following Jesus's death, securing his body, and the mysterious circumstances of his disappearance from a sealed and guarded room, urging him to explain.

6 Joseph recounted being imprisoned by them on the preparation day and remained there until midnight on the Sabbath. At midnight, as he prayed, the room was lifted, filled with light, causing him to fall. An angel helped him up, cleansed him with water, and surrounded him with a fragrant ointment. The angel encouraged Joseph, revealing himself to be Jesus, whom Joseph had cared for after his crucifixion. Jesus confirmed his identity, showing Joseph the burial site, and then miraculously transported Joseph home, instructing him to stay indoors for forty days as he would be visiting his brethren in Galilee.

Chapter 16

1 And when the leaders of the synagogue, the priests, and the Levites heard Joseph's words, they were overcome with shock and fell to the ground, fasting until the ninth hour. Nicodemus and Joseph comforted Annas, Caiaphas, the priests, and the Levites, saying: Get up and stand on your feet. Eat some bread and strengthen yourselves, for tomorrow is the Lord's Sabbath. They got up, prayed to God, ate and drank, and each went back to his own house.

2 On the Sabbath, the teachers, priests, and Levites gathered and asked each other: What is this disaster that has come upon us? We know his father and mother. Levi, the teacher, said: I know that his parents feared God, didn't withhold their vows, and paid tithes three times a year. When Jesus was born, his parents brought him here, offering sacrifices and burnt offerings to God. And when the great teacher Symeon held him in his arms, he said: Now, Lord, you let your servant depart in peace, for my eyes have seen your salvation, which you have prepared in the presence of all peoples, a light for revelation to the Gentiles, and the glory of your people Israel. Symeon blessed them and said to Mary, his mother: I bring you good news about this child. Mary asked: Good, my lord? Symeon replied: Yes, good. See, he is destined for the fall and rise of many in Israel and to be a sign that will be opposed - and a sword will pierce your own soul too - so that the thoughts of many hearts will be revealed.

3 They asked Levi, the teacher: How do you know these things? Levi said to them: Don't you know that I learned the law from him? The council asked him: We want to see your father. They summoned his father, questioned him, and he said to them: Why didn't you believe my son? The blessed and righteous Symeon taught him the law. The council asked: Rabbi Levi, is what you've said true? He answered: It is true. Then the leaders of the synagogue, the priests, and the Levites said among themselves: Let's send to Galilee for the three men who came and told us about his teachings and ascension, and have them explain how they saw him ascend. Everyone agreed to this, and they sent for the three men who had previously gone to Galilee, telling them: Say to Rabbi Addas, Rabbi Phinees, and Rabbi Aggaeus: peace be with you and all who are with you. Because there's been much questioning in the council, we've summoned you to this holy place, Jerusalem.

4 The men went to Galilee and found them sitting and meditating on the law, greeting them peacefully. The Galileans replied: Peace be upon all Israel. They asked: Why have you come? The messengers replied: The council calls you to the holy city of Jerusalem. Hearing this, the men prayed to God, ate and drank with the messengers, then set off peacefully to Jerusalem.

5 The next day, the council convened in the synagogue and questioned them: Did you actually see Jesus sitting on Mount Mamilch, teaching his eleven disciples, and did you see him ascend? The men confirmed: As we saw him ascend, so we have told you.

6 Annas said: Separate them and let's see if their stories agree. They separated them, and first called Addas, asking him: How did you see Jesus ascend? Addas replied: While he was still sitting on Mount Mamilch teaching his disciples, we saw a cloud overshadow him and his disciples. The cloud lifted him into heaven, and his disciples lay on the ground, face down. They questioned Phinees the priest in the same way, and he gave a similar account. They also questioned Aggaeus, who cor-

roborated the story. The council concluded: The law of Moses states: A matter must be established by the testimony of two or three witnesses. Abuthem, the teacher, said: It's written in the law: Enoch walked with God and then was no more, because God took him. Jaeirus, the teacher, added: We've also heard about the death of the holy Moses and haven't seen him; for it's written in the Lord's law: Moses died by the Lord's decree, and no one knows his grave to this day. Rabbi Levi asked: Why did Rabbi Symeon say, upon seeing Jesus, that this child is destined for the fall and rise of many in Israel and to be a sign that will be opposed? Rabbi Isaac stated: It's written in the law: I will send my messenger ahead of you, who will prepare your way before you, for my name is in him.

7 Then Annas and Caiaphas said: You have rightly quoted what is written in the law of Moses, that no one saw Enoch's death, and Moses's death is unmarked. But Jesus spoke before Pilate, and we saw him subjected to slaps and spit, crowned with thorns by the soldiers, scourged, and condemned by Pilate, crucified at Golgotha with two thieves, given vinegar mixed with gall to drink, and Longinus the soldier pierced his side with a spear. Our honorable father Joseph requested his body, and he claims Jesus rose again. The three teachers affirm: We saw him ascend into heaven. Rabbi Levi testified to what was spoken by Rabbi Symeon, saying: This child is destined for the fall and rise of many in Israel and to be a sign that will be opposed.

All the teachers told the people of the Lord: If this has happened by the Lord's doing, it is marvelous in our eyes. Know, O house of Jacob, it is written: Cursed is everyone who hangs on a tree. Another scripture warns: The gods who did not make the heavens and the earth shall perish.

And the priests and the Levites said to one another: If his memory lasts until the Jubilee, known as the Sommos or Jobel, understand that he will prevail forever and establish a new people for himself.

Then the leaders of the synagogue, the priests, and the Levites advised all of Israel, saying: Cursed be anyone who worships what human hands have made, and cursed be the one who worships any creature instead of the Creator. And all the people responded: Amen, Amen.

And all the people sang a hymn to the Lord, saying: Blessed is the Lord who has given rest to the people of Israel in everything He promised. Not one of His promising words to His servant Moses has failed. May the Lord our God be with us as He was with our ancestors; may He not leave us or forsake us. May He turn our hearts to Him, to walk in all His ways and keep His commands, decrees, and regulations given to our ancestors. And the Lord will be king over the whole earth on that day. There will be one Lord, and His name the only name, the Lord our King: He will save us.

There is none like You, O Lord. Great are You, O Lord, and great is Your name.

Heal us, O Lord, and we will be healed; save us, and we will be saved, for we are Your portion and inheritance.

And the Lord will not abandon His people, because of His great name, since the Lord has begun to make us His people.

And after singing this hymn, everyone went to their own house, glorifying God. For to Him belongs the glory, forever and ever. Amen.

Blessed be the Lord God who has given rest to all the people of Israel according to His promise. And may the Lord our God be with us as He was with our ancestors.

And they all went to their homes, praising God.

Then the teacher (Addas) said to the entire congregation: If all the things they have testified to happened in Jerusalem, they are from God, and we should not be astonished. The leaders of the synagogue, the priests, and the Levites said among themselves: It is written in our law: "His name shall be blessed forever; his place shall endure before the sun and his throne before the moon: through him, all the tribes of the earth will be blessed, and all nations will serve him; kings will come from afar to worship and exalt him."

Then Annas and Caiaphas separated the three individually and questioned them privately. They agreed, and all three gave the same account. The chief priests said: Our scripture states that every matter must be established by the testimony of two or three witnesses. Joseph thus admitted that he took care of his burial with Nicodemus and affirmed the truth of his resurrection.

Part II: Acts of Pilate
Chapter 17

1 And Joseph stood up and said to Annas and Caiaphas: It is truly astonishing that you have heard Jesus has been seen alive after his death, and that he ascended into heaven. However, what is even more astonishing is that he did not rise from the dead alone, but also raised many others from their graves, and they have been seen by many in Jerusalem. And now listen to me; we all know the blessed Simeon, the high priest who took the child Jesus into his arms in the temple. This Simeon had two sons, brothers, and we were all present at their death and their burial. Go, therefore, and look at their graves: for they are open, because they have risen, and now they are in the city of Arimathaea, praying together. And indeed, people hear them shouting, but they do not speak to anyone, they are as silent as the dead. But let's go to them and with all respect and kindness bring them to us, and if we ask them under oath, maybe they will tell us about the mystery of their resurrection.

2 When they heard these things, they all were joyful. Annas and Caiaphas, Nicodemus, Joseph, and Gamaliel went and did not find them in their grave, but they went to the city of Arimathaea and found them there, on their knees praying. They greeted them with kisses, and with all respect and in the fear of God, they brought them to Jerusalem into the synagogue. They locked the doors, took the law of the Lord, placed it in their hands, and

asked them under oath by the God Adonai and the God of Israel who spoke to our ancestors through the prophets, saying: Do you believe it was Jesus who raised you from the dead? Tell us how you were raised from the dead.

3 When Karinus and Leucius heard this oath, they trembled and groaned, troubled in heart. And looking up to heaven, they made the sign of the cross with their fingers on their tongues, and immediately they both spoke, saying: Give us each a piece of paper, and let us write what we have seen and heard. And they gave them paper, and each of them sat down and wrote, saying:

Chapter 18

1 O Lord Jesus Christ, the life and resurrection of the dead, allow us to speak of the mysteries of your majesty that you performed after your death on the cross, as we have been sworn by your Name. For you commanded us, your servants, not to reveal the secrets of your divine majesty which you performed in hell.

When we were gathered together with all our ancestors in the depths, in the darkness, suddenly a golden heat of the sun and a purple and royal light shone upon us. Immediately, the father of all humanity, along with all the patriarchs and prophets, rejoiced, saying: This light is the beginning of eternal light which promised to send us his co-eternal light. And Isaiah shouted and said: This is the light of the Father, the Son of God, as I proph-esied while I was on the earth: The land of Zebulun and the land of Naphtali, beyond Jordan, Galilee of the Gentiles, the people who walked in darkness have seen a great light, and those who lived in the land of the shadow of death, on them has the light shined. And now it has come and shone on us who sit in death.

2 And as we all rejoiced in the light that shone on us, our father Simeon came to us, and rejoicing, said to us: Praise the Lord Jesus Christ, the Son of God; for I held him in my arms in the temple when he was a child, and moved by the Holy Spirit I con-fessed and said to him: Now my eyes have seen your salvation, which you have prepared in the sight of all people, a light to reveal you to the nations and the glory of your people Israel. And when they heard these things, the entire multitude of the saints rejoiced even more.

3 And then someone who seemed like a dweller in the wilderness came to us, and everyone asked: Who are you? And he answered: I am John, the voice and the prophet of the Most High, who came before the face of his arrival to prepare his ways, to give his people knowledge of salvation by the forgiveness of their sins. And when I saw him com-ing to me, moved by the Holy Spirit, I said: Look, the Lamb of God, who takes away the sins of the world. And I baptized him in the Jordan River, saw the Holy Spirit descend-ing on him like a dove, and heard a voice from heaven saying: This is my beloved Son, with whom I am well pleased. And now I have come before him, descending to tell you

that he is about to visit us, the dawn from on high for us who sit in darkness and in the shadow of death.

Chapter 19

1 And when Adam, the first man created, heard that Jesus was baptized in Jordan, he cried out to his son Seth, saying: Tell your sons, the patriarchs and prophets, everything you heard from Michael the archangel, when I sent you to the gates of paradise to plead with God to send his angel to give you the oil of the tree of mercy to anoint my body when I was ill. Then Seth approached the holy patriarchs and prophets, and said: When I, Seth, was praying at the gates of paradise, behold, Michael, the angel of the Lord appeared to me, saying: I am sent to you from the Lord: I am appointed over the human body. And I say to you, Seth, do not distress yourself with tears, praying and pleading for the oil of the tree of mercy; to anoint your father Adam for his bodily pain: for you will not be able to obtain it until the last days and times, only when five thousand and five hundred (al. 5,952) years have passed: then shall the most beloved Son of God come to earth to raise the body of Adam and the bodies of the dead, and he shall come and be baptized in Jordan. And when he comes out of the water of Jordan, then he shall anoint with the oil of mercy all who believe in him, and that oil of mercy shall be for all generations of those who are born of water and of the Holy Spirit, unto eternal life. Then shall the most beloved Son of God, even Christ Jesus,

come down to earth and bring our father Adam back into paradise to the tree of mercy.

And when they heard all these things from Seth, all the patriarchs and prophets rejoiced greatly.

Chapter 20

1 And while all the saints were rejoicing, behold Satan, the prince and chief of death, said to Hell: Prepare yourself to receive Jesus who claims that he is the Son of God, whereas he is a man who fears death, and says: My soul is deeply sorrowful, even to death. And he has been a great enemy to me, causing me much harm, and many whom I had made blind, lame, mute, leprous, and possessed, he has healed with a word: and some whom I had brought to you dead, he has taken away from you.

2 Hell answered and said to Satan, the prince: Who is this that is so powerful, if he is a man who fears death? For all the mighty ones of the earth are subdued by my power, even those whom you have brought to me, subdued by your power. If, then, you are mighty, what kind of man is this Jesus who, though he fears death, resists your power? If he is so powerful in his humanity, truly I tell you he is almighty in his divinity, and no man can withstand his power. And when he says that he fears death, he aims to ensnare you, and woe shall be unto you for everlasting ages. But Satan, the prince of Tartarus, said: Why do you doubt and fear to receive this Jesus, who is both your adversary and mine? For I tempted him, and I have stirred up my ancient people, the

Jews, with envy and wrath against him. I have sharpened a spear to thrust him through, mixed gall and vinegar to give him to drink, and I have prepared a cross to crucify him and nails to pierce him: and his death is near at hand, so I may bring him to you to be subject to you and me.

3 Hell answered and said: You have told me that it is he who has taken away the dead from me. For there are many who, while they lived on the earth, have taken the dead from me, yet not by their own power but by prayer to God, and their almighty God has taken them from me. Who is this Jesus who by his own word without prayer has drawn the dead from me? Perhaps it is he who by the command of his word did bring Lazarus back to life, who was four days dead and stank and was corrupt, whom I held here as dead. Satan, the prince of death, answered and said: It is that same Jesus. When Hell heard that, he said to him: I adjure you by your strength and my own, do not bring him to me. For at that time, when I heard the command of his word, I quaked and was overwhelmed with fear, and all my minions with me were troubled. Neither could we keep Lazarus, but he, like an eagle shaking himself, leaped forth with all agility and swiftness, and departed from us, and the earth also which held the dead body of Lazarus immediately gave him up alive. Therefore, now I know that the man who was able to do these things is a God strong in command and mighty in humanity, and that he is the savior of mankind. And if you bring him to me, he will set free all those who are shut up in the hard prison and bound in the chains of their sins that cannot be broken, and will bring them to the life of his divinity forever.

Chapter 21

1 And as Satan, the prince, and Hell, spoke thus together, suddenly there came a voice as of thunder and a spiritual cry: Remove, O princes, your gates, and be lifted up, you everlasting doors, and the King of glory shall come in. When Hell heard that, he said to Satan, the prince: Depart from me and go out of my dwelling: if you are a mighty man of war, fight against the King of glory. But what have you to do with him? And Hell cast Satan out of his dwelling. Then Hell said to his wicked ministers: Close the hard gates of brass and put on them the bars of iron and stand firm, lest we who hold captivity be taken captive. 2 But when all the multitude of the saints heard it, they spoke with a voice of rebuke to Hell: Open your gates, that the King of glory may come in. And David cried out, saying: Did I not, when I was alive on earth, tell you: Let them give thanks to the Lord, for his mercies and his wonders to the children of men; he has broken the gates of brass and shattered the bars of iron in sunder? He has taken them out of their way of iniquity. And thereafter, in like manner, Isaiah said: Did I not, when I was alive on earth, tell you: The dead shall rise, and those in the tombs shall awaken, and those in the earth shall rejoice, for the dew that comes from the Lord is their

healing? And again I said: O death, where is your sting? O Hell, where is your victory?

3 When they heard that from Isaiah, all the saints said to Hell: Open your gates: now you shall be overcome and weak and without strength. And there came a great voice as of thunder, saying: Remove, O princes, your gates, and be lifted up, you doors of hell, and the King of glory shall come in. And when Hell saw that they cried out twice, he said, as if he did not know: Who is the King of glory? And David answered Hell and said: The words of this cry I told you when I was alive on earth: The Lord strong and mighty, the Lord mighty in battle. And with that, the Almighty Lord appeared in the form of a man and lightened the eternal darkness and broke the bonds that could not be loosed: and the help of his everlasting might visited us, who sat in the deep darkness of our transgressions and in the shadow of death of our sins.

Chapter 22

1 When Hell and death and their wicked ministers saw that, they were struck with fear, they and their cruel officers, at the sight of the brightness of such great light in their own realm, seeing Christ suddenly in their abode, and they cried out, saying: We are overcome by you. Who are you who are sent by the Lord to our confusion? Who are you who without any damage of corruption, and with the signs of your majesty unblemished, do in wrath condemn our power? Who are you who are so great and so small, both humble and exalted, both soldier and commander, a marvelous warrior in the shape of a servant, and a King of glory dead and living, whom the cross bore slain upon it? You who lay dead in the tomb have come down to us alive: and at your death all creation quaked and all the stars were shaken: and you have become free among the dead and do rout our legions. Who are you who set free the prisoners that are held bound by original sin and restore them to their former liberty? Who are you who shed your divine and bright light upon those who were blinded with the darkness of their sins? In the same manner all the legions of devils were struck with like fear and cried out all together in the terror of their confusion, saying: Where are you from, Jesus, a man so mighty and bright in majesty, so excellent, without spot and clean from sin? For the world of earth which has always been subject to us until now, and did pay tribute to our profit, has never sent to us a dead man like you, nor ever dispatched such a gift to Hell. Who then are you that so fearlessly enter our borders, and not only do not fear our torments but also try to take away all men from our bonds? Perhaps you are that Jesus, of whom Satan our prince said that by your death on the cross you would receive the dominion of the whole world.

2 Then did the King of glory in his majesty trample upon death, and seized Satan the prince and delivered him to the power of Hell, and drew Adam to him into his own brightness.

Chapter 23

Then Hell, receiving Satan the prince, with sore reproach said to him: O prince of perdition and chief of destruction, Beelzebub, the scorn of the angels and spitting of the righteous, why would you do this? You wanted to crucify the King of glory, and at his death did promise us great spoils of his death: like a fool you did not know what you were doing. For behold, now, this Jesus by the brightness of his majesty puts to flight all the darkness of death, and has broken the strong depths of the prisons, and let out the prisoners, and loosed those who were bound. And all who were sighing in our torments now rejoice against us, and at their prayers our dominions are vanquished and our realms conquered, and now no nation of men fears us anymore. And besides this, the dead who were never wont to be proud triumph over us, and the captives who never could be joyful threaten us. O prince Satan, father of all the wicked and ungodly and renegades, why would you do this? Those who from the beginning until now have despaired of life and salvation—now none of their wonted roarings are heard, nor does any groan from them sound in our ears, nor is there any sign of tears upon the face of any of them. O prince Satan, holder of the keys of hell, those riches which you had gained by the tree of transgression and the losing of paradise, you have lost by the tree of the cross, and all your gladness has perished. When you hung up Christ Jesus the King of glory you worked against yourself and against me. Henceforth you shall know what eternal torments and infinite pains you are to suffer in my keeping forever. O prince Satan, author of death and head of all pride, you ought first to have sought out matter of evil in this Jesus: Why did you venture without cause to crucify him unjustly against whom you found no blame, and to bring into our realm the innocent and righteous one, and to lose the guilty and the ungodly and unrighteous of the whole world?

And when Hell had spoken thus to Satan the prince, then said the King of glory to Hell: Satan the prince shall be in your power for all ages in the place of Adam and his children, even those that are my righteous ones.

Chapter 24

1 And the Lord reaching out his hand, said: Come to me, all my saints who bear my image and likeness. You who were condemned by the tree, the devil, and death, see now the devil and death condemned by the tree. And immediately all the saints were gathered together under the hand of the Lord. And the Lord, taking Adam's right hand, said to him: Peace be to you and all your children who are my righteous ones. But Adam, throwing himself at the knees of the Lord, begged him with tears and pleadings, and said loudly: I will exalt you, O Lord, for you have lifted me up and have not let my enemies triumph over me: O Lord my God, I cried to you and you have healed me; Lord, you have

brought my soul out of hell, you have saved me from those who go down to the pit. Praise the Lord, all his saints, and thank him for the memory of his holiness. For his anger lasts but a moment, and in his favor is life. In the same way, all the saints of God knelt and threw themselves at the feet of the Lord, unanimously saying: You have come, O redeemer of the world: what you foretold through the law and your prophets, you have now fulfilled in action. You have redeemed the living by your cross, and by the death of the cross, you have come down to us, so that you might save us from hell and death by your majesty. O Lord, as you have placed your glorious name in the heavens and set up your cross as a sign of redemption on the earth, so, Lord, establish the sign of the victory of your cross in hell, that death may no longer reign. 2 And the Lord extended his hand and made the sign of the cross over Adam and over all his saints, and he took Adam's right hand and ascended out of hell, and all the saints followed him. Then holy David exclaimed and said: Sing to the Lord a new song, for he has done marvelous things. His right hand has achieved salvation for him, and his holy arm. The Lord has made his salvation known, he has revealed his righteousness in the sight of the nations. And the whole multitude of saints responded, saying: Such honor have all his saints. Amen, Hallelujah.

3 And after that, the prophet Habakkuk cried out, saying: You went forth for the salvation of your people, to set your chosen ones free.

And all the saints answered, saying: Blessed is he who comes in the name of the Lord. God is the Lord and has made his light shine upon us. Amen, Hallelujah.

Similarly, the prophet Micah also exclaimed, saying: What God is like you, O Lord, pardoning iniquity and passing over transgression? And now you withhold your wrath as a testimony that you are merciful by choice, and you turn away and have compassion on us, you forgive all our iniquities and have cast all our sins into the depths of the sea, as you swore to our ancestors in days of old. And all the saints answered, saying: This is our God forever and ever, he will be our guide even to the end. Amen, Hallelujah. And so spoke all the prophets, recalling holy words from their praises, and all the saints followed the Lord, crying Amen, Hallelujah.

Chapter 25

But the Lord, taking Adam by the hand, entrusted him to Michael the archangel, and all the saints followed Michael the archangel. He led them all into the glory and grace of paradise. There, they were met by two men, elders with the appearance of ancient days. The saints, curious, asked: "Who are you, who have not experienced death in hell with us and now reside in paradise in bodily form?" One of them replied: "I am Enoch, who was transported here by the word of the Lord, and this man with me is Elijah the Tishbite, who was taken up in a chariot of fire. To this day, we have not tasted death. We are reserved for the coming of the Antichrist, to oppose him with signs and wonders from God, to be killed by him in Jerusalem, and then, after three and a half days, to be raised up alive into the clouds."

Chapter 26

As Enoch and Elijah were speaking thus with the saints, another man approached, wearing the humble attire of a thief, carrying on his shoulders the sign of the cross. When the saints saw him, they asked: "Who are you? Your appearance is that of a robber; and why do you carry the sign on your shoulders?" He answered them: "You have spoken truly, for I was a thief, committing all sorts of wickedness upon the earth. The Jews crucified me alongside Jesus, and as I hung there, I witnessed the wonders that occurred at the crucifixion of Jesus and realized that he was the creator of all and the almighty king. I begged him, saying: 'Remember me, Lord, when you come into your kingdom.' Immediately, he accepted my prayer, saying: 'Truly, I tell you, today you will be with me in paradise.' He then gave me the sign of the cross, instructing me: 'Carry this and go to paradise; and if the angel guarding paradise does not allow you to enter, show him the sign of the cross, and say to him: Jesus Christ, the Son of God, who is now crucified, has sent me.' When I did so and told the angel all these things, he immediately opened the gate, welcomed me in, and placed me on the right side of paradise,

saying: 'Wait here a little, for Adam, the father of all humanity, will enter with all his holy and righteous descendants, following the triumph and glory of the ascension of the crucified Lord Christ.' Upon hearing the words of the thief, all the holy patriarchs and prophets exclaimed in unison: 'Blessed be the Lord Almighty, the Father of eternal blessings, the Father of mercies, who has granted such grace to sinners and has restored them to the beauty of paradise and to your excellent pastures: for this is truly the life of the spirit most holy. Amen, Amen.'

Chapter 27

These are the divine and sacred mysteries that we, Karinus and Leucius, witnessed and heard. However, we were not permitted to divulge further the remaining mysteries of God, as commanded by Michael the archangel. He strictly instructed us, saying, "You shall journey with your brethren to Jerusalem and stay there in prayer, exalting and glorifying the resurrection of the Lord Jesus Christ, who has resurrected you from the dead alongside Him. You shall not converse with anyone, but remain mute, like those who cannot speak, until the time arrives when the Lord Himself allows you to reveal the mysteries of His divine nature." Furthermore, Michael the archangel ordered that we cross over the Jordan to a rich and fertile place, where many who were resurrected alongside us reside as a testament to the resurrection of Christ the Lord. We, who had been raised from the dead, were granted only three days to celebrate the Lord's Passover in Jerusalem with our living relatives, as a witness to the resurrection of Christ the Lord. We were baptized in the holy river Jordan and each received white robes. After the three days of celebrating the Lord's Passover, all who had risen with us were taken up into the clouds, crossed over Jordan, and vanished from sight. However, we were instructed to stay in the city of Arimathaea and continue in prayer.

These are all the things that the Lord commanded us to communicate to you: offer praise and confession to Him, and repent so that He may show mercy upon you. Peace be with you from the Lord Jesus Christ, the Savior of us all. Amen.

Upon completing their writings, Karinus and Leucius stood up; Karinus handed his writings to Annas, Caiaphas, and Gamaliel, while Leucius gave his to Nicodemus and Joseph. Suddenly, they were transformed, their appearance becoming exceedingly white, and then they were seen no more. However, their writings were discovered to be identical, not differing by a single letter.

When the Jewish assembly heard all these astonishing accounts from Karinus and Leucius, they said to one another, "Truly, all these events were orchestrated by the Lord, and blessed be the Lord forever, Amen." Overwhelmed and troubled, they left, striking their chests in fear and trembling, each returning to his own home.

Joseph and Nicodemus immediately reported all these discussions from the Jewish assembly to the governor. Pilate himself documented all the occurrences and statements made about Jesus by the Jews, securing all the records in the public archives of his judgment hall (praetorium).

Chapter 28

After these things, Pilate entered into the temple of the Jews and gathered together all the chief priests, the teachers, scribes, and doctors of the law, and went in with them into the holy place of the temple and commanded that all the doors be shut, and said to them: "We have heard that you have in this temple a certain great Bible; therefore, I ask you that it be presented before us." When that great Bible, adorned with gold and precious jewels, was brought by four ministers, Pilate said to them all: "I adjure you by the God of your fathers who commanded you to build this temple in the place of his sanctuary, that you hide not the truth from me. You know all the things that are written in this Bible; but tell me now if you have found in the scriptures that this Jesus, whom you have crucified, is the Son of God who should come for the salvation of mankind, and in what year of the times he must come. Declare unto me whether you crucified him in ignorance or knowingly."

And Annas and Caiaphas, when they were thus adjured, commanded all the rest that were with them to go out of the temple; and they themselves shut all the doors of the temple and the sanctuary and said to Pilate: "You have adjured us, O excellent judge, by the building of this temple to make manifest to you the truth and reason. After we had crucified Jesus, not knowing that he was the Son of God but supposing that by some chance he did his wondrous works, we made a great assembly in this temple; and as we conferred one with another concerning the signs of the mighty works that Jesus had done, we found many witnesses of our own nation who said they had seen Jesus alive after his passion, and that he was passed into the height of heaven. Moreover, we saw two witnesses whom Jesus raised from the dead, who declared unto us many marvelous things which Jesus did among the dead, which things we have in writing in our hands. Now our custom is that every year before our assembly we open this holy Bible and inquire the testimony of God. And we have found in the first book of the Seventy how Michael the angel spoke unto the third son of Adam the first man concerning the five thousand and five hundred years, wherein the most beloved Son of God, even Christ, should come; and furthermore, we thought that perhaps this same was the God of Israel who said to Moses: 'Make thee an ark of the covenant in length two cubits and a half, and in breadth one cubit and a half, and in height one cubit and a half.' For by those five cubits and a half, we have understood and known the fashion of the ark of the old covenant, for that in five thousand and a half thousand years Jesus Christ should come in the ark of his body; and we have found that he is the God of Israel, even the Son of God. For after his passion, we, the chief priests, because we marveled at the signs which came to pass on his account, did open the Bible, and searched out all the generations to the generation of Joseph, and Mary the mother of Christ, taking her to be the seed of David; and we found that from the day when God made the heaven and the earth and the first man, from that time to the Flood are 2,212 years;

Appendixes to the Acts of Pilate

Letter of Pilate to Tiberius

Jesus Christ, about whom I recently wrote to you, has been executed against my will. Such a pious and austere man has never been seen, nor will be again. However, there was a remarkable consensus among the Jews and their leader that he should be crucified, despite their own prophets and the Sibyls testifying against them, and signs appeared at his death which the philosophers said threatened the collapse of the entire world. His disciples, who are still alive, do not contradict their master's teaching, but are active in good deeds. Had I not feared a general uprising, the man might still be alive. He ends, weakly justifying his actions. Date, the 5th of of April.

Report of Pilate (Anaphora)

I have received a message, O most mighty, which fills me with fear and trembling.
He continues to report that in Jerusalem, a city within his province, the Jews handed over a man named Jesus to him, accusing him of many things they could not prove, especially of violating the Sabbath. The miracles are then described with some rhetorical flair, particularly in the case of Lazarus. Jesus was delivered to him by Herod, Archelaus, Philip, Annas, Caiaphas, and all the people.

At his crucifixion, the sun darkened; the stars appeared, and throughout the world, people lit lamps from the sixth hour until evening; the moon looked like blood, and the stars and Orion mourned the sin of the Jews. (Another version mentions that Abraham, Isaac, Jacob, the twelve patriarchs, Moses, and Job, who were seen by the Jews and many others 'whom I, too, saw', appeared in person and thus lamented.)

On the first day of the week, at the third hour of the night, there was a great light: the sun shone with unusual brightness, men in shining garments appeared in the air, and called out to the souls in Hades to come up, announcing Jesus's resurrection.

The light lasted all night. Many Jews vanished into the chasms created by the earthquake: and all the synagogues except one were destroyed. Overwhelmed by the alarm these portents caused, Pilate writes to Caesar.

Attached in one version is the 'Delivering up, Paradosis, of Pilate'.

Upon receiving the letter, there was great astonishment in Rome, and Caesar angrily ordered Pilate to be brought to him as a prisoner.

Upon his arrival, Caesar sat 'in the temple of the gods before all the senate, and with all his army and all the multitude of his power', and questioned Pilate: How could you dare, you most impious, to do such a thing, after witnessing such signs concerning that man? By your wicked audacity, you have destroyed the whole world.

Pilate placed the blame on the Jews, Herod, Archelaus, Philip, Annas, and Caiaphas. Caesar asked, Why did you give in to them? Pilate responded, The nation is rebellious and disobedient. Caesar retorted, You should have protected him and sent him to me, and not have capitulated and crucified someone who had performed all those mighty works you described in your report. It is clear he was the Christ, the king of the Jews.

When Caesar mentioned Christ, all the images of the gods fell down and turned to dust. This caused great consternation, and Caesar sent Pilate back to prison.

The next day, he sat in the Capitol with all the senate, and a similar dialogue occurred. Afterward, Caesar wrote to Licianus, the chief governor of the East, ordering him to enslave the entire Jewish nation and reduce their numbers because of their wickedness. Licianus carried out these orders.

Caesar then commanded that a ruler named Albius execute Pilate. As he was led to his death, Pilate prayed: Do not count me among the wicked Hebrews. Do not remember evil against me or against your servant Procla who stands here, whom you made to prophesy that you must be nailed to the cross. But forgive us and count us among your righteous ones.

A voice from heaven declared: All the generations and families of the Gentiles shall call you blessed, for in your days were fulfilled all these things that were spoken by the prophets concerning me; and you shall also appear as my witness (or martyr) at my second coming, when I shall judge the twelve tribes of Israel and those who have not confessed my name.

The prefect beheaded Pilate, and an angel of the Lord received his head. Upon seeing this, Procla, his wife, was filled with joy, and immediately died, and was buried with her husband.

The Letter of Pilate to Herod

It was not a good thing that I did at your urging when I crucified Jesus. I learned from the centurion and the soldiers that he had risen again, and I sent to Galilee and found out that he was preaching there to more than five hundred believers.

My wife Procla, along with Longinus, the believing centurion, and ten (or twelve) soldiers who had guarded the tomb, went out and found him 'sitting in a tilled field' teaching a large crowd. He saw them, spoke to them, and talked about his victory over death and hell. Procla and the others came back and told me. I was deeply distressed, and put on mourning clothes and went with her and fifty soldiers to Galilee. We found Jesus, and as we approached him, there was a sound in heaven and thunder, the earth shook and released a sweet fragrance. We fell on our faces, and the Lord came and lifted us up, and I saw the marks of the crucifixion on him, and he placed his hands on my shoulders, saying: All generations and families will call you blessed (as mentioned before), because in your time the Son of Man died and rose again.

The Letter of Herod to Pilate

It is with considerable sorrow—a sentiment echoed in the divine Scriptures—that I write to you.
My beloved daughter Herodias was playing by the water and fell in up to her neck. Her mother tried to save her by grabbing her head, which was then severed, and the water carried her body away. My wife sits with our daughter's head on her knees, weeping, and our entire household is engulfed in grief.
I am deeply troubled by the death of Jesus and haunted by my sins, including the killing of John the Baptist and the massacre of the Innocents. 'Since you are now able to see Jesus again, please make an effort on my behalf and intercede

for me: for the kingdom is granted to you Gentiles, according to the prophets and Christ himself.'
My son Lesbonax is in the final stages of consumption. I suffer from dropsy, and worms are emerging from my mouth. My wife has lost the sight in her left eye from constant weeping. The judgments of God are just, for we mocked the gaze of the righteous. Vengeance will fall upon the Jews and the priests, while the Gentiles will inherit the kingdom, and the children of light will be expelled.
And Pilate, as we are contemporaries, please ensure my family is buried with honor. It is preferable for us to be buried by you than by the priests, whose destruction is imminent. Farewell. I have sent you my wife's earrings and my own signet ring. I am beginning to face judgment in this world, but I dread the eternal judgment hereafter even more. This is temporary; that is everlasting.

The Letter of Tiberius to Pilate

This message was delivered to Pilate through the messenger Raab, who was dispatched with 2,000 soldiers to bring him to Rome.
Because you have passed a harsh and unjust death sentence on Jesus of Nazareth, showing no compassion, accepting bribes to condemn him, and verbally expressing sympathy while in your heart you betrayed him, you are to be brought back as a prisoner to answer for your actions.
I have been deeply troubled by the reports that have reached me: a woman, a follower of Jesus named Mary

Magdalene, from whom he is said to have expelled seven demons, has come here and recounted all his miraculous healings. How could you allow him to be crucified? Even if you did not acknowledge him as a God, you might at least have respected him as a healer. Your own misleading letter to me has sealed your fate.

Since you have sentenced him unjustly, I will sentence you and your accomplices justly.

Pilate, Archelaus, Philip, Annas, and Caiaphas were arrested.

Rachaab and the soldiers killed all the Jewish men, violated the women, and brought the leaders to Rome. On the way, Caiaphas died in Crete: the earth would not accept his body, and he was buried under a heap of stones.

According to the old law, if a condemned criminal saw the face of the emperor, he was to be spared: thus, Tiberius refused to meet Pilate, instead confining him in a cave.

Annas was encased in a fresh bull's hide, which, as it dried and contracted, crushed him to death. The other Jewish leaders were executed: Archelaus and Philip were crucified. One day, the emperor went hunting and chased a deer to the entrance of Pilate's prison. Pilate attempted to catch a glimpse of the emperor's face, but at that moment, the emperor shot an arrow at the deer, which flew through the window and killed Pilate.

The Death of Pilate

Emperor Tiberius, being gravely ill, heard about an extraordinary physician in Jerusalem, named Jesus, who cured all illnesses. He dispatched one of his officers, named Volusianus, to Pilate, instructing him to send this physician to him. Pilate was terrified, as he knew Jesus had been crucified. On his way back to the inn, Volusianus encountered a woman named Veronica and inquired about Jesus. She revealed the truth, causing him great sorrow, and to comfort him, she added that while Jesus was away teaching, she had wanted to always have a picture of him. She intended to bring a linen cloth to a painter for this purpose. However, Jesus met her, and upon learning of her wish, took the cloth from her and transferred the features of his face onto it. She told him this cloth would heal his lord: she could not sell it, but she would accompany him to Rome.

Volusianus and Veronica returned to Rome, and Tiberius, awaiting the arrival of the likeness, covered the path with silk cloths. He was instantly cured by merely looking at the image.

Pilate was arrested and brought before the emperor in Rome. At that time, he was wearing the seamless tunic of Jesus. Before the emperor, who had been furious with him, he became very calm. The emperor sent Pilate away, and his anger immediately flared up again. This occurred multiple times. Then, either inspired by divine revelation or following a Christian's advice, the emperor had Pilate stripped of the tunic, sent back to jail, and soon after, sentenced him to the most shameful death. Upon hearing this, Pilate took his own life with his knife. Caesar then had a millstone tied around his neck and cast him into the Tiber. Demons congregated in large numbers, and storms caused such disturbance that everyone was in great fear. Pilate's body was retrieved from the river and taken to Vienne (via Gehennae) on the Rhone, with the same disturbances occurring. From there, it was moved to be buried in the territory of Lausanne, but the disturbances persisted until the locals exhumed it and threw it into a well in the mountains, a place still rumored to be plagued by demonic occurrences.

In another version of this legend: Tiberius, severely ill, was informed by a Jew named Thomas about the miracles of Jesus, and sent a high-ranking officer, Volusianus, to fetch him from Jerusalem. The journey took one year and three months. Pilate and the Jews were terrified. Pilate was convinced by one of his soldiers that it was indeed the crucified Jesus they were referring to, and the proof of the resurrection was corroborated by Joseph of Arimathaea and others. Meanwhile, Pilate was imprisoned and forced to publicly confess his guilt.

A young man named Marcius then told Volusian that a woman from Tyre, Veronica (also known as Basilla in some early texts), had the likeness of Jesus, who had healed her of a hemorrhage three years earlier. Initially denying it, she eventually presented it under duress. Volusian venerated the image and threatened with punishment all those involved in Jesus' death. He then set off for Rome with Veronica and Pilate, arriving shortly after. Tiberius questioned

why Pilate had not been executed. Volusian explained he did not want to preempt the emperor's decision. Tiberius exiled Pilate to Ameria in Tuscany without meeting him. Volusian then presented Veronica and the image to Tiberius, who venerated it and was healed. Tiberius rewarded Veronica financially, created a precious shrine for the image, was baptized, and died some years later in peace.

The Vengeance or Avenging of the Saviour

There was a king named Titus under Tiberius, in Aquitaine, in a city called Bordeaux (Burgidalla). He had cancer in his right nostril, and his face was disfigured up to his eye.

There was also a Jew named Nathan, son of Naum, whom the Jews had sent to Tiberius with a treaty. Tiberius himself was suffering from fever, ulcers, and had nine kinds of leprosy. Nathan's ship was forced ashore at the city of Titus. When summoned, Nathan shared his story. Titus inquired if he knew anyone who could heal him. Nathan responded: If you had been in Jerusalem recently, there was a prophet named Emanuel, whose miracles, Passion, descent into hell, and resurrection were recounted. Titus exclaimed: Woe to you, Tiberius, for allowing such things to happen in your domain. I would have executed these Jews myself for destroying my Lord. Upon saying this, the wound from his face vanished, and he was healed, along with all the sick present. Titus proclaimed his faith in Christ and had Nathan baptize him.

Then, he called for Vespasian to come with all his forces. Vespasian arrived with 5,000 men and asked: Why have you summoned me? "To destroy the enemies of Jesus," Titus replied. So, they set off for Jerusalem. Frightened, Archelaus handed his kingdom over to his son and then killed himself. The son, allying with other kings, fortified Jerusalem. The city was besieged for seven years, leading to such desperation that the inhabitants resorted to eating dirt. Eventually, they decided to surrender, handing over the keys to Titus and Vespasian. Some were killed, some crucified upside down, pierced with lances, sold, cast lots upon, divided into four parts, and the remainder sold for thirty for a penny.

They then searched for the likeness of Jesus and found Veronica, who possessed it. Pilate was handed over to four squads of soldiers.

A message was sent by Titus to Tiberius to dispatch Velosian, instructing him to go to Jerusalem to find someone to heal him, promising half the kingdom in return.

Velosian arrived after a year and seven days, first meeting Joseph and Nicodemus. Joseph recounted the burial, his imprisonment, and his rescue by Jesus.

Then Veronica came forward, sharing her story of healing. Velosian arrested and imprisoned Pilate, placing him in an iron cage. Upon questioning Veronica, who initially denied having the likeness, she eventually admitted to possessing it, kept in a linen cloth, which she venerated daily. She presented it, and Velosian, in reverence, took it, wrapped it in a gold cloth, secured it in a box, and set sail for Rome. Veronica, leaving everything behind, insisted on accompanying him. They journeyed up the Tiber to Rome, taking a year to arrive.

Upon their arrival, Tiberius summoned Velosian, who recounted the entire story, including the destruction of the Jews. Tiberius then requested the likeness, which upon being presented, he venerated, and his flesh was cleansed as he prayed. He then inquired if anyone present had seen Christ and knew how to baptize. Nathan was summoned, baptized Tiberius, who then praised God and was educated in the Christian faith's doctrines.

The Golden Legend

This account begins with Pilate sending a messenger, named Albanus, to Caesar to defend himself regarding the condemnation of Jesus. Albanus ends up in Galicia and is brought before Vespasian, who got his name because he had been troubled by a wasp's nest in his nose since childhood. Vespasian told Albanus: You come from the land of the wise; you must cure me. Albanus responded: I am not a physician. Vespasian then said: You must cure me or face death. Albanus replied: There was a man who could have healed you with just a word; he expelled demons and resurrected the dead. He was Jesus of Nazareth, whom the Jews executed out of jealousy. If you believed in him, you would be healed. Vespasian declared: I truly believe he is the Son of God and that he can heal me. Instantly, the wasps exited his nose, and he was cured. Vespasian vowed to go to Tiberius to secure forces to destroy the city and nation of the Jews. After spending some years assembling an army, he laid siege to Jerusalem. The Christians, having been warned by the Holy Spirit, had already fled to Pella.

The narrative then introduces a meeting between the historian Josephus and Vespasian, during which Josephus prophesies Vespasian's rise to the empire, which subsequently occurs. Following this, we learn of Titus falling ill from the joy of his father's victory, and being healed by the placement of a slave he despised next to him at the dining table, a scheme devised by Josephus. The story continues with the famine in Jerusalem and the horrifying tale of a woman named Mary who resorts to cannibalism. Ultimately, the city falls, and the Jews are sold at the price of thirty for a penny.

The discovery of an elderly man embedded within a very sturdy wall follows; this man is Joseph of Arimathea. According to the Gospel of Nicodemus, after being freed by Jesus, he was imprisoned once more by the Jews for continuing to preach the gospel and had since been miraculously sustained with light and food from heaven.

STORY OF JOSEPH OF ARIMATHAEA

Chapter 1

1 I, Joseph of Arimathaea, who requested the body of the Lord Jesus from Pilate, was imprisoned by the Jews for this reason. These are the people who challenged their lawgiver Moses, and by failing to recognize their God, crucified his Son.

Seven days before the passion of Christ, two condemned robbers were transferred from Jericho to Pilate, accused of the following crimes.

2 The first, Gestas, would rob and murder travelers, suspend women by the feet and sever their breasts, consume the blood of infants: he did not acknowledge God nor adhere to any law, but was violent from his early days.

The other, Demas, was a Galilean who ran an inn; he would rob the wealthy but assist the poor, even burying them, similar to Tobit. He had committed thefts against the Jews, for he stole (plundered) the law itself in Jerusalem, and stripped the daughter of Caiaphas, who was a priestess of the sanctuary, and he even took the mystical deposit of Solomon which had been placed in the sacred site.

3 Jesus was also captured in the evening on the third day before the Passover. However, Caiaphas and the multitude of Jews did not celebrate the Passover but were in great sorrow because of the theft from the sanctuary by the thief. And they summoned Judas Iscariot who was the nephew of Caiaphas, and had been convinced by the Jews to become a follower of Jesus, not to embrace his teachings, but to betray him. They paid him a didrachm of gold daily; and as one of Jesus' followers, named John, states, he had been with Jesus for two years.

4 On the third day before Jesus was captured, Judas proposed to the Jews: Let us gather a council and claim that it was not the robber who took the law, but Jesus. Nicodemus, who had the keys to the sanctuary, objected: for he was an honest man. However, Sarra, the daughter of Caiaphas, shouted that Jesus publicly declared, 'I can destroy the temple'. All the Jews exclaimed: We believe you. For they regarded her as a prophetess. Thus, Jesus was apprehended.

Chapter 2

1 On the following day, being Wednesday, at the ninth hour, they brought him into Caiaphas' hall, where Annas and Caiaphas asked him: "Why did you take away the law?" He remained silent. "Why would you destroy Solomon's temple?" Again, he did not answer. 2 In the evening, the crowd sought Caiaphas' daughter, intending to burn her because the law was stolen, and they could not observe the Passover. But she said: "Wait a bit, my children, and let us eliminate Jesus, then the law will be recovered, and the feast can be observed." Then, Annas and Caiaphas secretly gave gold to Judas, saying: "Repeat what you previously stated, that it was Jesus who stole the law." Judas agreed but insisted: "The people must not learn of this from you: release Jesus, and I will convince them." So, they deceitfully released Jesus. 3 At dawn on Thursday, Judas entered the sanctuary and announced to all the people: "What will you give me if I hand over to you the one who destroyed the law and robbed the prophets?" They replied: "Thirty pieces of silver." However, they were unaware that he was speaking of Jesus, as many believed him to be the Son of God. And Judas received the thirty pieces. 4 Between the fourth and fifth hours, he went out and found Jesus walk-

ing in the street. By evening, he had secured a group of soldiers. As they proceeded, Judas indicated: "The one I shall kiss, arrest him: he is the one who stole the law and the prophets." He approached Jesus and kissed him, saying: "Greetings, Rabbi." They then took Jesus to Caiaphas and interrogated him. "Why did you do this?" but he gave no response. Nicodemus and I left the seat of the corrupt and refused to be part of the council of sinners.

Chapter 3

1 They subjected Jesus to many cruel acts that night, and at dawn on Friday, they handed him over to Pilate. He was condemned and crucified alongside the two robbers, Gestas on the left, Demas on the right. 2 The one on the left shouted at Jesus: "Look at the evils I have committed on earth; had I known you were the king, I would have sought to kill you as well. Why do you call yourself the Son of God and yet cannot save yourself in this time of need? Or how can you help others who pray to you? If you are the Christ, come down from the cross so that I might believe in you. But now, I see you not as a man but as a wild beast trapped and dying alongside me." And he continued to speak against Jesus, blaspheming and gritting his teeth at him: for he was ensnared by the devil. 3 But Demas, on the right, witnessing the divine grace of Jesus, began to exclaim: "I recognize you, Jesus Christ, as the Son of God. I see you, Christ, adored by countless angels; forgive the sins I have committed:

do not let the stars or the moon accuse me when you judge the world: for it was at night that I plotted my misdeeds. Do not allow the now darkened sun to reveal the wickedness of my heart: for I have nothing to offer for the forgiveness of my sins. Death approaches me because of my sins, but forgiveness is with you: save me, Lord of all, from your fearsome judgement. Do not let the enemy consume me and claim my soul, as he does with the one on the left; for I witness how the devil joyfully takes his soul, and his body disintegrates. Do not send me to join the Jews, for I see Moses and the patriarchs in deep sorrow, and the devil gloating over them. Therefore, before my spirit leaves, command, O Lord, that my sins be erased, and remember me, a sinner, in your kingdom when you reign from the great throne of the Most High and judge the twelve tribes of Israel: for you have prepared severe punishment for your world for your sake."

4 After the thief spoke, Jesus said to him: "Truly, I tell you, Demas, today you will be with me in paradise: but the sons of the kingdom, the descendants of Abraham, Isaac, and Jacob, and Moses, will be thrown into the outer darkness: there will be weeping and gnashing of teeth. But you alone shall stay in paradise until my second coming when I will judge those who have not acknowledged my name." And he instructed the thief: "Inform the cherubim and the powers that guard the flaming sword, which guards the garden since Adam, the first man, resided in paradise and disobeyed, not keeping my command-

ments, leading to his expulsion—but none of the former humans shall see paradise until I return a second time to judge the living and the dead." And he proclaimed thus: "Jesus Christ the Son of God, who descended from the heights of heaven, who emerged from the bosom of the invisible Father without separation, and came into the world to become flesh and to be nailed to the cross, to save Adam whom I created: to my powers, the archangels guarding the gates of paradise, the servants of my Father, I decree and command that the one crucified with me be allowed entry, to receive forgiveness of his sins for my sake, to be clothed with an incorruptible body, to enter paradise, and to reside where no other man has ever dwelled."

And with these words, Jesus passed away on Friday at the ninth hour. Darkness covered the entire land, and a great earthquake occurred, causing the sanctuary to collapse and the pinnacle of the temple to fall.

Chapter 4

1 And I, Joseph, obtained the body and placed it in my new tomb. The body of Demas was not found; Gestas' body appeared dragon-like.
I was imprisoned by the Jews on the evening of the Sabbath.

2 On the evening of the first day of the week, at the fifth hour of the night, Jesus appeared to me with the thief from the right side. There was a brilliant light; the house lifted from its four corners, and I stepped outside: first I saw Jesus, and then the thief, who was delivering a let-

ter to him. As we traveled to Galilee, there was an immense light, and a sweet fragrance emanated from the thief.

3 Jesus sat down at a certain spot and read the following: "The cherubim and the six-winged beings, commanded by your divinity to guard the garden of paradise, convey this message through the hand of the thief who was crucified alongside you by your arrangement. When we observed the nail marks on the thief crucified with you and the light from the letters of your divinity, the fire diminished, unable to withstand the brightness of the mark, leaving us in great awe and causing us to shrink back. We had heard that the creator of heaven, earth, and all creation had descended to the lower regions of the earth for the sake of Adam, the first man. We saw the unblemished cross, with the thief radiating light, shining sevenfold brighter than the sun, causing us to tremble. We heard the tumult below the earth, and the servants of Hades echoed our sentiments: 'Holy, Holy, Holy, is He who was in the highest from the beginning.' And the powers exclaimed, proclaiming, 'Lord, you have revealed yourself in heaven and on earth, bringing joy to the ages and rescuing your creation from death.'"

Chapter 5

1 As I accompanied Jesus and the robber to Galilee, Jesus's appearance transformed entirely into light, and angels attended to him while he spoke with them. I remained with him for three days, without any of the disciples present.

2 During the days of unleavened bread, his disciple John arrived, and the robber was nowhere to be seen. John inquired about his identity, but Jesus remained silent. John expressed: "Lord, I know you have loved me since the beginning: why do you not reveal who this man is to me?" Jesus responded: "Are you seeking to uncover secrets? Do you lack understanding? Can you not sense the scent of paradise permeating this place? Do you not recognize who he was? The thief from the cross has inherited paradise: truly, I tell you, it belongs solely to him until the grand day arrives." John requested: "Allow me to see him."

3 Suddenly, the thief reappeared, causing John to fall to the ground, for the thief now resembled a powerful king, adorned with the cross. A voice from a multitude declared: "You have entered the paradise prepared for you: we are assigned to serve you by the one who sent you until the grand day." Subsequently, both the thief and I, Joseph, disappeared, and I found myself back in my home, seeing Jesus no more.

I have witnessed and recorded all this so that everyone might believe in Jesus and abandon the law of Moses, instead, to believe in the miracles and signs of Christ; and by believing, attain eternal life and enter the kingdom of heaven.

For to Him belong glory, power, praise, and majesty, forever and ever. Amen.

Made in the USA
Columbia, SC
13 July 2024

38586238R00119